139982

HUMANISTIC FOUNDATIONS OF EDUCATION

WITHDRAWN
...AM COLLEGE LIBRARY

edited by

Carl Weinberg

University of California at Los Angeles

370.112
Wei

Prentice-Hall, Inc., Englewood Cliffs, N.J.

© 1972 by Prentice-Hall, Inc.,
Englewood Cliffs, New Jersey.

All rights reserved. No part of this book may be
reproduced in any form or by any means without
permission in writing from the publisher.

13-447771-5

Library of Congress Catalog
Card Number: 77-161913

10 9 8 7 6 5 4 3 2 1

PRINTED IN THE UNITED STATES OF AMERICA

Prentice-Hall International, Inc., *London*
Prentice-Hall of Australia, Pty. Ltd., *Sydney*
Prentice-Hall of Canada, Ltd., *Toronto*
Prentice-Hall of India Private Limited, *New Delhi*
Prentice-Hall of Japan, Inc., *Tokyo*

contents

introduction

Humanism is a common word today both in and out of academic circles. This does not mean, however, either that it is overused or that it is used very differently by different people. The chapters of this book are about many versions of humanism. This is a necessity, for humanism, like love, is a concept which resists classification. Experiencing love provides more understanding than analyzing it. So it is with humanism as well.

If we pause to indicate the precise nature of humanism, we will surely not be performing a humanistic task, for we would be saying that humanism involves some standard prescription for defining itself and the tasks intending to represent it. Because humanism is an experience or perspective on life or education, it must define itself without a standard definition. If I, for example, define myself as a scholar, or a male, or a moral man, then I make it convenient for others to detect contradictions in myself; I force people to look for consistencies, and perhaps even see them because they expect to see them. On the other hand, if I merely say I am a human being, then there can be no contradictions or mind sets, for then I can be expected to be anything within the wide range of the human potential. This, too, is the case for humanism: it can be anything that human beings can be. There is only one thing it cannot be, as I cannot be: it cannot be nonhuman, which separates it from the majority of academic products which are precisely that—nonhuman.

I have rarely read a paper in history, philosophy, sociology, or psychology that did not sound as if it had been done by a very fine and complex computer. Most papers in education that intend to shed some light on learning seem divorced from the human experience of the authors. This is not merely because the papers are written in the third person; it is because the writers believe they are somehow separate from their observations. The pretense of objectivity, the self-righteous claims of detachment that are so apparent in the academic task, are not only delusion, but they distract us from seeing and exploring the enormous potential inherent in subjective scholarship. Subjectivity does not mean a soft-headedness, or intuitive belief. It means, rather, that persons become aware of their relationship to what they are observing and how their own experience transforms the material with which they work.

Humanism, then, for the purposes of this book, consists of bringing the person and the material he describes into some sort of meaningful relationship. It will be my purpose to attempt to prepare the reader for each reading by describing what I believe to be the special humanistic understanding of each author. In each of the three chapters that I have contributed, I have taken a slightly different approach to the humanistic task. When I deal with sociology, I am mostly concerned with application of scientific knowledge to human needs. When I talk about literature, I approach humanism from the perspective of coming to know oneself and to grow through this knowledge. When I write about guidance, I take the clinical view of humanism, which is a special perspective of mental health and how it is produced. Prior to each chapter, I will attempt to analyze its humanistic thrust. The reader should not try to anticipate the specific humanistic version of each chapter, other than to expect that the author will make himself known in the writing so that knowledge and personal context begin to conjoin. This is the foundation of humanistic wisdom which our present academic world seems to have lost sight of.

Now I wish to say a word about how this book was conceived and why it was conceived. Initially, it should be noted that I have taught the standard stuff in the standard way for several years and became quite as bored as my students. I found that the only way to overcome boredom in the American university is not to exist in it as a bureaucrat, not to simply play out a series of static impersonal roles in the office, in the laboratory, and in the classroom.

Now my students' boredom and mine ended at precisely the same time, and this was not coincidental. I discovered that the way to experience the joys that were possible in the university was to bring myself into real contact with both my knowledge and my students. In describing to them how I believe I know something, I communicate an understanding of it. In talking about what I know, I communicate a set of lifeless ideas that fail to awaken any but the most disciplined and sterile minds. I know, for example, that social institutions change slowly. By recounting my personal experiences with the bureaucracy of which both students and I are a part, they begin to understand something about the interaction of persons and institutions. This idea, then, of bringing ideas into human perspective seems to be the way to make classes interesting and meaningful and it occurred to me that it should make a book the same.

Another reason why this book became a reality had to do with my belief that poor education had much to do with the pathetic state of human existence in our society. If students can get something more out of foundations courses than a booklet full of lecture notes, they might figure out something they could do to make schools and schooling better for children, who have it almost as bad as adults. Two years ago, many of the secondary schools and a large number of universities in this country were shut down, closed to students. This is sad, not just because schools were closed, but because they had to be. The rationality that has guided the educational enterprise for many years seems to have run out of solutions to the basic problems. Educational leaders are asking "What do students want?" There seems no clear method to the madness. The fever will spread throughout the country. We can't diagnose it. The dinosaur is dying. Where have we failed?

We haven't. We did the best we could with the tools we had and the structure within which we had to work. We in the university, responsible for the training of teachers for the network of educating institutions, can smile and say that they wouldn't listen and now are paying the consequences. We had all the good ideas, the innovations, the correct attitudes, the experimental techniques dying for lack of a good try. But they, the school people down on the "firing line," all they cared about was control, the status quo, protecting the equilibrium.

Is the mess really out there? If so, then why are the troops in our own back yard restless? Why do they riot, protest, sit in? Why are college students fainting from the pressure and smothering from the irrelevance? The word of the day is out: relevance. What is it? Most students can tell us. It is simply a feeling that what one is doing is what one has to do. It is a congruence of a person with his activities. It is believing that one's position does not deprive him of his dignity as a human being. It is knowing that one's integration with his institution is not based on impersonal rules of order and control, but on the belief that the institution is offering him what he needs in the way that he needs it.

This is why the schools are closed and closing, why students everywhere are beginning to smell the blood of the beast that has enslaved them. It is no longer possible to preserve the old structures in education. Students don't want them anymore. They are ready and willing to consult their humanness regarding the tasks we ask them to perform, and the conditions under which they must perform them. And if either tasks or conditions do not meet their criteria for how they are willing to exist in the long or short run, they will turn us down and wait for us to rethink our problem.

Our problem in professional schools of education is the same. We must find some way to link our programs to these emerging life forces that students now feel, to fulfill a commitment to themselves and others to be personally and socially responsible. If this is our problem, it is also our salvation. Aren't these the kinds of students we want? But in the past, very few of these students looked towards schools of education as a source of preparation for such commitment. Educationists must share in the blame, for they take no moral stand on the failure of schools to innovate and prepare students for living better in a difficult society. Nor do they attempt to reconstruct their own establishment in order to attract a different population from the one they currently attract. Are they so insecure about their intellectual capacities and professional posture that they shy away from recruiting students who will challenge them to do their job in a better or more significant way?

This foundations book is intended for persons either beginning the study of education or exposing themselves to a first course in order to evaluate their interests and future plans. Much is usually determined by the foundations course. Students decide upon their interests, and those interested decide upon the intensity of their commitment. Foundations courses are important, not only as building blocks to the development of a professional self, but also in the way in which the study of professional education is assessed within the academic community. This does not mean an evaluation of the quality of scholarship, although this is a part, but—of critical significance to our concerns—an evaluation of the relevance of the learning experience to the student's sense of himself. If there is anything upon which we need to build that will communicate our notion of a foundations book, or course, or experience, it is a sense of self. College students are becoming aware of their needs as independent human beings, and their evaluation of instruction begins and often ends with the question, "Is this important to me?" The foundation of the development of the professional self must rest upon this sense of importance. Students must sense that education and teaching are important and that the knowledge they receive maintains this standard of importance. The image of education departments, usually fostered by these foundations courses, is not good at this time. Perhaps we, as professional educators, have not dealt with this question of implicit human value. And if we do not, what more can we expect of the teachers we produce? If our students can be stimulated, even inspired by the humanistic frontiers presented in our foundations courses, then they will communicate their new awarenesses to their peers, many of whom might be potential recruits.

Our task is greater now than before, because students are more demanding than in the past, and more critical of that which they feel to be an irresponsible view of their needs and capacities. They are beyond the concern about courses being interesting. Although they insist upon this as a minimum, they want also to feel that their studies will help them to evolve as persons and perform effectively in useful social tasks. As we think about a foundations course, or book, we must begin to conceive of an experience which will bring students to the point of recognizing in themselves, and in our ideas, something that is relevant to the notion of important human purposes and important human involvement.

Perhaps university education is itself not relevant in this sense. Behind the ivy-covered walls there exists a sense of detachment and isolation. The affiliation of students with their colleges does not carry the sense of pride that it once did—not if football teams, sororities, and academic standards can no longer confer what students consider to be a meaningful identity. Students everywhere in the world are carrying the brunt of the burden to bring about social change, to effect an egalitarian evolution. These grand ideas are adequately translated by students into personal commitments at a microscopic level. Students are coming to believe that whatever little thing they do in pursuing their commitment to be personally responsible in effecting change, they should do well. They are willing to learn how to think, but they want to see the relevance of thought to action.

Action is a cohering experience. Those who have worked and learned with others recognize that their efforts are rewarded by latent outcomes. Even when their action programs fail, they realize that they have grown in their ability to relate to others. They also recognize that they are not alone in experiencing alienation and wanting to do something about it.

Students are beginning to recognize that the most viable force for bringing about social reconstruction is the institution of the school. Education is the answer to problems of poverty, race relations, mental illness, and personal alienation. Many of the students who acknowledge this are working in other disciplines. They are willing, even eager, to participate in solving problems of inequality and neglect, but they refuse to move into education departments, to subject themselves to courses which are not only irrelevant, but also uninteresting.

Most students do not consider education as an area of commitment, although many are willing to view it as a place where one can qualify for a job. These are not the people who will make the major difference in channeling the power of education towards building a healthy world. Educationists are their own worst enemies insofar as they do everything in their power to limit the impact that schools can have. Students must be able to see that an educational career can be a self-fulfilling mission, and that the studies they undertake towards preparing themselves to do mankind's work is exciting business, and directly linked to their future task. This does not mean that every lecture or discussion in educational psychology must be implicitly tied to improving reading scores, or some other predetermined educational objective. But it must be tied to some process, the goal of which may always be unclear, but never really in doubt. We want students to be able to conceive of structures in which they can be integrated in a meaningful way, and we are certain that this kind of integration —of student with knowledge or with others—will provide the foundation for personally determined growth.

This book is intended to help students "turn on" to education. In many, if not most circles, there are sufficient educational technocrats and ivory-tower scholars to force departments of education to shy away from such a soft, abstract, and non-respectable process. Critics suggest that students are already too "turned on," that they need to be trained to act and think rationally. We don't wish to argue against rationality per se. But we do want to suggest that perhaps rationality has turned students off precisely because it did not include affective education. The emphasis upon cognitive education will be given a giant boost when it becomes linked to the concerns of the whole person. Foundations courses will, of course, continue to emphasize content, but, more important, they will begin to relate this content to student concerns.

The authors were asked to talk about their areas of interest and specialization in such a way as to excite students about the human potentialities in the study of education. Scholars, like students, are beginning to question the viability of an educational process unrelated to personal quests. They, too, wish to extend their own concerns about relevance beyond the limitations of traditional scholarly achievement. They want to know what ideas, knowledge, techniques, questions, and assumptions within each area are important, in the sense of being meaningfully related to student growth and commitment. Within this book they have done so, and in so doing endanger their institutional mandate. In the long run, we hope that our more academically-oriented critics will come to see that taking an applied view of knowledge reinvests the educational process with personal significance.

Although many students refuse to be drawn from their very predictable and comfortable routines, enough students have demanded to see some relationship between their academic efforts and their personal growth to shake the university bureaucrats out of their complacency. Students who cannot find this relationship in the university are willing to look elsewhere. There are not many alternatives outside the traditional institutions, but there are some. There are the Free Universities and the number of these is growing. There are the communes in Vermont, Colorado, New Mexico, California, and elsewhere. There are the urban collectives, where groups of students live and study together. There are the political organizations that are attempting to recruit workers and students alike to collective action to improve official local and national policy. And there is the random life of the streets, where young people shift in and out of the occupational market as their survival needs demand. Still, however, the university remains as the most viable place where young people may attempt to discover some meaningful existence.

Within the next ten or twenty years people on college campuses will make few major changes in the established structures of our society. In the schools of education we will still continue to produce bodies who will staff the public schools. And we will produce administrators able to keep the lid on, so that those who receive a very poor education will not cause us much difficulty because of it. But if this is to be the density of education in this country, at least those of us who wish to make changes will be able to say that we did not participate in maintaining the old functions of grinding out a legion of alienated students who then become alienated workers. Schools could change if teachers would dare to change them. But this requires commitment and wisdom. Wisdom is rare everywhere. It differs from knowledge insofar as it involves making sense of knowledge within the context of a life style. Wisdom is understanding how your knowledge fits into how you need to live your life. We think this is what students are searching for.

Wisdom cannot be taught or communicated as substantive knowledge can. Wisdom can only be demonstrated or seen in the personal adaptations of wise men. The persons whom I asked to contribute chapters for this book have shown me sparks of that kind of wisdom and I hoped that they would be able to infuse some of these sparks into their writing. To greater or lesser extents they have succeeded. They have succeeded where they have been able to explain their ideas in personally important ways. They have failed where they have retreated behind their substantive knowledge and did not show the personal context that generated these ideas. The reader will have to assess for himself the extent to which the authors were able to communicate themselves through their ideas.

Students seeking wisdom are seeking a sense of believing that one's activities are congruent with one's values and abilities. Most students who pass through programs in schools of education are not forced to worry about this congruency. They are satisfied to earn credits and degrees. Students who identify themselves as future teachers usually wonder about how they are going to do what they are required to do, rather than how to do what they must do to grow as persons and professionals.

Each author was asked to consider his area of specialization in terms of its relevance to human concerns rather than its relevance as an academic discipline. Academic disciplines are a set of conventions about how to gather and report information that is pertinent to a group of traditionally related problems. It has, for example, been a convention within the behavioral sciences to work on problems that were intellectually interesting, but which were irrelevant to the solution of human or social problems. The interest in the application of knowledge for human betterment is one aspect of humanism we emphasize in this book. We do not want to consider the dominant paradigms nor theoretical issues involved in understanding the structure of a field of study. We do not assume that understanding the conventional principles in the study of philosophy or history, for example, is adequate for understanding how to apply these principles to human problems. Our concern is with action, with involvement, and with commitment, and our responsibility to effect these goals is reflected in the chapters. The promise of producing a new generation of educators intensifies our commitment to our current task.

One way of looking at the problem the authors were asked to deal with is to consider the difference between the effectiveness of stating an idea and experiencing one. Experiencing ideas is another version of contemporary humanism, one that is central to the pedagogical task. By students infusing themselves and their own particular experiences with ideas into the writing, it was hoped that they might grasp a sense of the kind of thing they would need to do to understand. If we are talking about learning, for example, what experience can we suggest to help students experience learning? How can students know a bureaucracy, a value, an interpersonal approach to school organization, a curriculum structure, a counseling goal, a research process or the educational significance of a short story? We know that it is not enough just to tell them. We have been doing this for too long, and our "significant" contributions lay clearly written in students' notebooks without having made an imprint on the mind. We want to somehow convey experience: ours—the only one we know.

The humanistic approach to the study and practice of education is one which views students and their teachers as more important than their educational objectives. What teachers want for students, and what students come to believe they want for themselves, is defined by tradition and by the institutional conceptions of how people learn. Schools are places to teach people to fit into conventional social patterns. Students are assigned culturally valued roles in which they play out their lives on one or two notes.

Humanistic education views the child as a potential orchestra, and encourages him to experiment with every instrument and every theme that is in him. Anything less is to regard the child and education as limited to that which we are sure we can produce with our current resources. This conception of education diminishes the quality of teaching and learning to the lowest common denominator.

Schools have evolved into an institutional arrangement bent upon preserving itself against the discord of too many instruments playing in opposite directions. Schools are run by a bureaucracy committed to maintaining the system in equilibrium. It is difficult to accommodate disparate student drives and maintain this equilibrium at the same time; therefore, it becomes convenient to shut off human emotion during the education process and rely exclusively upon the intellect. Education has too long been almost wholly rational, without any consideration of the emotions and how these can be linked to learning. Students may "learn" about democracy, trust, truth, or society without ever being permitted to experience them. Experiences involve feelings, and feelings have been traditionally denied legitimacy as educational tools. Our stabilizing social structures—law, government, the family, the school—cannot endure an educational process where students learn in a cognitive as well as an affective manner. These stabilizing structures are maintained because people who live in terms of them believe and accept them and resist the anxiety of doubt. Persons appear to prefer order to disorder, conformity to nonconformity, law to justice, comfort to pain, and being given answers to seeking them. They also appear to prefer bondage to freedom. It is easier to believe in the wisdom of tradition and convention than to be set adrift to discover one's own sense of truth, order and personal fulfillment.

The problem for the old patterns of education and socialization is to be viable enough to resist all attempts to question their legitimacy. For once our educational processes are questioned, the beliefs produced by these processes are threatened. Can we afford to have students question democracy, efficiency, work, our moral codes? If we cannot, it is only because we have never known these values as truths. We have only "learned" them as patterns which others respect, and we are taught to respect those others because they are our significant carriers of tradition.

The sense of personal commitment comes not from evaluating the content of ideas, but from evaluating the process of learning about them. If democracy as we know it is to be a viable condition of social life, it must be experienced. Anyone who has lived under both a totalitarian and democratic regime can communicate the experience of the differences that he has learned. I am talking about a way of learning about the world—a humanistic method which leads to humanistic outcomes, like acceptance and cooperation and resistance of all attempts to dehumanize. If education is a preparation for life, then students should have the opportunity to experience as many forms of group life as it is possible to stimulate within a classroom. If a belief in democracy emerges from that educational experience it will be permanent, because the whole person was involved in the learning process. Do we trust the foundation values of our truths enough to permit students to learn them rather than simply accept them?

History will surely show that the attacks upon our way of life from within our own society were not upon our goals, but our process of attaining them.

The process of education as we are best able to describe it in a sociological and philosophical frame of reference, aims to produce workers and moral citizens. Technology is pressed into continuous service to do old things in new and more efficient ways. Teaching machines, moveable partitions, indirect lighting, videotapes, and a long run of other technological innovations have not brought us any closer to a humanistic concept of learning. Institutions of learning seem to conceive of students as sheep and the teacher as shepherd. In our ghetto schools, teaching has been informally defined as discipline, as the control of behavior, and our most operational innovations are those which relate to controlling groups and individuals. In our suburban schools we have allowed competition for grades to ravage the spirit of education while we improve our facilities to allocate depersonalized high school students to impersonal college environments.

While the institution of the school appears to be approaching a state of monolithic impersonality, beyond the control of either the participants or the community, we university educators go about the business of preparing teachers to staff the classrooms. We provide them with a set of teaching tools and a way of evaluating student needs and student achievement. But we do not challenge our education students to question the assumptions that underlie the teaching process they are about to serve. We do not encourage them to combine commitment to teach with commitment to change the whole concept of teaching and learning as we know it. We may teach them, for example, how to objectify the behaviors they wish to produce in the classroom, but we do not encourage them to question the possibility of not having any objectives at all. We have our students study education as if certain goals and means were somehow inviolable and they often come away discouraged because we haven't clearly taught them how to conceptualize either goals or means meaningfully. When these new teachers step before the class for the first time, they usually do so with anxiety, uncertain of how to accomplish specific teaching goals. As they look about them and pick up the first cues they perceive to help them reduce their discomfort, they are then well on their way to perpetuating the status quo.

The humanistic approach to training teachers can be a model for teaching children, and teachers will be able to do it only if they understand their own experiences and how these have changed them, as well as how they have been educated. Teacher trainees are taught to believe that theory can be distinguished from practice and most of their criticisms about the way they were prepared to conduct a classroom are related to this lack of integration between these principles. These frustrated and angry disciples of our training programs assume that college instructors failed them by not illustrating better this linkage between theory and practice. Within the present structure of educational programs, however, affective processes are not demonstrated. Teaching is a humanistic as well as a technological process, and if we demonstrate this process, our teacher trainees will experience it. Then we will begin to close the imaginary gap between theory and practice.

The assumptions underlying educational process will be stated and questioned again and again in the following pages. The major assumption which humanistic education categorically rejects states that learning is an interaction between knowledge and the mind. Although this view of learning may lead to many levels of conceptual thinking, it does not provide the student with a way to experience meaning or joy in his learning. This, too, is the goal of education. It is the only objective that we can confidently predict will permit the school to play a significant role in approaching the major humanistic tasks of our time.

A SPECIAL NOTE TO STUDENTS

Many of you, perhaps most, are headed towards a classroom where you will be, for a short time, the most significant person in the child's world. What you give him, what you have to give him, may constitute the important catalyst in his life. In an age where education is the only elevator to the fortieth floor, your sense of responsibility may be the difference between his riding or taking the stairs.

It all boils down to a teacher's sense of responsibility. If our courses bore you, if we fail in our efforts to make you see, and even appreciate, the significance of our knowledge, if we are unable to show you the relationship between knowledge and professional educational life, then we've blessed many of you with a mediocre career. It is unlikely that you will be able to give to your students any more than you have received from us.

This book tries to communicate the relationship between ideas and persons who work with them. The authors you will read were chosen because they are persons who have either discovered or are close to discovering what it means to be separate from one's professional responsibility, and are in the process of integrating that responsibility with their personal commitments. Most of the authors are deeply involved, at some cost to their academic productivity, in issues which concern them as citizens. They are engaged in setting up programs to make the university exist on a more relevant plane, in programs to improve the quality of education in nonwhite communities, and in a personal plan to relate to students and colleagues in a humanistic and socially responsible manner.

In each of their separate chapters the authors were asked to do two things: communicate both what they know and what they personally see as the value of knowing it. If they do not communicate the importance of their knowledge, then they will not have communicated their knowledge. If they do not communicate a sense of the relevance of their studies to the important issues of the day, they will not have communicated themselves.

Sometimes a person can strain himself trying to excite or delight, inform or reform his students, and he fails to establish contact. In this case, the question you, as students, need to ask of yourselves is: Am I open to the study of education or am I simply passing through on the way to a degree, marriage, or just a job? If the latter is the case, and we should fail to inspire you, at least we will have been true to our own sense of responsibility. This is the best we can manage. We cannot attack your motivations in the same way that you can challenge ours. After all, you as the consumer of our teaching have the right to reject the product. We only hope that rejection comes after, if it comes at all, rather than before the fact of our teaching attempts.

The chapters in this book are divided in line with the content specialties of the authors. We could have chosen snappy titles to dress up the book in new wrapping, but if we aren't communicating anything new, you would know it. The fact is, the persons writing these chapters are specialists in specific areas of study. The value of this book is precisely that persons representing diverse interests can come together at this point of considering how one communicates interest and a sense of relevance about the study and practice of education.

We ask you to consider a new concept of the study of education, although we realize most of you have never been exposed to the old, except, perhaps, in the way you yourselves have been taught. If you have no complaints about your own educational history, then we have to ask you to consider the plight of those who were not as well trained to accept what they received in good faith, and also consider the crisis of our time. This crisis is represented by the confrontation of those who receive with those who give. Whether the product be values, knowledge, or economic goods, persons are no longer buying in good faith. On the campus and on the city streets the consumer is wary and impelled to question the merchandise. Is it worth anything to me, or will it just get in the way of my social, personal, or economic development? You as students have the responsibility to improve the content of the courses you take and the books you read by rejecting what does not meet your standards. We are all students and we are all teachers, and the best—perhaps the only—thing we really have to offer each other is the way we, from our varied perspectives, have experienced learning. This is what is new about our approach. It is new because now we are talking about the way we experience the world of education, not the standard way that we view it through the perspectives of our disciplines. This approach may not be new at all to many of you. You may recognize, in those teachers who you remember as being important in your lives, the quality of being involved in what was being communicated. You will probably remember that you were given an experience and not cold, impersonal facts or ideas. It is knowledge enriched by experience and refined by human decisions that is important for us as persons, not scholars, to know, that awakens in us our sense of dedication and commitment. The authors have made their presentations according to these kinds of decisions. It makes their professional lives sensible to them, and hopefully, it will make their professional lives sensible to you.

1
philosophy and education

Thomas Robischon

TOM ROBISCHON, in my opinion, is an integrated man. More than any of us, his writing reflects who he is. This is a difficult thing to do: to successfully integrate oneself so that the professional and the personal come together. Most of us are struggling to achieve this. Tom, I believe has already made it.

Tom is very much in the "movement," and he is also a very fine scholar and writer. He is the ideal person to start us off. As I read Tom's chapter I began to understand what experience has to do with understanding, which is what I think humanistic education is all about. Tom has thrown himself wholeheartedly, as usual, into living his beliefs. So take my word for it, as you read through his writing, trying to get a grip on what he is saying, that Tom comes to his conclusions and understanding more from the kind of life he has lived than from the works he has read. He has learned what ideas mean by living them, and this is what he proposes for others. His personal philosophy is as integrated as he is, bringing together the world of knowledge and the world of intuition, the world of meaning and the world of personal commitment.

Tom's humanism is all encompassing. It ranges from the need to understand to the need to get involved, including the need to bring all parts of oneself and one's world into harmonious congruity. You will get a sense of all of his beliefs and commitments as you go through the pages. You will understand, if you do your part, what it means to think, do, and be philosophy. You are charged with the responsibility to make sense of philosophy within a personal, rather than an academic framework. Many people study philosophy but very few bring it to life in the way that he suggests, or in the way that he does.

Tom's career is very much in jeopardy, as are the careers of most academics who presume to live what they teach. Hopefully the university can become a place where people like Tom can survive; and if it does, then it will be because people like Tom made it possible. If you should understand what he is saying in his chapter and if this kind of thinking has any impact upon the academic community, the university may someday be transformed from the sterile bureaucracy it has become into the humanistic learning center that people like Tom envision.

Unlike many of his colleagues who see only that the American university is doomed, Tom retains an uncanny optimism. This too should come through in his writing. Many of his colleagues treat him like a "token nut" that every department needs to maintain their image. This would be enough to demoralize most of us, and it has taken its toll of Tom. Nonetheless, he works always to the point of fatigue to bring his students far beyond the point where most of his colleagues leave them. As he says, he sees the human and academic condition as gravely deprived; but always, in the same breath he reminds us that the human condition is vastly improveable. All it takes is to believe, to understand, and to do. In this chapter, the groundwork for all three is laid before us.

Is not the public itself the greatest of all sophists, training up young and old, men and women alike, into the most accomplished specimens of the character it desires to produce? . . . And I have said nothing of the most powerful engines of persuasion which the masters in the school of wisdom bring to bear when words have no effect. As you know, they punish the recalcitrant with disfranchisement, fines, and death . . . How could the private teaching of any individual sophist avail in counteracting theirs? It would be great folly even to try; for no instruction aiming at an ideal contrary to the training they give has ever produced, or ever will produce, a different type of character—on the level, that is to say, of common humanity; and you may be sure that, in the present state of society, any character that escapes and comes to good can only have been saved by some miraculous interposition.

Plato, *The Republic*

There are those who say Plato is as right today as he was in his own day over 2000 years ago. Perhaps you are one of these people. Can "common humanity" be educated according to an ideal that is different from what their society wants? Is it only by a "miraculous interposition" that those few characters escape and come to good? And what about you? Do you consider yourself one of those who has escaped and "come to good," or are you among the "common humanity" who have been educated by the "greatest of all sophists" according to *its* desires? And where do you stand on these questions as they bear on your future role as a teacher?

These are ancient questions, and they have an urgency about them today. Education (as formal schooling) has never been as widespread as it is today, and probably has never been so widely questioned. And the questions are Plato's: Must education for most young people be an indoctrinating (and thereby impersonal and alienating) experience? Can we hope for only a few at any time to escape this (by some miraculous intervention)? What do you think it would be like for you to be educated? What can we reasonably hope for in education?

Let us begin with a typical philosophical ploy by asking a question about meanings: What do we mean by "dehumanized, irrelevant, alienating education"? What do we mean by "humanizing" education? Does it strike you as odd that we should be talking about *humanizing* education? Of all human endeavors, is there any other that has so often and so widely been identified with man's humanity? Education is of humanity, by humanity, and for humanity, isn't it?

But now, another philosophical question confronts us. To answer the question about the humanity of education (or the lack of it) we are going to have to first answer the question "what is education?" And this question has a deceptive look. Like so many other questions of this type ("What is freedom?" "What is truth?" "What is love?") it looks like a simple question with a simple answer. But if you were to ask the next five people you encounter, "What is education?" I should consider it unusual if you found (1) that what they say raises no further questions in your mind; or, even if you found their answers satisfactory, (2) that any two of them were in agreement. And I venture to say this would be true of educators as well as laymen.

Let's try five philosophers of education whom I will choose at random as if they were the next five people I were to encounter. Here comes William K. Frankena who tells me that the term "education" in this question is ambiguous. Before he can answer my question he must know what it is I am asking about. Am I asking about the *activity* of educating carried on by teachers and others? Am I asking about the *process* of being (or becoming) educated which goes on in students? Am I asking about the *result* of the activity and the process? Or am I asking about the discipline or field of inquiry that studies the activity, process, and result, and is taught in schools of education?

Already we can see the question is a bit less simple than we thought. But Frankena now can give us his answer. If we are asking about the activity of educating when we ask "What is education?" Frankena would say it "is the use of certain kinds of methods to foster excellences or desirable dispositions..."[1] Do any further questions occur to you? I find there is one important question I have to ask: *Which* "excellences or desirable dispositions"? Frankena's reply would be that a philosophy of education will tell us which excellences and dispositions to foster. But *whose* philosophy of education? And why that one?

Frankena has described three historical philosophies of education— Aristotle's, Kant's and Dewey's. What do they tell us the excellences and dispositions are, or should be? They tell us a lot of things; but, unfortunately for our purposes, a lot of different things. Here are some as Frankena summarizes them:

> Aristotle and Kant both distinguish intellectual and moral excellences, Aristotle exalting the first and Kant the second. Dewey attacks the distinction.... They also distinguish theoretical and practical reason, Aristotle giving primacy to the first and Kant to the second. Again, Dewey attacks the distinction.... The three have different criteria of what is right. ...In his conception of intellectual excellence Aristotle exalts the kind of intuitively and demonstratively certain knowledge in mathematics, physics, and metaphysics. Dewey denies that we can have this kind of certainty or should even seek for it.... Kant largely agrees with Dewey.... Aristotle says that it is happiness...contemplation, in direct opposition to Kant, who says that it is good will. Against both, Dewey insists that

---

[1] William K. Frankena, *Three Historical Philosophies of Education* (Chicago: Scott, Foresman and Co., 1965), p. 6.

neither contemplation or good will is unconditionally good—for him there is no disposition or activity that can be said always to shine by its own light regardless of its setting.... Kant, however, talks as if the mere possession of certain *dispositions* (i.e., "perfections") is the ultimate end, whereas Aristotle and Dewey insist that the end must be certain kinds of intrinsically desirable *activities* or *experiences*.[2]

Even if these philosophers accepted Frankena's answer to our question, it is clear they still would differ in some basic ways.

Let's ask some more. Paul Arthur Schilpp says education is "the process of guided development (growth) of the individual (and society) in his rational, moral, and spiritual capacities."[3] George Kneller says much the same thing when he says education is "any act or experience that has a formative effect on the mind, character, or physical appearance of an individual," and, in a technical sense, education is handing down a cultural heritage, values, skills, knowledge, by means of schools and other agencies.[4] Kingsley Price says "education" refers to the process of deliberately transmitting the arts and sciences and of fostering contributions to them.[5] And Louis Arnaud Reid describes it as "a purposive activity towards ends which are (rightly or wrongly) deemed to be good."[6]

Reid's parenthetical "rightly or wrongly" suggests further questions. Whether it is dispositions, excellences, growth development, cultural heritage, arts, sciences, values, skills, or knowledge being referred to, we have to go on to ask: *Which* dispositions and excellences? Growth *of what* and *for what*? *Which* values, sciences, skills and knowledge? *Whose* cultural heritage and arts?

We don't seem to have gotten very far. We set out to clarify what "dehumanized" (and "humanizing") education is, and found we had to ask what education is. And this led to further questions! But before you give up, I wonder if there is something we might see now that we did not see before, not just about these answers to our question, but about education. In asking who is to decide which dispositions, excellences, values, skills, and so on are to be fostered in education (assuming that *is* what education is), we can go on to ask whether the students should decide any of this and, if so, to what extent. It's a question I am sure you have heard many times. Do

2 Frankena, *Three Historical Philosophies,* pp. 193–94.
3 Paul Arthur Schilpp, "The Distinctive Function of 'Philosophy of Education' as a Discipline," *Educational Theory* 3, no. 3 (July 1953): 261.
4 George F. Kneller, *Foundations of Education* (New York: John Wiley, 1963), p. 64.
5 Kingsley Price, "What Is a Philosophy of Education?" *Educational Theory* 6, no. 2 (April 1956): 88.
6 Louis Arnaud Reid, *Philosophy and Education* (New York: Random House, 1962), p. 17.

you think that most people who have raised (and answered!) the question have seen it as part of a philosophical question that goes to the very nature of education?

But other questions arise. I said earlier that questions like "What is education?" have a deceptively simple look. Then I went on to illustrate how you can get a variety of answers to questions like this by showing how five philosophers have answered the question. But there is something else about this type of question. Just what are we asking for in such a question? The form of the question suggests we are asking about a fact: what in fact is education? Did you think that is what these philosophers were telling you when they said what they did? Why ask philosophers about facts when there are social scientists to ask? And if it is a factual question we are asking, why did the philosophers come up with so many different answers? Furthermore, while I did not include everything they said, no evidence was cited by them for their answers, something we might have expected from someone making factual statements.

Well, if it is not a factual answer, what kind of answer is it? To answer that, we have to decide what kind of a question it is. (Don't despair! We are working our way out of the woods.) What is it we are asking for when we ask "What is education?" We cannot expect to receive a clear answer to that if we are not clear what the question is, can we? And so, when we consider the answers philosophers (and others) give to questions of this sort, we often cannot be sure how they have interpreted the question.

Let us assume that philosophers do *not* think they are answering a factual question. Then what do they think they are doing? This too is not always clear! Until they tell us what reasons they have for us to accept their answers, we do not know what kind of answer they think they are giving. And many do not give us these reasons. Let's look again at Frankena's answer. He noted that the *term* "education" was ambiguous, and showed how it could be used in four different ways to refer to four different *things*. When he went on to give us four answers corresponding to these different uses of the word, it seems clear to me that he was not giving us just four different meanings of the word "education," nor was he giving us analyses of four different *concepts* of education. He seemed to be telling us *what education is* as an activity, a process, a result, and an academic discipline. But isn't that a factual description? But why should he as a philosopher be doing this when we have the social scientists to tell us these things? We seem to be back where we started!

The same questions can be raised about the answers given by Schilpp, Kneller, and Reid. Price, however, does something else. He begins his answer by talking about "education." By putting it in quotes, he is talking about the *word* "education," and so he goes on to say it "refers to. . ." But if that is all Price is doing, we still can ask why philosophers, more than anyone else, should spend their time telling us what words refer to.

PHILOSOPHY AS AN ACTIVITY

There is much more to this question of what the business of philosophy is. I raise it here in order to illustrate some of the questions that can be raised about the answers philosophers (and others) give to a question like "What is education?" But I want to do something more than that. I want to suggest that there is a serious philosophical question here, a question that, while not strictly about facts, still is not independent of the facts, but in its greater import seeks an *understanding* of those facts. In this respect, philosophy is not a body or source of facts at all, but rather a way of looking at facts, at what goes on around us. But that doesn't get us very far. We still have to know what that way of looking is. Also, which facts do we look at? What kind of understanding is sought through philosophizing?

Let us return to the philosophers and the answers they gave to my question. While they differed to some degree, I wonder if you detected a rather remarkable agreement among them. Reid's answer gives us one hint: "a purposive activity towards ends which are (rightly or wrongly) deemed to be good." Frankena spoke of "excellences or desirable dispositions." Schilpp referred to "guided development (growth) of the individual (and society)." Kneller spoke of "a formative effect." And Price spoke of the arts and sciences. I wonder if you see what I do in these answers? Do you think any of these philosophers would include in their answers to the question "What is education?" aims and purposes that they deemed to be *bad*? Reid's parenthetical remark suggests that a person may be wrong in what he deems to be a good activity in education. But do you think that a person would continue to hold that view if he *knew* he was wrong? Would anyone telling you what he thinks education is, tell you that it is intended to be something bad? Does it seem consistent to you to say that a person has been educated (meaning not just having gone to school, but really educated) and that he is none the better for it?[7] When we think of education doing what we want it to do—as an ideal, norm, or standard—education seems to have something to do with bettering a person, with making him in some sense (and of course *which* sense is all important) a better person. And even though our educational activity may not achieve this, or achieve it only in part, do we not still *want* our education to do this?

If you are willing to grant this, then I think I can explain at long last why I would identify education with man's humanity, and why I suggested it might be odd to speak of "humanizing" education (even though it may turn out that that is what we have to do). If we are talking about

---

[7] See R. S. Peters, *Ethics and Education* (Glenview, Ill.: Scott, Foresman, 1966), p. 3.

bettering human beings when we talk about educating them, then that means to me deliberately bettering them as *human* beings. It may be one of humanity's distinctive marks. But whether you are willing to go that far or not, I hope you will agree that something very much like this is what we might identify as the humanistic element in education. And if we can agree to that, we can also then see what we are talking about when we speak of a "dehumanized" education: an education that is not only not bettering people, but that is in some distinct way harming them, or making them worse.

EDUCATION AS A HUMAN ENDEAVOR

Unless I am off on some trip of my own, we seem to have arrived at something like the following. As a human endeavor, education at its best seeks to make better human beings out of us (and we would want to add, our society, too). But what "better" means here, what constitutes making a human being (and a society) better—and the equally important question of what means we use to achieve this aim—is not so easily agreed upon. Different people at different times have answered these questions differently. Is there any reason to believe they will not continue to do so? So too, if we talk about our failure in education to better people, if we say we are dehumanizing people, we say we are not only failing to make people better, we are making them worse. But what "worse" means here, what constitutes making a human being worse—and the equally important question how this is done when all along we think we are making them better—is not so easily agreed upon. (Perhaps you detected still other questions: Is the betterment of persons always a betterment of society? Is the converse true? If they differ, how do we resolve the conflict?)

Still, the meaning of these words apart, there are a lot of people—in and out of education—who are disturbed about what they call dehumanized, irrelevant, alienated education, and who have spoken eloquently and at length about it. But no matter how many there are, and how well they have spoken, if you do not sense these wrongs for yourself, it is of little use to speak about what education could, or should, be. Before we can do that in anything other than an academic way (in the bad sense of that word), *you* must see that possibility—and that includes the need—of education being some other way. And you will see that possibility only if you have seen education in a different way from that which your socialization has led you to see it.

EDUCATION AS SOCIALIZATION

Edgar Z. Friedenberg has described socialization as "the systematic extinction of alternatives, the reduction of the potentially unassimilable view or disruptive thought to the level of the literally *unthinkable*."[8] Its complementary function is indoctrination, but because we don't like that word we call it "transmitting our cultural heritage."

> Education...seems to consist primarily in communicating just this information (what may be thought or must be thought, what alternatives society will allow and even encourage); it does not seek to convince but to indicate subtly but clearly which interpretation of reality will be tolerated. Both repression and indoctrination work toward the same end: increased social stability on terms set by those currently in power and consistent with the moral tradition they endorse; at the cost of alienating us from those of our feelings and insights that might impede the process.[9]

Does that sound at all like the schooling process you have been through? Does it come as a shock to be told that your education has been largely a manipulative process designed to shape and control you? Are you surprised to learn that the noble educational function of transmitting the culture is in reality a prolonged indoctrination?

Perhaps my questions display an ignorance of the level of awareness of you who belong to another generation. In teaching experience, however, I have often encountered something akin to shock when I have suggested such things to my students. And so I find myself wishing at this point that I could hear from you. It makes little sense to talk about humanizing education if you do not think education needs humanizing. On the other hand, why should I bore you with a philosophical discussion of dehumanized, alienated education when you are already painfully aware of it, and may be among its walking wounded? Therefore if you find the following paragraphs of dubious worth, I hope you will give them no more attention than they deserve. But it does make good philosophical sense to be sure your reader has a reasonably clear idea of the problem you are addressing yourself to, even if he may doubt how real the problem is.

It strikes me that a strong case can be made for the proposition that education in most places, and at most times, has as a major aim the socialization of the young. (Not all the young, of course, only a selected portion. Not even in the United States have we been able to accomplish it with all.) I doubt that few students of education would argue with this. What they would differ about is their conception of this socializing, and whether it can be justified. Some claim that all cultures depend upon socialization as the means of maintaining themselves, a process of conscious and unconscious assimilation and internalization in the young of the ac-

---

[8] Edgar Z. Friedenberg, "Current Patterns of Generational Conflict," *Journal of Social Issues* 25, no. 2 (April 1969): 30.

[9] Friedenberg, "Current Patterns of Generational Conflict," p. 30.

cumulated knowledge, beliefs, values, and mores of their culture. These would be the dispositions and excellences Frankena speaks of, the "ends which are (rightly or wrongly) deemed to be good," as Reid puts it, that a culture would build its education around. Burton R. Clark has described how formal schooling became involved in this:

> ...formal schooling became a necessity as the home and the community became ineffectual, even incompetent, in training the young for adulthood through informal contact. A new class of cultural agents—the teachers of the commoners—grew up. The changing nature of knowledge and work brought the children of the common man into the schoolhouse and gave to the schools a greatly broadened and deepened role in cultural transmission and continuity.[10]

"Socializing," "transmitting the culture"—however you describe this function of schooling—may have bought our society stability and continuity (though this is apt to be overstated by both those who find this function desirable and those who do not). But it is increasingly being questioned whether we are paying an acceptable price for this stability and continuity. Irrelevance and alienation are the two most often heard statements of that price. There are many accounts of what this means in concrete schooling experiences, and many descriptions of the connection between the irrelevance and alienation and the socializing function of the schools. I find the account of it in the 1962 *Port Huron Statement* of the Students for a Democratic Society still relevant, even though minor qualifications might now be called for:

> ...students are breaking the crust of apathy and overcoming the inner alienation that remain the defining characteristics of American college life. If student movements for change are rarities still on the campus scene, what is commonplace there? The real campus, the familiar campus, is a place of private people, engaged in their notorious "inner emigration." It is a place of commitment to business-as-usual, getting ahead, playing it cool. It is a place of mass affirmation of the Twist, but mass reluctance toward the controversial public stance. Rules are accepted as "inevitable," bureaucracy as "just circumstances," irrelevance as "scholarship," selflessness as "martyrdom," politics as "just another way to make people, and an unprofitable one, too."
>
> Almost no students value activity as a citizen. Passive in public, they are hardly more idealistic in arranging their private lives.... There is not much willingness to take risks (not even in business), no setting of dangerous goals, no real conception of personal identity except one manufactured in the image of others, no real urge for personal fulfillment except to be almost as successful as the very successful people. Attention is being paid

[10] Burton R. Clark, *Educating The Expert Society,* quoted in David A. Goslin, *The School in Contemporary Society* (Glenview, Ill.: Scott, Foresman, 1965), p. 3.

to social status...much too, is paid to academic status. But neglected generally is real intellectual status, the personal cultivation of the mind...[11]

There have been changes, of course. While a study of student protest in 1967–68 showed that only about 2 percent on a given campus could be described as "activists," they could draw on an additional 8 to 10 percent depending on the issues, and these numbers are rising steadily, though not spectacularly.[12] A Gallup Poll in May 1969 reported a new, highly vocal breed of student on the campus, who speaks like this:

> We are disenchanted with the ideologies of the adult population today, with their belief that a large Buick says something important about one's self. The urge of people for self-aggrandizement repels us. Furthermore, we don't go along with the "hard work mystique"—the notion that if one works hard he is therefore a good person.[13]

But still apathy and alienation remain. The *Port Huron Statement* claims that the extracurricular and the curricular organization of our schools reinforce one another in developing these attitudes.

> ...apathy is not simply an attitude; it is a product of social institutions, and of the structure and organization of higher education itself. The extracurricular life is ordered according to *in loco parentis* theory, which ratifies the Administration as the moral guardian of the young. The accompanying "let's pretend" theory of student extracurricular affairs validates student government as a training center for those who want to spend their lives in political pretense, and discourages initiative from more articulate, honest, and sensitive students. The bounds and style of controversy are delimited before controversy begins. The university "prepares" the student for "citizenship" through perpetual rehearsals and, usually, through emasculation of what creative spirit there is in the individual.[14]

THE COSTS OF AN EDUCATION

What then are the advantages of going to college? (And this question, like others we are raising, could apply to other levels of schooling, could they not?) A professor of education at Michigan State University, W. Harold

---

11 Students for a Democratic Society, *The Port Huron Statement* (n.p., n.d.), pp. 7–8.

12 Richard E. Peterson, *The Scope of Organized Student Protest in 1967–1968* (Princeton, N.J.: Educational Testing Service, 1968), p. 39.

13 "Today's Student New Breed in 6 Respects," *Los Angeles Times,* 26 May 1969, p. 6.

14 *The Port Huron Statement,* p. 8.

Grant, may have been doing something more than kidding when he pointed out that only one of every four students in college gets a degree; that there are twice as many suicides among college students as among the general population; that college students have fifty percent more emotional problems than the general public; that there is little or no correlation between grades in college and later success; and that at least one person has claimed that if a student invested the equivalent of the costs of four years of college, he would have larger lifetime earnings than if he attended college. Professor Grant summed it up this way: By attending college, you have a better chance of

> Becoming a dropout;
> Going crazy;
> Killing yourself;
> Learning irrelevant things; and
> Losing money.[15]

Speaking specifically of the curricular organization of our schools, the SDS *Port Huron Statement* brings us back to our question, "What is education?"

> The academic world is founded in a teacher-student relation analogous to the parent-child relation which characterizes *in loco parentis*. Further, academia includes a radical separation of student from the material of study. That which is studied, the social reality, is "objectified" to sterility, dividing the student from life—just as he is restrained in active involvement by the deans controlling student government. The specialization of function and knowledge, admittedly necessary to our complex technological and social structure, has produced an exaggerated compartmentalization of study and understanding. This has contributed to: an overly parochial view, by faculty, of the role of its research and scholarship; a discontinuous and truncated understanding, by students, of the surrounding social order; a loss of personal attachment, by nearly all, to the worth of study as a humanistic enterprise.[16]

Our question "what is education?" is then asking for something more than what actually goes on in our schools. Important as that is—and I have given a partial account of that part that so many today find unsatisfactory— we are looking for something more. We need to know the facts, but we also need to have understanding of those facts. Now I am going to suggest that in order for us to understand what goes on in education, we need to be

---

15 "Q.E.D.—The Advantages of the Higher Learning," *The Chronicle of Higher Education,* 21 April 1969, p. 1.

16 *The Port Huron Statement,* pp. 8–9.

aware of its possibilities at any given time, of alternatives to what it is. We need to know not only what it is and has been, but how it might be related to human purpose, to *your* purposes, in new, more satisfying ways.

But to do this I must ask of you something that you may not have done too much thus far in your schooling. (Again I feel the need to hear from you, for you may be one who has done this a great deal.) I am asking you to reflect on your educational experience—what you have done, what you are doing now and planning to do—as part of your values and purposes, and that means your choices. I am not thinking so much about those immediate, short-range purposes and choices, usually of a vocational or practical nature, important as they can be. I refer to the deeper purposes and choices that we associate with a philosophy of life, with ideas of what a good life for you might be, your life worth living.

In doing this it would be appropriate, I think, to begin with Jean Paul Sartre. Sartre is concerned with that condition we sometimes call apathy. It is the experience of something wrong, perhaps profoundly wrong, but accompanied by a lack of commitment to do anything about it. Sartre speaks of the person who can not even imagine that he can exist in a different situation:

> It is on the day that we can conceive of a different state of affairs that a new light falls on our troubles and our suffering and that we *decide* that these are unbearable. A worker in 1830 is capable of revolting if his salary is lowered, for he easily conceives of a situation in which his wretched standard of living would be not as low as the one which is about to be imposed on him. But he does not represent his sufferings to himself as unbearable; he adapts himself to them not through resignation but because he lacks the education and reflection necessary for him to conceive of a social state in which these sufferings would not exist. Consequently *he* does not act. . . . He suffers without considering his suffering and without conferring value upon it. To suffer and to *be* are one and the same for him. . . . Therefore this suffering cannot be in itself a *motive* for his acts. Quite the contrary, *it is after he has formed the project of changing the situation that it will appear intolerable to him.* [my emphasis] This means that he will have had to give himself room, to withdraw in relation to it, and will have to have effected a double nihilation: on the one hand, he must posit an ideal state of affairs as a pure *present* nothingness; on the other hand, he must posit the actual situation as nothingness in relation to his state of affairs. He will have to conceive of a happiness attached to his class as a pure possible—that is, presently as a certain nothingness—and on the other hand, he will return to the present situation in order to illuminate it in the light of this nothingness and in order to nihilate it in turn by declaring: "I *am not* happy."[17]

[17] Jean Paul Sartre, *Being and Nothingness* (New York: Philosophical Library, 1956; and London: Methuen and Co. Ltd., 1957), pp. 435–36. Reprinted by permission of the publishers.

Sartre is saying here that no factual state can by itself motivate an action. Facts are not enough. (Sartre distinguishes action—human action—from events, occurrences, simple reactions, none of which is characterized by freedom, choice, human purpose and projects, or valuing.) No simple awareness of what is the case, of the facts, can by itself tell you what is lacking, what is missing; or, put another way, of what could be, of possibility. There must be something more. But what is it?

EDUCATION AND FREEDOM

Sartre says it is human consciousness which is the source of that "nihilation" he speaks of that is, in turn, the source of human action by which we modify the world, arrange means in view of an end and produce anticipated results. It is by

> ...a pure wrenching away from himself and the world that the worker can posit his suffering as unbearable suffering and consequently can *make of it the motive* for his revolutionary action. This implies for consciousness the permanent possibility of effecting a rupture with its own past, or wrenching itself away from its past so as to be able to consider it in the light of a nonbeing and so as to be able to confer on it the meaning which *it has* in terms of the project of a meaning which it *does not have*. Under no circumstances can the past in any way by itself produce *an act.* . . . In fact as soon as one attributes to consciousness this negative power with respect to the world and itself, as soon as the nihilation forms an integral part of the *positing* of an end, we must recognize that the indispensable and fundamental condition of all action is the freedom of the acting being.[18]

So it is freedom we are talking about. The human act, Sartre says, is the free act. But not everything humans do is an action, so not everything we do is free. And not even all those times when we think we are free.

It will be the theme of the rest of this paper that your education thus far, and the education you will be expected to participate in as a teacher, are not only *not* designed to help students achieve the awareness and reflective ability that Sartre here associates with the freedom of the acting being, but that both of these educations usually have as their result something quite the opposite. It is the dehumanizing in education that makes us poorer persons than we are and might be.

I am confident that I can set all of this forth, but I am not so confident that this will mean anything more for you than an academic exercise. In the end, you have to make the "double nihilation" Sartre speaks of. You have to see how education (ideally) might be, and see it as "a pure

[18] Ibid.

present nothingness;" but also (the second nihilation) you have to see your present education, including the education you are being trained for, also as a nothingness. This, I suggest, is philosophizing, something you may have been doing for some time now. William James once described philosophy as the art of developing alternatives. What I am claiming here is that your education has not helped you to learn how to do this. You may at times have caught glimpses of alternatives; you may even at times have been able to bring these to an illumination of your present. But largely, I daresay, it has been for you, as for so many others, an exercise in futility. Somewhere along the line the vital nerve has been cut between the illumination and the act. A sense of frustration, of alienation, of lack of integration ensues. It is my hope that the nerve can be restored; that the blocks can be removed and action once more turned on, as we say. For it is in our natures to be active, not inactive and hungup. The SDS *Port Huron Statement* suggests one way is which your schools have failed you:

> Students leave college somewhat more "tolerant" than when they arrived, but basically unchallenged in their values and political orientations. With administrators ordering the institution, and faculty the curriculum, the student learns by this isolation to accept later forms of minority control. The real function of the educational system—as opposed to its more rhetorical function of "searching for truth"—is to impart the key information and styles that will help the student get by, modestly but comfortably, in the big society beyond.[19]

I would like to suggest—with some diffidence—that perhaps this is where you find yourself in your education. To what extent would you say your education has enabled you to conceive of situations other than those that have confronted you? I am not speaking of imagining or dreaming. Sartre is speaking not only of seeing possibilities, but of *making them your project*. Not only must you see how things could be other than what they are. The very seeing of this must be turned against things as they are (or, as Sartre says, it must "nihilate" what is now into nothingness and thereby illuminate it). You must give value to what you see. To make the possibility your project is *to choose it*, to make it part of you, in a far deeper and more committed way than simply seeing it, reading about it, or being told it. But how much of your education would you say has become a part of you? If what you have seen as possibility is not relevant to you and your condition, can you make it your project? If what you have seen is largely or exclusively theoretical, can you relate it to your practice by choosing it for yourself? If what you have seen is a cognitive, overly intellectualized version of reality (highly or exclusively verbalized, quantified, analytical),

[19] *The Port Huron Statement,* p. 9.

but your feelings, desires, and impulses tell you something else, can you choose that for yourself?

What I am suggesting by these questions is not particularly new. I am suggesting that in your education only a part of you has been involved. Thought, theory, cognition have dominated your education (especially your "higher" education) at the expense of your action, practice, and feelings. Sometimes—perhaps a lot of the time—you live a segregated life, fragmentized, and compartmentalized. You are the product of a tradition we identify as Platonistic and Cartesian in which the conflicts and differences between thought and feeling have been resolved largely in favor of thought and against feeling.

EDUCATION AND ALIENATION

Friedenberg and others have suggested that the use of drugs among the young has intensified the seemingly never-ending conflict of thought and feeling between

> those individuals whose sense of personal security is derived chiefly from reliance on order and control, and perpetually threatened by feeling, impulse and human messiness; and those who feel safest when they are in closest touch with their feelings, but are perpetually threatened by repression and constraint. But this conflict bears most heavily on the young, who are not only most exposed to and permitted fewer defenses against socializing forces, but especially subject to the least liberal elements in society. School personnel and probation officers are selectively recruited from the respectable and relatively "uptight" working and lower-middle classes.[20]

And so I find myself wondering whether this conflict is not one that you find in your own experience, resolved only temporarily, and at times with understandable resentment on your part, by going along with an education that is biased toward the intellectual or mental side of the conflict. And if it remains thus, I wonder if you will carry it over into your thinking and practice as a future teacher. Will you perpetuate the conflict and continue to resolve it in your teaching the way it was resolved for you? Will you continue to be part of the problem? Or do you dare to break out of your socialized bondage, dare to "nihilate" your present, dare to exercise your freedom (instead of running away from it), dare to philosophize? It may be the only alternative to the alienation, irrelevance, and frustration you feel. It may be the only alternative to your unwitting continuation as a teacher of what was wrong in your education. If that is not

20 Friedenberg, p. 31.

your alternative, that is your choice, and you carry the burden of its consequences. And you remain part of the problem.

I am suggesting—and I wonder if its boldness startles you—that only in philosophical reflection will you find the alternatives to not just dehumanized education, but a dehumanized life. In *The Politics of Experience,* R. D. Laing says:

> We are born into a world where alienation awaits us. We are potentially men, but are in an alienated state, and this state is not simply a natural system. Alienation as our present destiny is achieved only by outrageous violence perpetrated by human beings on human beings.[21]

In proposing that we begin with philosophizing, I am proposing with Laing that we develop "a thoroughly self-conscious and self-critical human account of man"; that our "humanity is estranged from its authentic possibilities"; that it is an "essential springboard for any serious reflection on any aspect of present interhuman life" to realize that "our alienation goes to the roots." And finally, I think I am proposing what Laing does when he says: "No one can begin to think, feel or act now except from the starting point of his or her own alienation."[22]

But now I wonder if your scepticism (not to say puzzlement and even boredom) has overwhelmed you. There is much suspicion among the young, especially the militant, radical, "New Left" young, about proposals of this sort, especially when they come from over-thirty academicians. And I think there has been good reason for this suspicion of theory, ideology, and philosophy. (After describing the aims and tactics of a radical campus group, a militant student responded to the questions of my seminar in philosophy of education with "Don't give me that old philosophical bullshit.") The suspicion and rejection is justified if the proposal to philosophize is simply one more means of socializing, alienating, and indoctrinating. Intellect has been a source of alienation, a means of controlling and manipulating for just about as long as it has been around, and often among people with the best intentions, like liberal politicians, philosophers, and educators.

What I propose here then is not something to be studied, but something to do. Least of all do I offer it as a product of my philosophizing (or anyone else's), or as a doctrine. I offer philosophizing as a way to develop perspective, a contribution, hopefully, as a way to your enlightenment. It is not offered as a practical guide, either to life or to teaching. In an expression of a philosophical temper that is rare among professional philosophers, Everett J. Kircher said that the alternative to ivory-tower, irrelevant philosophy (and I would add, education) is not ultimate commitment to a

---

[21] R. D. Laing, *The Politics of Experience* (New York: Pantheon, 1967), p. xv.

[22] Ibid., p. xiv.

particular doctrine that directs practical affairs. He warns us of the danger lurking in the desire for commitment, including that in this volume. The "doctrinally uncommitted" teacher, Kircher says, doesn't know what the best, most reasonable commitment is, even though he may know more than others about what they have been, and the arguments for and against them. He has more knowledge than his students, but he also has wisdom, which means that with all his knowledge, he does not finally know. And when students sense this, it sets them *at one* in their wonderment with the teacher. It sets them free.[23]

PHILOSOPHY AS PROCESS

There is something else we should beware of. Kircher points out the temptation among scholars—especially among philosophers—to look for the overall system, the comprehensive world-view. Academics notoriously share a proclivity to generalization (which itself is a generalization), a desire to come up with *the* answer to a question or problem, especially when the reforming zeal is running high, as it is these days. We dream of exclusive adequacy, he says, and taken with the other proclivities we are driven to treat our philosophies (and our education) as doctrinal and indoctrinating. We can even do this with a philosophy (and education) of (and for) *freedom*.

So whatever uniqueness there is in what I offer here, I would not want to generalize it into a doctrine, for to do so, Kircher warns, is to attempt to deprive my readers of "the freedom to engage life with integrity each on his own terms."[24] I do not lament the fact that we have no one common philosophy to guide us. I do lament the fact that there are many who find it exceedingly difficult to work out a philosophy for themselves. We do not need in education a philosophy that wins the day over all others. As Kircher says, to expect that is a declaration of war, not an invitation to philosophize. What we need is more philosophizing, not more philosophies; more philosophers, not more disciples.

My proposal, then, is that we begin with philosophizing, and that we must begin, as Laing says, from the starting point of your own alienation. And where is that? I have already suggested the segregation, the divisions within your life between your thought and action, intellect and feeling. (The division is perpetuated in the myth of the "objective" examination.) We could talk about such things as theory and practice, intellect and feeling, how they are divided, and how this all comes out in education. But I am

---

[23] Everett John Kircher, "Philosophy of Education—Directive Doctrine or Liberal Discipline?" in *What Is Philosophy of Education?* by Christopher J. Lucas (New York: Macmillan, 1969), pp. 101–3.

[24] Ibid., p. 98.

going to suggest that we begin with a philosophical inquiry into your freedom and values, for I believe this is where you will find your alienation. What can be more fundamental to your condition than the question of the extent to which, and in what way, you can be free, and the goods you would be most desirous of pursuing in that freedom?[25]

TOWARDS PERSONAL FREEDOM

And so our topic is your freedom. We must see if we can say what that is, and whether it is possible. Surely there has been no word, no idea, in recent political and social affairs throughout the world that has received more use (and abuse!). But what is it that people think of when they speak of freedom? What experiences would *you* associate with it? I propose we begin here.

Would you say you have had experiences which might be called "freedom experiences"? And have you had experiences which might be called (awkwardly) "un-freedom experiences"? What we are looking for are experiences which only an idea of freedom can help us understand, and with this idea we can cultivate more of these experiences. For freedom seems to be good to us; at least always our own freedom is, if not always the other person's. But what will be your idea (and reality) of freedom?

I daresay your first response would be an idea of being able to do what you want to do. The feelings of physical and psychological constraint and restraint are familiar to us. Sigmund Freud once described what he claimed to be an inescapable fact about civilization:

> The liberty of the individual is no gift of civilization. It was greatest before there was any civilization, though then, it is true, it had for the most part no value, since the individual was scarcely in a position to defend it. The development of civilization imposes restrictions on it, and justice demands that no one shall escape those restrictions.... What makes itself felt in a human community as a desire for dreedom may be their revolt against some existing injustice.... But it may also spring from the remains of their original personality, which is still untamed by civilization and may thus become the basis in them of hostility to civilization.[26]

---

[25] In what follows I am indebted to William L. Reese and his book *The Ascent From Below* (Boston: Houghton Mifflin, 1959). It is within the spirit of Reese's approach to philosophizing that we should adopt it here but differ with him in the conclusions we come to. And that goes for your differing with me in your conclusions. Indeed, what we are about to do will be useless if you are not led by it to begin the search for your own position on your freedom and values.

[26] Sigmund Freud, *Civilization and Its Discontents* (New York: Norton, 1961), pp. 42–43. Reprinted by permission of W. W. Norton and Hogarth Press, Ltd.

...it is impossible to overlook the extent to which civilization is built up upon a renunciation of instinct, how much it presupposes precisely the non-satisfaction (by suppression, repression or some other means?) of powerful instincts. This "cultural frustration" dominates the large field of social relationships between human beings.[27]

When we think of education as one of the civilizing agents a society uses, it is difficult to deny much of what Freud says. There is some question, however, whether suppression and repression is, as he claims, a necessary condition of civilization. (And note that Freud admits that the freedom of precivilization "had for the most part no value.") Whether or not they are inescapable parts of civilization, repression and suppression do occur, so much so that for most people in our society (especially for those over thirty) it is simply unquestioned that the young must be socialized into society, and that this must be accomplished by any means necessary. As Laing said, "We are born into a world where alienation awaits us."

Common sense seems to support the idea that the ability to do what you want to do is a large part of freedom—the ideal and the reality. But common sense is notoriously untrustworthy. How much, and what part, of the idea is it?

Beyond this question lie others raised by Freud's view of the repressive nature of civilization. Must this ability to do what we want to do be curbed? And if so, when is this curbing justified and when is it not justified? (Even if we were to agree fully with Freud, we still would not have to accept all curbing of this ability as justified, would we?) In the western liberal tradition it is said "your freedom ends where my nose begins." This common sense idea by itself, however, tells us nothing about how we determine where the noses in society begin. There is more to us than our physical noses. Where does the "nose" of our person or personality begin? Where does the "nose" of the university or college begin? And whose "nose" is being encountered when my young friends and students are put in jail for refusing to kill in a war?

As it stands, then, the idea doesn't tell us much about the extent of our ability to do what we want to do when it runs up against the demands of society (justified or unjustified) for stability and continuity. But there are still other problems. Is it enough that society merely leave you alone to "do your thing"? Would not—does not—such a freedom mean that the privileged person will have a better and easier go of it than the non- or unprivileged (not to mention the "underprivileged")? Isn't this practically a guarantee that the elites in a society remain (and become ever greater) elites? That "the rich get richer and the poor get poorer"? Is this not the aim of certain Southern politicians desirous of keeping things as they are when they proclaim that leaving Negroes free to choose to attend all-white

27 Ibid., p. 44.

schools meets the requirements of equal educational opportunity? Is this not the freedom of a class society, a status-seeking society? And is it not fairly easy to connect such a society with alienation and unjust inequality?

Perhaps you will agree then that we need more than the removal of obstacles, restrictions, oppressions and coercions if freedom as "the ability to do whatever you please so long as you harm no one else" is going to meet the demands of other parts of our lives. As it stands, it is a negative freedom, the freedom of the rugged individualist, the freedom of the born competitor, the freedom of getting-out-and-getting-yours-while-the-getting-is-good and the-devil-take-the-hindmost. This kind of freedom can be destructive of shared values and experiences. It strikes me as pretty much the reality and —more unfortunately—the ideal of freedom we have in our society.

What is needed then is not only the absence of restrictions on our ability to do what we want to do, but the power to carry out our projects. What good is freedom from restriction when the power that not only lets us but aids and abets us in doing what we want to do is missing?[28]

But now a paradox confronts us. In our society today we are confronted with what is the greatest possibility (including ability and power) in the history of man of doing things we want to do, of "doing our thing," whatever that may be. Not only are we able to pursue a wide variety of wants, and more of us able to do it, but we are able to create or develop new wants. And yet, never perhaps have the people of an age been so alienated and isolated, so *dis*satisfied, so much in search of something more substantial! Why? Is there something missing in this widespread freedom that we have to pursue what we want?

It is no accident that the "laissez faire freedom"—the freedom to do what you want, of being able to satisfy your wants—grew up with the utilitarian ethic that evaluates alternative courses of action by their consequences, and evaluates those consequences by the amount of pleasure or satisfaction they bring. The one seems to require the other. But the utilitarian ethic, and the "laissez faire freedom" that goes with it, leaves us with the position that the satisfaction of *any* desire is justifiable (so long as you don't harm another, of course). Not only does a utilitarian society like ours seek the maximum satisfaction of wants, but it goes on to the deliberate production of new wants. Production in our society is a means to

---

[28] I am not telling the whole story, nor am I intending to do so. There is a vast body of writings on another aspect of the idea of freedom that is generally known as "the free will problem." Many who have adopted the liberal idea of freedom have at the same time held that our wants, desires, et al, are not a matter of independent, self-determined choices, but are made for us once and for all, by environment and heredity. In my discussion here I am assuming that this is not the case, that in some meaningful sense we do have control over our wants, and we can change them, and act on them. These are necessary conditions for the activity of philosophizing that I am urging on you here. But any fuller treatment of this would require arguments for these propositions.

consumption, but our consumption is a means to production! As one writer has said, ours is a society "in which everything is done for the sake of something else and nothing for its own sake."[29] Nothing for its own sake. Not love, not happiness, not learning, not persons. The failure philosophically lies in the failure of the utilitarian ethic to provide a *critique* of wanting, a critique of desire and satisfaction.[30]

> But there is something more ominous. Such a society inevitably arranges human beings according to their function; it also inevitably arranges them hierarchically. This follows from the causal means–end model. Since the process is a causal chain, there must be some who can see further along the chain than others. Some mind the levers of social change, some pull them. And at either end of the scale there are those who decide which levers are to be pulled and those who simply *are* levers. This causal, manipulative view of human change belongs essentially to our modern world. It is post-Christian; it belongs to a world where the images of the lever and the machine dominate.[31]

Do you see where this is leading? We began with the idea that something deep in our experience connects freedom with being able to do what you want to do. We have seen the adoption of this idea of freedom, and the organization of a society consonant with it, in our own society, our utilitarian society. Nothing is so widespread among my students than the idea that *any* action can be justified so long as it is a person doing what he wants to do and he is hurting no one else. Perhaps this is a necessary first, though negative, stage in a movement away from a social and religious ethic of moral suppression and repression. If this is your idea, or something like it, are you ready for the larger consequences MacIntyre points out? Do you see what such a freedom does to the individual? How it has turned individuals into means to be manipulated and exploited, while all the time justifying itself on the utilitarian principle that the individual's needs, wants, desires, or whatever, are being satisfied, and no one is being hurt? That is good, isn't it? Or am I overstating the case?

Let me return to two things. The utilitarian society, we have said, is characterized by an organization that treats human beings according to their function (that is, as means and not as ends in themselves), and arranges them in a hierarchy (as leaders and followers, "ins" and "outs," successes and failures, elites and proles, rich and poor, Mister Charleys and niggers). Secondly, in such a society everything is done for the sake of something else,

29 A. C. MacIntyre, "Against Utilitarianism," in *Aims of Education,* ed. T. H. B. Hollins (Manchester: Manchester University Press, 1967), p. 9. Reprinted by permission.

30 Ibid., p. 8.

31 Ibid., p. 9.

nothing is done for its own sake, for nothing has value except as a means to some further end (which in turn becomes the means to still some other end). What is most disturbing in all of this is the possibility that the utilitarian society has turned the satisfaction of desire into something "which helps us to love Big Brother." The danger in Orwell's *1984*, MacIntyre claims, is that it makes us believe that Big Brother will seem like a tyrant when, in fact, he will more likely seem like a brother and a friend.[32]

And so the question of what your freedom will be—not only in idea, but in ideal and in reality—has led directly into the question of what your values are. And does it not seem appropriate that the two should go together? What good are values if we are not free to pursue them? But what good is it to be free to pursue them if our values are not worth the pursuit? Here we confront a second aspect of our alienation. We are bewildered by a confused and confusing mixture of values or goods with no idea which is better or more worthy than the other, and no idea of how we might decide that—or whether it is even worth deciding. What really is important in a society in which one good is as good or worth having as another? What then are our values, *your* values? And do you find any need, and any basis, for a *critique* of those values?

EDUCATION AND HUMAN BETTERMENT

Education, we agreed in the beginning, embodies the ideal (in idea if not in practice) of human betterment. But *which* idea of human betterment? Plato said that for most young people it would be the idea of that "greatest sophist of all," the public. Few are able to escape being bettered according to that idea, and then only by some miraculous intervention. What I am proposing now is that the source of that intervention is *you*, and only you. (Actually, as it turned out, Plato thought the same thing, except he assumed that only a very few of you were at any time capable of this intervention, and then only by means of a society that supposedly was designed to make that possible. I say "supposedly," because on one reading of Plato he can be taken to be saying that acting on these assumptions will in the end be self-defeating.[33]) The source of the intervention, I am suggesting, lies in what Sartre described as that double "nihilation," that source of human action by which we modify the world, the education and reflection by which you see possibilities and make them your projects. And that, I have said, is philosophizing.

Let's go back to the critique of value that MacIntyre finds missing

---

[32] Ibid., p. 11.

[33] See Michael Young, *The Rise of the Meritocracy* (Baltimore: Penguin Books, 1967).

in our utilitarian ethic. A good part of the history of utilitarianism is involved in the attempt to find such a critique. The best known philosophical inheritor of the utilitarian tradition was John Stuart Mill. Mill could not believe that all pleasures counted equally, nor could he accept the idea that the satisfactions of a pig and the satisfactions of a Socrates were equally worthwhile. There were "higher" and there were "lower" pleasures, he proclaimed; some are worthier than others; some ought to be pursued, and some ought not to be pursued. But which are the "higher" and which are the "lower"?

Here Mill faltered. He referred us to "intelligent" human beings, persons "of feeling and conscience," beings of "higher faculties." In so doing he failed to see the possible bias in these beings, as well as a circularity in his argument. (Who is a being of "higher faculties"? Why, one who chooses the "higher" over the "lower" pleasures.) Mill had introduced the idea that we must have a critique of pleasure, but he offered us little basis for that critique.

If, then, yours is the utilitarian ethic that I suspect it is, where do you stand on this need for a critique of your values? Are they worthy enough as they stand? Would you find it sufficient if you were simply to be aided and abetted in pursuing your values as they are? It is the "as they are" that I am wondering about. What are your values as they are? What do you really want? It strikes me that we must attend now to this long delayed question.

But there are two things we still must be clear about before we begin. Reese speaks of both of them:

> Clearly, no one can tell us what in fact we value; but many...would claim that they can tell us what we ought to value. I now deny that this is possible. Why is it not possible? Everyone remarks...how the values of the world are changing. Now, when the values of the world are changing at a quickened tempo, this must be the rule: Each man is the measure of his values. Excellent, but then let man measure! If each man is the measure this is not to say there is no measure. It is to say rather that there is no alternative: each of us must decide the important values for himself. ... Man is the measure; therefore, let no one force a set of values on your life. Or therefore, do not condemn another because his values are unlike your own. But not: Man is the measure; therefore, everything is proper. This widely advertised conclusion does not follow. It may arise from our emptiness; it does not follow from our rule.[34]

No one but yourself can tell you what you value, *and* what you ought to value. Each man is the measure. But this does not mean there can not be, or should not be, measuring. And that is what we are seeking: the mea-

---

[34] Reese, *Ascent from Below,* pp. 83–84.

sure, the critique, of your own values. And in this, and in your freedom, lies the source of that "miraculous intervention" by which your education, and that of your future pupils, will be a humanized education.

It is no easy task to make explicit your values. (Try it, if you haven't already.) Yet it is a necessary first step to developing alternatives. Is it possible that the principal reason for this difficulty lies in the fact that we are rarely encouraged or allowed to develop such an explicit awareness of ourselves? Reese suggests five ways in which we might come to this awareness, and these are my versions of them.

First, you can become aware of the value of words you use in your conversation. And you can become aware of the values that you often (perhaps unwittingly many times) associate with facts. The courthouse over there is some sort of fact, but what values do you automatically associate with it? Your school is a fact: ah, but what values (and disvalues) do you associate with it? ("The TV program will be educational," the man said; "but," he hastened to add, "it will be entertaining too!")

Second, what were the values of your early life, that time when value attitudes and dispositions were impressed upon you without your knowledge, and without any judgment on your part? Many of your values came from these early years, did they not?

Third, if you would know what your values are, examine the decisions you make and have made, especially those important decisions that made a difference in your life. In choice and in action our values come out.

Fourth, having come this far you should find yourself in possession of quite a mixture of values. Can you now arrange them in an order of importance, placing those most important apart from those less or least important? Which values are means to other values, and which—if any!—seem to be intrinsic values, worth pursuing for their own sake? I am not talking here about which values you *ought* to value. Which *do* you value? In questioning yourself this way you should begin to uncover those values that you want for themselves alone. As Reese says, in constantly asking yourself why you value this over that, if the answer is that you value it because you do, then you may have come upon a "final value," something desired for itself alone.

Finally, the way in which we spend our time should tell us something about our values. How much of your day do you spend with your instrumental values, and how much time do you devote to those "final values"? Is your life, your society, your world, so arranged that the far greater portion of your time is spent with those values you acknowledge as instrumental, values that are means to other values and thus derive their value from them (which in turn may themselves be instrumental means to still further ends)?[35]

[35] Ibid., pp. 49–55.

If what we have said about our utilitarian society is true, then I suspect you will go through these five ways to find your values and come out something like this: If ours is a society in which we treat one another functionally and hierarchically—as means and never as ends; if in our utilitarian ethic every value has its worth in being the means to something else so that there is little or nothing of final value or intrinsic worth; and if the educational system of this society is the socializing (indoctrinating and repressing) process Friedenberg and others have said it is; then is it any wonder that you should find yourself spending the greater part of your time with values of only instrumental or utilitarian worth? And if that is the case, is it any wonder that you—like so many of us—should find something missing, something *un*satisfying in the pursuit of your satisfactions?

And MacIntyre shows, I think, that all of this can be found in our educational system:

> It is clearly functional and hierarchical. The selection methods throw their shadows back into the earliest years of a child's schooling. You are graded by ability and ability is understood functionally. Our educational system, like our social system, is a matter of grooves and ladders. Of grooves because the route the individual takes is determined by factors largely beyond the individual's control. He is sorted out by the luck of the draw in terms of geographical situation, and local authority policies, and in so far as his conscious effort is involved it is in climbing the appropriate ladder to the appropriate rung—and no further. Everything is dominated from the top...[36]

Ends disappear in this hierarchical arrangement of our educational system:

> The universities do what they do partly because of what the schools do. And the schools do what they do partly because of what the universities do. Each has the other as an alibi...such ends as our educational system serves are of two kinds. On the one hand they are the ends of practical utility imposed from the outside.[37]

The second kind of aims are the unclear and uncertain aims of the teachers. Even in the arts and humanities the criterion for what ought to be done lies in what has been done, and the hard, verifiable, testable fact is always preferred to the practice of critical discrimination.

We return to education—to your education, that is—and to Plato. If education (in the sense of formal schooling) is one of society's major means of socialization, and if socialization is what Friedenberg and others claim, can there be any hope that the education will change without commensurate change in society? Maybe not. And yet, in some areas at least,

[36] MacIntyre, "Against Utilitarianism," p. 15.
[37] Ibid., p. 16.

we know the educational system can and does influence change in its society. Some people do survive their education and go on to become critics of their society. MacIntyre's education would aim at more of this by helping "people to discover activities whose ends are not outside themselves..."[38] But what are these activities "whose ends are not outside themselves"? (We never do seem to be done with questions in philosophy!) MacIntyre says "all intellectual inquiry," meaning "critical ability" which "serves nothing directly except for itself, no one except those who exercise it."

Lest you think this is another of those overly-intellectualized views of educational activities (i.e., activities worthwhile in themselves), MacIntyre says that in strengthening the values of "rational critical inquiry" (and weakening the prevailing social values), education's task is above all that of teaching "the value of activity done for its own sake." And this will only be partially done if

> it is restricted to rational inquiry in the narrower sense; for rational inquiry in the narrower sense will not remain rational. Unless the feelings too are sifted and criticized, the feelings are simply handed over to unreason. We have to allow those whom we teach to remake themselves through their activity. And if we do this, we shall be educating those who may in the end help to remake society itself. For critical inquiry is not utilitarian; it is not functional; it is not hierarchical; it demands independence of mind and feeling; it demands all that our society tends to deny us. Above all critical inquiry is not an academic retreat; for its maintenance presupposes rebuilding a particular kind of community.[39]

This idea of education as an end in itself is not a terribly new idea. It is the idea of education for human betterment. Its most important element—the element least honored in what our education thus far has been and continues to be—is the participation of the learner in constructing his own purposes, his own worthwhile activities. While such an education sets human betterment as its purpose, what constitutes human betterment—the question we began with so long ago—is not decided by the system, but is the product of the teacher-student relationship, of *each* teacher-student relationship. Over thirty years ago John Dewey described what this meant as "opposed" to traditional education:

> To imposition from above is opposed expression and cultivation of individuality; to external discipline is opposed free activity; to learning from texts and teachers, learning through experience; to acquisition of isolated skills and techniques by drill, is opposed acquisition of them as means of attaining ends which make direct vital appeal; to preparation for a more or less remote future is opposed making the most of the opportuni-

---

38 Ibid., p. 19.
39 Ibid., p. 21.

ties of present life; to static aims and materials is opposed acquaintance with a changing world.[40]

Many have argued that this was tried long ago and found wanting. But Dewey has often been the target of criticisms blaming him for things he never proposed. *Experience and Education* includes several warnings Dewey made to people who had taken up his ideas but with serious lapses in their understanding of them.

Here I feel my work should stop. If Dewey sounds like your bag, his books are there to be read, along with competent criticisms of them. I tread closely to that area where you must begin to make the double "nihilation," where you must move beyond awareness that something is wrong and begin to develop your own alternatives and make them your project. The difference between alternatives that are told to you, and alternatives that are your own, rests upon your struggle with your alienation, where your thought and feeling, your freedom and values, and your philosophizing begin.

In Plato's *Republic* there is an allegory of his idea of the education of philosophers. I would recommend it to you as the ideal of a humanistic education, or of any education that is worthy of the name. It is a description of man's ascent from the relative darkness of his uneducated moral and intellectual condition (and I would add, his alienated condition), to enlightenment and freedom. From being chained in a position that forced him to observe only shadows on the wall of a cave, and led him to mistake those shadows for truth and reality, man is led to awareness of truth and reality, to enlightenment, but not without struggle and pain. He is led by the philosopher-teacher who has himself made it out of the cave and has returned to the cave as teacher. (Bernard Malamud's "Fixer" says the only purpose in being free is to help others become free. Plato insists that all who make it out of the cave must be required—even forced, if need be—to return to the cave to do this.) The way in which Plato has his teacher par excellence, Socrates, describe this function of the teacher-philosopher is pertinent to what we have said here:

> ...we must reject the conception of education professed by those who say that they can put into the mind knowledge that was not there before—rather as if they could put sight into blind eyes...this capacity is innate in each man's mind, and...the faculty by which he learns is like an eye which cannot be turned from darkness to light unless the whole body is turned; in the same way the mind as a whole must be turned away from the world of change until it can bear to look straight at reality.... Then this business of turning the mind round might be

40 John Dewey, *Experience and Education* (New York: Collier Books, 1963), pp. 19–20.

made a subject of professional skill, which would effect the conversion as easily and effectively as possible. It would not be concerned to implant sight, but to ensure that someone who had it already was turned in the right direction and looking the right way.[41]

Plato did not leave it at that. Nor can we. "What is at issue," Socrates goes on to say, "is the conversion of the mind from the twilight of error to the truth, that climb up into the real world which we shall call true philosophy." Few would disagree with that as the nature or purpose of education. But when it comes to determining what sort of studies have this effect, you encounter much disagreement. Plato thought there were certain subjects that were inherently educational, others that were not worthy of education at all. That tradition persists to this day, especially in higher education. But the idea that this inherently educational subject matter was to be externally imposed, with little or no participation of the learner, is not part of Plato's thinking. It represents, I think, an exaggeration and mistaken view of the teacher's ability and purpose.

Several years ago, Rupert C. Lodge argued that no one really teaches anyone anything. We all teach ourselves. All the teacher can do is provide suitable environments, stimulate, and assist an already questioning mind. Thus stimulated, the student solves his own problem. If the spark in his mind is to grow into flame, Lodge said, we must let him solve his problems. Only then will the student pass beyond docility, acceptance, and dependence. Only then will he become educated, capable of facing and participating in solving the problems of his own day. Only if students can feel from the inside what it has been like to participate hopefully in important issues, will they be able to throw themselves intelligently and wholeheartedly into the movements of their own time.[42] It is not the generally accepted idea of education or of training teachers, is it?

The way to begin then is with asking questions. Without "an already questioning mind," no learning takes place. Bertrand Russell said the philosopher's contribution to teachers is not in the answers he gives but in the questions he raises, because if they are good questions they will enlarge our conception of what is possible, enrich our imagination, and diminish our dogmatic assurance. If any of what I have said here has started a question in your mind, and if it is a good question, then I shall feel I have shown what a philosopher and a teacher can contribute to humanizing education. And what you as a philosopher-teacher can contribute to the education of your students.

41 Plato, *The Republic,* trans. H. D. P. Lee (London: Penguin Books, 1958), p. 283.

42 Rupert C. Lodge, "The Essence of Philosophy of Education," *Educational Theory* 3, no. 4 (October 1953): 355.

2

a humanistic history of american education

Sol Cohen

SOL COHEN projects his humanism from the stance of the intellectual and scholar. He is, perhaps, more of a scholar than any of the other contributors. He makes for us a remarkable adaptation to the task because, while holding on to his commitment to the discipline and to the professional posture of the conventional historian, he considers both himself and his discipline in terms of the contemporary scene.

Sol, like so many of us, is very worried about the problems of contemporary society. This comes through in his chapter. But unlike some of us, he compounds his worries by maintaining his loyalty to some of the more permanent aspects of scholarship. Unlike myself, and probably Reidford and Robischon, he is quite unwilling to throw the baby out with the bathwater. He still believes that the teacher does have a legitimate body of subject matter to impart to students, and a duty to assign them specific tasks and evaluate their performance. But he does not assume these stances easily. He is torn by the possibility that he may be wrong.

I have seen Sol struggle with the need to define his role in the humanistic "movement." I stood with him in a crowd as radical students attempted to picket the recruitment office where students were protesting the presence of recruitment people from the Dow Company, manufacturers of napalm. Unlike the others in the crowd, he was suffering from indecision, asking himself whether he should join the picketers, perhaps at a potential cost of his job, and finally doing so.

But the job to Sol has never gotten the upper hand as it has with most of our bureaucratic colleagues. I have seen him tender his resignation on at least two occasions when he felt his principles were being violated. And I have seen him, in his very mild manner, with his typical eloquence, go before a meeting of all his colleagues and denounce them for their inability to take a moral stand in a time that calls for moral leadership. And this, too, is his version of the role of the intellectual leader, which most of our colleagues find to be outdated. Sol thus emerges as a man who distinguishes himself by his allegiance to two standards, excellence and moral commitment, anguished because, around him, he senses too little allegiance to either.

In Sol's contribution, he takes the same position that I do in my chapter, "The School, the Society, and the Individual." He asks the historian, as I ask the sociologist, to employ his skills in a more "relevant" manner. That is, he asks that the historian find in the present the seeds for his study, to illuminate the past in such a way as to reveal the heart of present social disruptions. What is the school's role in improving social conditions? What has it been? How has the school been involved in doing man's good work as well as his dirty work?

Sol provides us with an example of the kind of work that he feels historians should do. This example accomplishes three tasks: it is instructive as to the new approach to history that he is calling for; it is informative as history of education, tracing a very important segment of that history; and it throws some light upon the dynamics of problems that concern us all.

Look for the parallels to our current conflicts and disorganizations in the Industrial Education movement at the end of the nineteenth century. And look also for Sol's very special way of calling for us all to unravel the mystifications that surround both the past and the present. Consider the issue of "differentiation in the name of democracy" and supply yourself with a similar list of mystifications from the annals of our history and our education. Ask yourself about any reform movement from the annals of our history and our education: Who wins? Who loses? Whom do I want to win?

Sol still believes that professors should wear ties when they lecture to students. But if Sol were told that he had to wear a necktie or put his job on the line, then he would put his job on the line. He believes in conventions, but not when they interfere with freedom. A mental necktie, which I am sure many of my colleagues will add to their dress during this time of reaction against student dissent, Sol will never wear, and that, I believe, is what counts.

NEW PERSPECTIVES IN THE HISTORY OF
AMERICAN EDUCATION

Sociologist Max Weber has described our age as one of disenchantment. One of the characteristics of our time is a certain disenchantment, a certain skepticism, especially about the absolutism of human knowledge. We are moving to a critical and cautious assessment of what it really means to "know" something. Richard Hofstadter refers to playfulness as one of the characteristics of the intellectual. And to speak of the playfulness of ideas is to reveal a disenchantment with absolutes. The disillusionment of many with Lyndon B. Johnson came about partly because he employed a rhetorical style consisting of simplistic, absolutist ethical categories to describe an ambiguous and complex military venture. The young of whatever age speak of keeping one's "cool." It would be a mistake to call this disenchantment, what philosopher Morris I. Berger calls "the new skepticism," a pessimistic or antihumanistic response to the world. Rather, contemporary critical thought stems from the hope of improving man's condition and state of understanding. "Telling it how it is" is the challenge and the need. It is my challenge and my need as person and as historian.

For more than three-quarters of a century the history of American education has had a promising future and a disappointing present as a subject of investigation. This is not to say there is not a voluminous literature on the subject; there is. Unfortunately, too much of it is parochial, anachronistic, and out of touch with main currents of contemporary scholarship. As Professor Bernard Bailyn stated, at a time of deep public concern over the schools: "The role of education in American history is obscure. We have almost no historical leverage on the problems of American education."[1] Why? Because, Bailyn continues, those who have taught the history of education—and written the textbooks—have viewed the subject not as an aspect of American history writ large but rather as a device for communicating an appropriate ideology to a newly self-conscious profession. Hence their scholarship proceeded in a special atmosphere of professional purpose, almost totally isolated from the major streams of twentieth century historiography. The result has been "a foreshortened chronicle of pedagogical institutions so caught up in anachronisms as to make (historical) explanation impossible."[2] The facts, or many of them, are there, but they form no

---

[1] Bernard Bailyn, *Education in the Forming of American Society: Needs and Opportunities for Study* (Chapel Hill: University of North Carolina Press, 1950), p. 4. See also Fund for the Advancement of Education, Committee on the Role of Education In American History, *Education and American History,* The Fund, New York, 1965.

[2] Bailyn, *Education in the Forming of American Society,* p. 4. See Lawrence A. Cremin, *The Wonderful World of Ellwood Patterson Cubberley: An Essay on the Historiography of American Education* (New York: Bureau of Publications, Teachers

significant pattern. We know little about education as a creature of social forces; less about the impact of education on American society. What is wanted is a new history of education, humanistic in character, broadly conceived, and closely allied with the fields of social and intellectual history.

Two traits will distinguish the new historian from his predecessors in the field of educational history. These traits are his use of broader historical references and his wider, more humanistic, professional commitment. The new historian of education will attempt to trace the sanctions and sources of education through society and ideology rather than attempt to write educational history as the story of formal institutions. While he employs broader historical references, the new historian of education may increasingly display his second trait—a professional commitment that is freer in its intellectual concerns than the interests of his predecessors. The latter were governed by their commitment to aggrandizing the educational profession. But, in the words of Wilson Smith,

> the new historian is likely to think of our educational past in terms that reveal his close kinship to humanists and to social scientists. . . . From his historian's vantage point he can well afford to use some of the hypotheses and methods of the ecologist, the demographer, the philologist and semanticist, or the sociologist, whenever they appear to offer new insights or to substantiate old ones. . . . Indeed, the new historian of education himself may be trained or employed in an academic field outside of history, yet come temporarily to the history of education with an outlook that dispels cant and fruitless preconceptions. . . [3]

The new historian of education will still be "useful," and "functional," but in ways significantly different from the older generation of historians. For the new historian of education, as Smith concludes, will see his own role first as that of being a representative of humane learning in our industrialized and specialized society.[4] It remained for Lawrence A. Cremin in 1961 to exemplify just such a new history of education.[5] Great historians enlarge the sphere of available evidence. By discovering new historical materials, they enrich the terrain of historical inquiry. This is precisely Cremin's contribution. Cremin locates progressive education as part of that broader turn-of-the-century burst of social and political reform called the

---

College, Columbia University, 1965). In this study Cremin also wisely points out that charges of isolationism and parochialism can be hurled at many in the field of history in general.

[3] Wilson Smith, "The New Historian of American Education," *Harvard Educational Review* 21 (Spring 1961): 138.

[4] Ibid., p. 143.

[5] Lawrence A. Cremin, *The Transformation of the School: Progressivism in American Education, 1876–1957* (New York: Knopf, 1961).

Progressive Movement. Progressivism was America's response to the challenge of urbanization, industrialization, and immigration. Progressive education was the educational manifestation of the progressive movement. Nothing is foreign to Cremin: child care, marriage and the family, immigration, the rise of the city, social Darwinism, science and technology, the arts, Greenwich Village bohemianism, Freudianism, the New Deal, the conservative revival since World War II. By placing progressive education squarely in the mainstream of American social and intellectual history, Cremin has enlarged the sphere of available evidence, discovered "new" sources for history of education, and thereby given us our first major interpretation of the progressive movement in American education.

The past decade has witnessed a surge of writing in the history of education that is broad in scope, humanistic in character, solid and mature in its use of the tools and apparatus of historical scholarship.[6] And recently, several of our more venturesome practitioners have demonstrated how methods and insights borrowed from the social sciences can provide significant new approaches to the history of education. I have in mind David Tyack's study of the relationship of bureaucratic processes in the Portland school system at the turn of the century and progressive education, Michael Katz's examination of bureaucratic structure and educational innovation in mid-nineteenth century Massachusetts, and Charles Bidwell's extremely sophisticated use of sociological and statistical tools to analyze the relationships between school control and moral training and social structures in the Northeast during the Jacksonian period.[7]

---

[6] Jack K. Campbell, *Colonel Francis W. Parker, The Children's Crusader* (New York: Teachers College Press, 1968); Patricia Albjerg Graham, *Progressive Education, From Arcady to Academe: A History of the Progressive Education Association* (New York: Teachers College Press, 1967); Edward A. Krug, *The Shaping of the American High School* (New York: Harper & Row, 1964); Claude A. Bowers, *The Progressive Educator and the Depression: The Radical Years* (New York: Random House, 1969); Geraldine Joncich, *The Sane Positivist: A Biography of Edward L. Thorndike* (Middletown, Conn.: Wesleyan University Press, 1968); Robert Middlekauf, *Ancients and Axioms: Secondary Education in Eighteenth Century New England* (New Haven, Conn.: Yale University Press, 1963); Clarence J. Karier, *Man, Society, and Education* (Glenview, Ill.: Scott, Foresman, 1967); Henry J. Perkinson, *The Imperfect Panacea: American Faith in Education, 1865–1965* (New York: Random House, 1968); Theodore Sizer, *Secondary Schools at the Turn of the Century* (New Haven, Conn.: Yale University Press, 1964); Michael B. Katz, *The Irony of School Reform: Educational Innovation in Mid-Nineteenth Century Massachusetts* (Cambridge, Mass.: Harvard University Press, 1968).

[7] David Tyack, "Bureaucracy and The Common School: The Example of Portland, Oregon, 1891–1913," *American Quarterly* 19 (Fall 1967): 475–98; Michael B. Katz, "The Emergence of Bureaucracy in Urban Education: The Boston Case, 1850–1884," *History of Education Quarterly* 8 (Summer 1968): 155–88; Charles E. Bidwell, "The Moral Significance of the Common School: A Sociological Study of Local Patterns of School Control and Moral Education in Massachusetts and New York, 1837–1840," *History of Education Quarterly* 6 (Fall 1966): 50–91; Frank F. Cobun, "The Educational Level of the Jacksonians," *History of Education*

Despite the renaissance in history of education of the past decade, there are still some reservations or, more positively, some further and urgent needs and opportunities for historians of American education. First, we have sadly neglected the writings of foreign observers of American education, writings which unlock a rich store of information and insights on the American school system. Professor William Brickman has long labored in this area and it is high time to exploit his labors.[8] In fact, to our loss, we have neglected the comparative approach to American educational history in general. After all, the intellectual and economic interests of the great nations are closely interwoven and therefore a serious change to the educational system of any one of them is certain sooner or later to concern the rest. For example, the study of educational developments in America in the twentieth century in the light of certain social changes common to all the Western powers: industrialization, urbanization, population changes, might profitably be pursued. For the unrest in education characteristic of this century is not unique to America, but is characteristic of England, Germany, and France as well.[9] Then, not only does our educational history neglect any international or comparative approach, it hardly does justice to American regionalism. For example, so far as historians of education are concerned, the American West is uninhabited: no Mexican-Americans, Indians, Japanese, Chinese, Negroes; no cities like Los Angeles or San Francisco or Seattle; no schools. No region of the United States has been so neglected by historians of education as the region west of the Rockies.[10] My most serious reservation, however, is that the new history of education is too tame, too safe, too bland; it is a conservative historiography. For all the new history of

---

Quarterly 7 (Winter 1967): 515–20; Timothy L. Smith, "Immigrant Social Aspirations and American Education, 1880–1930," *American Quarterly* 21 (Fall 1969): 523–43; Jonathan Messerli, "To Broaden Schooling Was to Narrow Education," *Notre Dame Journal of Education* 1 (Spring 1970): 5–16; Maxine Greene, *Public School and Private Vision* (New York: Random House, 1965).

8 E.g. William W. Brickman, "An Historical Survey of American Educational History," *Paedogogica Historica* 11 (1962): 5–21; Steward E. Fraser and William W. Brickman, eds., *A History of International and Comparative Education; Nineteenth Century Documents* (Glenview, Ill.: Scott, Foresman, 1963). See also Sol Cohen, "English Writers on the American Common Schools, 1884–1904," *The School Review* 76 (June 1968): 127–46.

9 Sol Cohen, "Sir Michael E. Sadler and the Sociopolitical Analysis of Education," *History of Education Quarterly* 7 (Fall 1967): 281–94. There is much to learn from books like George Z. F. Bereday, *Comparative Method in Education* (New York: Holt Rinehart & Winston, 1964); and Robert J. Havighurst, *Comparative Perspectives on Education* (Boston, Mass.: Little, Brown, 1968), and Philip H. Coombs, *The World Educational Crisis: A Systems Analysis* (London: Oxford University Press, 1968).

10 E.g. Earl S. Pomeroy, *The Pacific Slope: A History of California, Oregon, Washington, Idaho, Utah, and Nevada* (New York: Knopf, 1965); and Moses Rischin, "Beyond the Great Divide: Immigration and the Last Frontier," *Journal of American History* 55 (June 1968): 42–53.

education, the verdict of Bailyn still stands: "The role of education in American history is obscure. We have almost no historical leverage on the problems of American education." Thus, the new historian of education, afraid of being called tendentious or partisan like the generation against whom he is reacting, or overreacting, has been far too cautious in exploring the theme of conflict in American education. Our new history of education is an innocent history of education, innocent of education as an arena of strife and conflict. John Higham's strictures about the homogenizing of history should be pondered by all students of education:

> The emphasis on consensus and continuity has softened the outlines and flattened the crises of American history. A certain tameness and amiability have crept into our view of things; perhaps the widespread interest in myths comes partly from a feeling that realities are simply not as interesting. The conservative frame of reference is giving us a bland history, in which conflict is muted, in which the elements of spontaneity, effervescence, and violence in American life get little sympathy or attention, . . . scholarship is threatened with a moral vacuum.[11]

It is precisely this moral vacuum at which J. H. Plumb directed these eloquent and angry words:

> As the historian has grown mountainous in scholarship, he has shrunken as a man. He has ceased to be a combatant in the battle for truth. Aping a nonexistent Providence, his cult of objectivity has been nothing more than a treason to the intellect. By squeezing morality out of history, he is committing professional suicide, leaving the biting social and intellectual criticism which should be his milieu to the rare satirist or philosopher, the Orwells and the Russells, or to the little reviews. . . . We erect pyramids of papers, concentrate on the growth and delay of estates, reconstruct the ideology of an age with precision and care and antiseptic indifference to what was perpetrated in its name. All these are undertaken with the minimum of consideration for the pain and suffering of humanity, or for its blindness, stupidity, and addiction to cant. . . . What historians have forgotten is that facts, either human or social, become inescapably moral facts.[12]

This neglect of conflict, this indifference to "moral facts" has left us unprepared even to explain, let alone to cope with, the strife and division—ethnic, religious, social, ideological—characteristic of American education today.

There are at least three legitimate conditions for reinterpretation in history: (1) the discovery of new source materials; (2) the impact of new

[11] John Higham, "Beyond Consensus: The Historian as Moral Critic," *American Historical Review* 67 (April 1962): 616.

[12] J. H. Plumb, "Where are Tacitus, Plutarch, Voltaire?" *Saturday Review,* 26 November 1966, p. 29. © 1966 Saturday Review, Inc.

theories, new methods, new academic disciplines; and (3) the asking of new or different kinds of questions of the historical data, old or new. The major questions historians of education have been asking this past decade have had to do with how education is related to broader currents in American intellectual life. It's high time to begin asking different sorts of questions—questions having to do with power, strategies, stakes, interests; questions having to do with the consequences of educational principles and practices for who get what, when, and how much of the good things in life such as money, status, jobs, culture.

In general, a totally artificial conception of the nature of public education prevails in America. There is a tendency in America—a tendency encouraged by educationists, and apparently shared by historians of American education—to believe that educational reformers are motivated by only the loftiest purposes and that educational policy making is dictated by the loftiest democratic values, or by advances in the "science" of pedagogy, or by the inexorable force of "progress," or by some process of ratiocination uncontaminated by mundane motives, and that school decision-makers are neutral and disinterested. But education cannot be divorced from political or social contexts. As political scientist Bernard Crick has observed: "Pure education is pure nothing; its claimants have only neglected to study the political and social conditions of its existence and presuppositions." Education is a field supremely loaded with "value." Indeed, education is a realm of clashing values, an arena, a battlefield in which competing interests—ethnic, racial, religious, social class—jostle for power and influence. Yet the theme of conflict has largely been ignored. For example, of any reform movement in education we should be asking questions of this sort: Who wants it? Why? What strategies and slogans are used to get what they want? Are they successful and under what conditions and with what consequences? We should be asking questions of the following sort: Who profits? Who loses? Who is advantaged? Who is disadvantaged? A slogan one often comes across in the study of reform movements in urban education is "Take the schools out of politics and politics out of the schools." The widespread acceptance of this slogan has simply resulted in making the operations of school decision-makers less visible, to the detriment of questioning accountability and responsibility. And historians of education have been loathe to contradict the slogan and define or locate responsibility. We know all too little about such important matters as: Who has the power? Where is this power located? How is it exercised? Whose interests are served? That is not to suggest that there has not been any confrontation with questions of power and conflict among historians of education. Of course there has.[13]

---

[13] Professors Tyack and Katz and Bidwell in their studies of bureaucracy are implicitly concerned with questions of power and control. Claude Bowers has sharply portrayed ideological conflict in the thirties. Raymond E. Callahan has critically ex-

But we need more of the same and, more explicitly, a picture of history of education in the bold hues of conflict. With the understanding that those who read these words will do as I say and not as I do, I offer the following as a sample of what can be done if one asks questions of the historical data of the kind I have suggested above. Let us take, for example, the industrial education movement, an extremely important phase of the progressive education movement.

THE INDUSTRIAL EDUCATION MOVEMENT: NEEDS OF THE CHILDREN

The industrial education movement began in a desultory way in the late 1870s as a demand for manual training in the elementary grades and trade training on the high school level. In the 1880s and 1890s a few vocational or manual training high schools were established, some public, more private. Many public high schools began to add vocational courses to their programs, and elementary schools began gradually to expand their offerings in manual training.[14] But it was a case of too little too late. In 1906, with the publication of the Report of the Massachusetts Commission on Industrial and Technical Education, and the organization later that year of the National Society for the Promotion of Industrial Education, the movement began in earnest. Bankers, businessmen, industrialists, philanthropists, social workers, educators, all jumped on the bandwagon. Few movements in the history of American education have taken so sudden and so powerful a hold on the minds of school reformers. Some impatient partisans were of a mind to issue ultimatums. "The truth is," warned Robert A. Woods, head resident of South End House, Boston, in 1907, "that industrial education is coming. Those that do not put themselves in line to reap its advantages may even have some of its force turned against them."[15] By 1908 the National Education Association rang with oratory and resolutions on behalf of industrial education. "We are besieged," declared one state school superintendent, "with public documents, monographs, magazine articles, reports of

---

plored the exercise of administrative power in his *Education and the Cult of Efficiency* (Chicago: University of Chicago Press, 1962). And earlier there is, of course, George S. Counts, *School and Society in Chicago* (New York: Harcourt, Brace Jovanovich, 1928); and Merle Curti, *The Social Ideas of American Educators* (New York: Scribner's, 1935).

[14] See Edward A. Krug, *The Shaping of the American High School* (New York: Harper and Row, 1964), chap. X; Lawrence A. Cremin, *The Transformation of the School: Progressivism in American Education, 1876–1957* (New York: Knopf, 1961), pp. 39–41, 50–56. The recently published Berenice Fisher, *Industrial Education: American Ideals and Institutions* (Madison: University of Wisconsin Press, 1967), locates the industrial education movement in the broadest perspective yet.

[15] Robert A. Woods, "Industrial Education From the Social Worker's Standpoint," *Charities and the Commons* 19 (5 October 1907): 852.

investigations too numerous to mention. . . ."[16] Another school administrator said it was a "mental epidemic," like the free silver crusade or the Klondike gold fever.[17] It was truly an amazing phenomenon, whose ramifications were very wide indeed. The industrial education movement involved the child labor and compulsory education movements, the junior high school movement, vocational guidance, the neighborhood school concept and more, the very way Americans had traditionally conceived of the public schools.

The connection between the industrial education movement and the child labor and compulsory education movements is extremely close. Until the late nineteenth century, child labor was not only acceptable but praiseworthy. But child labor in industrial society was another matter. For many of the estimated 1,750,000 children between the ages of 10 and 16 employed in gainful occupations in 1900 (some placed the figure much higher), there was no benevolent system of apprenticeship education but a system of cheap, easily discarded labor which depressed the wages of adults and broke the spirits and bodies of the children. In the early 1900s, spurred on by the muckraking of John Spargo, Robert Hunter, Edwin Markham and others, progressives launched a crusade against child labor.[18] The point to emphasize here is that from the beginning all those concerned with the child labor problem insisted on the centrality of the schools in any program of child labor reform. It wasn't enough to shut the child out of the factory, he had to be pulled into the school. One of the initial aims of child labor reformers was to establish fourteen years as the minimum age of school leaving. As one reformer put it, "the movement for compulsory education everywhere goes hand in hand, and must go hand in hand, with the child labor movement."[19] Compulsory education was the solution to the child labor problem.

The achievement of the child labor and compulsory education move-

16 H. C. Morrison, "Vocational Training and Industrial Education," *Educational Review* 36 (October 1908): 242.

17 John J. Marrinan, "Vocational Education for the Rural School," *Educational Review* 46 (June 1913): 39.

18 John Spargo, *The Bitter Cry of the Children* (New York: Macmillan, 1906); Robert Hunter, *Poverty* (New York: Macmillan, 1904), pp. 223–60; Edwin Markham, Benjamin B. Lindsay, and George Creel, *Children in Bondage* (New York: Hearst International Library, 1914); Jeremy P. Felt, *Hostages of Fortune: Child Labor Reform in New York State* (Syracuse, N.Y.: Syracuse University Press, 1965); Robert H. Bremner, *From the Depths: The Discovery of Poverty in the United States* (New York: New York University Press, 1956), pp. 76–80, 212 ff.

19 Felix Adler, "Child Labor in the United States and its Great Attendant Evils," *Annals of the American Academy of Political and Social Science* 25 (May 1905): 428. See also Owen R. Lovejoy, "The Function of Education In Abolishing Child Labor," ibid., 32 (July 1908): 80–91; Lewis W. Parker, "Compulsory Education, the Solution of the Child Labor Problem," ibid.: 92–100; Sol Markoff, *The Changing Years: The National Child Labor Committee, 1904–1954* (New York: National Child Labor Committee, 1954), p. 7.

ments comprise one of the greatest triumphs of the progressive era, as school enrollment figures testify. Public elementary school enrollment climbed from about 12,500,000 in 1900 to about 16,000,000 in 1910, while the average number of days per pupil per semester climbed in this decade from 86.3 to 113. But if the schools were to help solve the problems of child labor and child welfare, of immigration, and congestion of population, the children had not only to be got into the schools but kept there as long as possible. This was a cardinal article of the progressive creed. But here the schools were failing. Children were leaving school in large numbers as soon as they could. It was estimated that only 40 to 50 percent of the children finished the eight grades of elementary school. Only 8 to 10 percent finished a high school course. Between the ages of 13 and 15 more than 50 percent of the children dropped out of school, most of them in the sixth and seventh grades.[20] One of the major problems of the pre-World War I generation of school reformers became that of halting this "premature" school leaving. While investigators disagreed somewhat on the statistics, all agreed that the school dropout rate was high. And there was surprising unanimity on where the blame lay for this deplorable situation. The investigators dismissed poverty (although, even in good times, Robert Hunter concluded in 1904, as many as 10 million were in poverty), unsympathetic or incompetent teachers (An NEA report of 1910 revealed that of 600,000 public school teachers, 300,000 had no special preparation for their work.), ineffective compulsory education laws (Even as late as 1918, for practical purposes, compulsory education laws didn't affect children over 14.), and fastened on the curriculum. They said the curriculum wasn't meeting the interests or needs of the children, and it wasn't suited to their intellectual capabilities.

One of the best-publicized findings to come out of the report of the Massachusetts Commission on Industrial Education was that of the "two wasted years" between the ages of 14 and 16. The Commission discovered thousands of children between these ages out of school, out of work, or working at low-paying, dead-end jobs, a problem to themselves and the community. The situation of these children was "the most important question which faces the educational world today."[21] Why were they out of school? This is a difficult question to answer. The Commission's chief investigator stated the opinion of most school officials: the schools were at

[20] For example, Leonard P. Ayres, *Laggards in Our Schools* (New York: Russell Sage Foundation, 1908); Edward L. Thorndike, *The Elimination of Pupils from School*, U. S. Bureau of Education Bulletin no. 4 (Washington, D.C., 1908); George D. Strayer, *Age and Grade Census of Schools and Colleges*, U. S. Bureau of Education Bulletin no. 5, (Washington, D.C., 1911); George D. Strayer, *Educational Administration: Quantitative Studies* (New York: Macmillan, 1913), pp. 12–13.

[21] Columbia University, Teachers College, *Report of the Massachusetts Commission on Industrial and Technical Education*, Educational Reprints no. 1 (New York, 1906), pp. 25, 30–31.

fault, school didn't appeal to children, and "the great lack is in the system, which fails to offer the child of fourteen continued schooling of a practical character."[22] What the children desired was vocational education. This view was to gain immediate and widespread acceptance. Thus, the editor of *Manual Training Magazine* dismissed out of hand the exigencies of poverty, inadequate teachers, and ineffective compulsory education laws as possible explanation of why children left school. He wrote: "Children leave school because they do not like to go to school, because the work is distasteful to them and offers them little or nothing that they conceive to be of value in their lives. It is useless to attempt to explain the great loss in school attendance on other grounds."[23] If children were offered industrial training, the schools' holding power would be enormously increased. Since there was little empirical evidence in support of this proposition, advocates hedged, asserting that if industrial training was not what the children wanted, it was what they needed.

At the turn of the century, American school reformers began to note the appearance in the public schools of that vast category of the population known as the "masses." And the masses, the vast majority of school children, they were convinced, were destined to follow manual pursuits. For Nicholas Murray Butler, the question of vocational education was the question of "adapting by far the larger proportion of the population to their environment."[24] Similar sentiments were echoed by leaders in public education before annual meetings of the National Education Association. The superintendent of schools of North Carolina in 1910 spoke for many when he pointed out, that 90 percent of the people in the United States make their living by industrial pursuits. Scarcely 5 percent ever reach the college or university. What America needs, he concluded, was a system of public education adapted to "the industrial masses, who are the people."[25] For the children of the masses, the whole system of public education had to be reshaped along vocational lines to help them better to adjust to the life they were purportedly destined to lead.

But the argument was also advanced that vocational training was needed because it was the only kind of education these children could

22 Ibid., pp. 18, 44, 87.

23 "Why Children Leave School," *Manual Training Magazine* 14 (April 1913): 360; Helen M. Todd, "Why Children Work: The Children's Answer," *McClure's Magazine* 40 (April 1913): 74; "What Children Who Leave School Really Need," *The Survey* 30 (24 May 1913): 273–74; Lovejoy, "The Function of Education in Abolishing Child Labor," pp. 84–86.

24 Nicholas Murray Butler, *Vocational Education: An Address* (Chicago, Ill., 1913), p. 6.

25 James Joyner, "Some Dominant Tendencies in American Education," *Journal of Proceedings and Addresses,* National Education Association (1909): 53–54; Lorenzo D. Harvey, "The Need, Scope, and Character of Industrial Education in the Public Schools," ibid. (1910): 80.

understand and appreciate, the kind of education best suited to their intellectual capacities. As one studies the writings of diverse school reformers of this period it becomes apparent that no sooner had the problem of mass education made its appearance than they began to assume a vast deterioration in the school's clientele, though it was seldom put so bluntly. As early as 1899 John Dewey was proclaiming, "in the great majority of human beings the distinctively intellectual interest is not dominant. They have the so-called practical impulse and disposition."[26] In 1904 G. Stanley Hall called attention to "the great army of incapables" in the public schools.[27] Investigators of the dropout problem reinforced these doubts about the intellectual potential of the school's population. Leonard Ayres in 1908 in his extremely influential *Laggards in Our Schools* concluded that the course of studies in our city school systems "are adjusted to the power of the brighter pupils. They are beyond the powers of the average pupils, and far beyond those of the slower ones."[28] This dim view of the capacities of the children was shared by some leaders of the social settlement movement. In 1911 two leading social workers asserted:

> So far as consecutive application to accepted cultural studies is concerned, *full disclosure of the facts shows comprehensive lack not only of background but of latent instinct.* Among people whose powers are fundamentally manual, and whose prospects lie chiefly in the direction of those powers, educational service must necessarily be turned into channels of industrial training. [Italics mine.][29]

For the academically inept, the unscholarly, the misfits, which is to say, the new clientele of the public school, the solution was industrial training. This argument had great appeal and, like the proverbial bad penny, kept turning up.[30]

THE INDUSTRIAL EDUCATION MOVEMENT: NEEDS OF SOCIETY

The school reformers' stated concern with the needs and interests of children can, however, be overemphasized; the needs and interests of American industrial society no less than those of the children conspired to demand

---

[26] John Dewey, *The School and Society* (Chicago, Ill.: University of Chicago Press, 1900), p. 42.

[27] G. Stanley Hall, *Adolescence,* 2 vols. (New York, 1904), 2: 510.

[28] Ayres, *Laggards in Our Schools,* pp. 5, 7, 88; Thorndike, *The Elimination of Pupils from School,* p. 10; Strayer, *Age and Grade Census of Schools and Colleges,* pp. 139–40.

[29] Robert A. Woods and Albert J. Kennedy, *The Settlement Horizon* (New York: Russell Sage Foundation, 1911), pp. 136–37.

[30] Krug, *The Shaping of the American High School,* pp. 227 ff.

industrial education. With dramatic suddenness, by the last year of the nineteenth century America emerged as the world's foremost industrial nation, and a powerful rival to England and Germany in world trade. The epithets, "American peril" and "American menace"—terms frequently employed by Europeans to describe this new giant in their midst—amply testifies to this phenomenon.[31] Americans seemed to awaken somewhat later than the rest of the world to this new fact of international life. It was a great awakening. Nothing, said an official of the U. S. Bureau of Education in 1904, has tended to open the eyes of Americans more than the consternation and concern of European nations. To Europeans the "American peril" is a real one. No American, he concluded, does not take pride in this forced tribute to American strength and greatness.[32]

Such sentiments could unloose visions. In volume of output, a Congressional commission noted in 1915, the U. S. leads the four great manufacturing nations of the world. But, it continued, we had only begun to contest for world markets. Pointing to the more than one and a half billion people living outside the Big Four but dependent upon them for manufactured goods, the commission observed," the rewards offered in this world trade are beyond comprehension."[33] If rivalry in trade and commerce was destined to be the warfare of the future, as many were predicting, then Americans were determined to carry off the victor's share of the spoils. At last, declared one school man, America is coming into her own. She is coming to recognize a twofold ideal—"industrial supremacy and perfected democracy. . . . Industrial supremacy is America's rightful ideal."[34] Now the question of the recruitment and proper training of a new-style army, an industrial army, assumed in the United States the same urgency it was assuming in England, and had assumed a generation earlier in Germany.

The officers for this new army, the lieutenants and "captains of industry," would be recruited and trained in the engineering and scientific and

31 Edward J. Kirkland, *Industry Comes of Age: Business, Labor, and Public Policy, 1860–1897* (New York: Holt, Rinehart & Winston, 1961), chap. XIV; Richard H. Heindel, *The American Impact on Great Britain, 1898–1914* (Philadelphia: University of Pennsylvania Press, 1940), chap. VII; Harry Cranbrook Allen, *The Anglo-Saxon Relationship Since 1783* (New York: St. Martin's Press, 1959), pp. 110 ff.

32 Howard J. Rogers, "The Relation of Education to Industrial and Commercial Development," *Educational Review* 23 (May 1902): 493.

33 U. S. House of Representatives, *Report of the Commission on National Aid to Vocational Education,* 2 vols. (Washington, D.C., 1914), 1: 11.

34 Alvin E. Dodd, "Better Grammar Grade Provision for the Vocational Needs of Those Likely to Enter Industrial Pursuits," *Manual Training Magazine* 11 (December 1909): 98. See also Andrew S. Draper, *Our Children, Our Schools, and Our Industries* (Albany, N.Y.: New York State Education Department, 1907), p. 88; Frank T. Carlton, *Education and Industrial Evolution* (New York: Macmillan, 1908), p. 136; Ellwood P. Cubberley, *Changing Conceptions of Education* (Boston: Houghton Mifflin, 1908), pp. 49–50.

business schools. Here was no problem. But industry desperately needed privates (it was estimated that the country's labor force required at least one million additions annually). In the candid terminology of the time, what the new industrial order needed was "the training of recruits for our leading mechanical industries"; the service of an army of semi-skilled workers who would "adjust nicely (to) the industrial machine"; "high privates who can adequately meet unexpected situations and an industrial rank and file who shall rise to the possibilities of the less skilled type of work"; an army of privates, obeying orders, "keeping step, as it were, to the tap of the drum."[35] In other words, what the schools had to provide was an education with an industrial bias—one which would predispose the children to enter the factories and manual trades, impress them with the "dignity of labor," and equip them with "industrial intelligence." They would require some facility with handling tools and machines, basic literacy to enable them to read and understand directions, and discipline enough to enable them better to conform to the requirements of large-scale, rationalized, factory routine.[36] The privates, the rank and file, would be recruited and drilled in the public schools.

Many complained, however, that the American boy was uninterested in manual occupations; to him, mechanical labor was just a little bit servile. Worse yet, the American public school did little to make such work more enticing. Indeed, the schools positively tended to unfit youth for such work. In the course of his Annual Message to Congress in 1907, Theodore Roosevelt declared: "Our school system is gravely defective insofar as it puts a premium upon mere literacy training and tends therefore to train the boy away from the farm and the workshop."[37] American public schools were too literary in their spirit, scope, and methods. In an address to the NEA, the Commissioner of Education for New York State complained:

> Our elementary schools train for no industrial employments. They lead to nothing but the secondary school, which in turn leads to the college, the university, and the professional school, and so very exclusively to the professional and managerial occupations.[38]

---

[35] For example, Hanus, "Industrial Education," *Atlantic Monthly,* January 1908, p. 60; Woods, "Industrial Education From the Social Worker's Standpoint," pp. 854–55; Carlton, *The Industrial Situation,* p. 69; David E. Wells, *Recent Economic Changes* (New York, 1888), p. 93. See also the discussion of the problem of recruiting and training of workers in Kirkland, *Industry Comes of Age,* chap. XVI.

[36] See the general discussion in Paul H. Douglas, *American Apprenticeship and Industrial Education* (New York: Columbia University Press, 1921), p. 76; and Kirkland, *Industry Comes of Age,* chap. VIII.

[37] Quoted in Krug, *The Shaping of the American High School,* p. 225.

[38] Andrew S. Draper, "The Adaptation of the Schools to Industry and Efficiency," *Journal of Proceedings and Addresses,* National Education Association (1908): 70. See also James E. Russell, "The School and Industrial Life," *Educa-*

The public schools were criticized for encouraging ambitions to soar too high. This same educational leader asserted that the program of the public school and the influence of the teachers, acting upon our national temperament and aspirations "have led an undue proportion of youth to literature and scientific study which too often ends either in idleness or insipidity, or in professional or managing occupations for which they are not well prepared which are already overcrowded."[39] While the dean of Teachers College, Columbia, thoughtfully inquired in 1906:

> How can a nation endure that deliberately seeks to raise ambitions and aspirations in the oncoming generations which in the nature of events cannot possibly be fulfilled? If the chief object of government be to promote civic order and social stability, how can we justify our practice in schooling the masses in precisely the same manner as those who are to be our leaders?[40]

There was a crying need for labor. Many Americans were apprehensive that if the schools were not given an industrial bias, there would be no one to tend the machines or go down into the mines. Adults would, but would their children? And if the latter did, how efficient would they be? After all, the children of today were the workers of tomorrow. As the United States Commissioner of Education asserted in 1909, during an address to the NEA, "There is no doubt that industrial education is needed to perpetuate the prosperity of our industries. This aspect of the case has been widely discussed and may simply be taken for granted here."[41]

At first the main thrust of the industrial education movement was aimed at the high schools. Very shortly, however, the limited value of this objective became apparent. Not only had the children to be recruited into the vocational high schools or into vocational tracks in comprehensive high schools but, more important, children weren't staying for the high school course. They were leaving in large numbers before the end of the eighth

---

tional Review 38 (December 1909): 439; Charles R. Richard, "The Problems of Industrial Education," *Manual Training Magazine* 8 (April 1907): 127; Paul H. Hanus, "Industrial Education," p. 60.

39 Draper, "The Adaptation of the Schools to Industry and Efficiency," p. 69. See also Draper, *Our Children, Our Schools, and Our Industries,* p. 56.

40 James E. Russell, "The Trend in American Education," *Educational Review* 32 (November 1906): 39. See also Russell, "Democracy and Education; Equal Opportunity for All," *Journal of Proceedings and Addresses,* National Education Association (1908): 157.

41 Elmer Ellsworth Brown, "Industrial Education as a National Interest," *Journal of Proceedings and Addresses,* National Education Association (1909): 288. See also Frank T. Carlton, *The Industrial Situation: Its Effects Upon the Home, the School, the Wage Earner and the Employer* (New York: Macmillan, 1914), pp. 65–66; Frank F. Bunker, *Reorganization of the Public School System,* U. S. Bureau of Education Bulletin no. 8 (Washington, D.C., 1916), p. 115.

grade. The problem was one of keeping them in school up to the eighth grade and exposing them to some form of vocational training before they left. In other words, by 1907 or 1908 the problem of vocational training in the public schools had become the problem of the elementary schools. The problem became one of adjusting the work of the elementary school for those who, upon graduation, or for those who, upon dropping out before graduation, entered the world of work. Out of the search for some solution to this problem came the theory of "differentiation."

The upper grades were to differentiate between the needs of those children preparing for high school and higher education, and those children whose education would be terminated with the elementary school. The editor of *Manual Training Magazine* called for the organization of "intermediate industrial schools," or "junior industrial high schools." Others (Russell and DeGarmo and Leavitt) proposed that the upper grades of the elementary schools, the seventh and eighth grades, be devoted to "prevocational" education; Ben Johnson, that the upper grades offer alternative courses of study: general, commercial, and vocational.[42] Once in motion, the drive for differentiation inevitably would impinge upon the lower grades. The statistics on early school leaving, if nothing else, ensured that it would. As early as 1907, one of the leaders of the National Society for the Promotion of Industrial Education urged a modification of the elementary school program beginning in the sixth grade.[43] In 1908, the NSPIE at its Chicago meeting came out for the introduction of "elementary industrial education in some form."[44] In 1910 the Superintendent of Schools of Cleveland, Ohio, introduced a plan of differentiated courses of instruction beginning in the fifth grade in the public schools of that city.[45] And by 1910, in the public schools of Gary, Indiana, the superintendent of schools, William Wirt, was actually demonstrating a scheme of vocational training beginning in the fourth grade. By 1915 John Dewey and many other pro-

---

[42] "Elementary Industrial Education," *Manual Training Magazine* 10 (October 1908): 165; James E. Russell, "The School and Industrial Life," *Educational Review* 38 (December 1909): 437; Charles DeGarmo, "Relation of Industrial to General Education," *School Review* 17 (March 1909): 152; Frank M. Leavitt, "Industrial Education in the Elementary Schools," *Manual Training Magazine* 9 (June 1908): 378–79; Ben W. Johnson, "Industrial Education in the Elementary School," *Journal of Proceedings and Addresses,* National Education Association, 1910, pp. 253–60; Draper, "The Adaptation of the Schools to Industrial Efficiency," 76–77; Krug, *The Shaping of the American High School*, pp. 237–41.

[43] James P. Haney, "Vocational Work for the Elementary School," *Educational Review* 39 (November 1907): 339–40.

[44] James P. Haney, "The National Society For the Promotion of Industrial Education," *Manual Training Magazine* 11 (October 1909): 33–34.

[45] William H. Elson and Frank P. Bachman, "Different Course For Elementary School," *Educational Review* 39 (April 1910): 361–63; William H. Elson and Frank P. Bachman, "Need of Different Elementary School Courses," *Elementary School Teacher* 10 (December 1909): 202.

gressives would be singing the praises of the Gary plan.[46] The enthusiasm for differentiation reached its peak at the Cincinnati meeting of the Department of Superintendence of the NEA in 1915 with the passing of a resolution bestowing approval on the "increasing tendency to establish beginning with the seventh grade, differentiated courses of study aimed more effectively to prepare the child for his probable future activities."[47] According to the record, only one educator, Superintendent Maxwell of New York City, spoke out against the resolution. He found the notion unacceptable that children of twelve and thirteen were prepared to choose their future course of instruction and presumably their life's work.

Partisans of vocational training agreed with Maxwell that youngsters were hardly prepared to wisely choose their course of studies and their life's work. This is where vocational guidance enters the picture. Implicit in the notion of differentiation is the elective principle. And implicit in the principle of election (a principle which, incidentally, by 1915 had been in retreat on the college level for at least a decade), is the wise guidance of children. Children needed direction; industry needed recruits. Out of these imperatives came the vocational guidance movement. The same people were active in both movements; their objectives were identical. In November 1910 the first National Conference on Vocational Guidance and the National Society for the Promotion of Industrial Education met concurrently in Boston. Felix Adler, Paul Hanus, Robert Archey Woods, S. McCune Lindsay, Charles R. Richards and David Snedden were among the more than 300 delegates from more than 35 cities who mingled at both conferences and discussed ways of adjusting the public schools to the social and industrial needs of the day.[48] Training labor for industry went hand in hand with vocational guidance, a fact which is forgotten today.[49]

With the drive for industrial education picking up more and more momentum each year, another problem arose. The high school was, or was

46 Winthrop D. Lane, "Education and Work: A Twilight Zone," *The Survey* 29 (23 November 1912): 227–28; John Dewey and Evelyn Dewey, *Schools of Tomorrow* (New York: Dutton, 1962), chap. 10. Examples of "prevocational" work in grades six to eight may be found in Frank M. Leavitt, *Examples of Industrial Education* (Boston: Ginn, 1912), chap. 10.

47 National Education Association, *Journal of Proceedings and Addresses* (1915): 256–57.

48 The 1913 Convention of the National Society for the Promotion of Industrial Education became the occasion for the organization of the National Vocational Guidance Association. See, for example, Meyer Bloomfield, "Vocational Guidance and Industrial Education," *The Survey* 25 (26 November 1910): 319–29; John M. Brewer, *History of Vocational Guidance: Origins and Early Developments* (New York, 1942), pp. 137–41; Krug, *The Shaping of the American High School*, p. 242.

49 Charles Prosser, Secretary of the NSPIE, declared that vocational education and vocational guidance are necessary in meeting the problem of fitting the great mass of our people for useful employment. "Each is the handmaiden of the other and each is indispensable to the success of the other," *Journal of Proceedings and Addresses*, National Education Association (1912): 647.

fast becoming, the educational ideal of the middle class throughout the country. It was necessary to assure these parents who looked forward to sending their children to academic high schools that vocational training was not intended for their offspring. Vocational guidance was one answer; the "neighborhood school" concept was another. It was as evident then as now that families of roughly similar social rank tend to inhabit the same neighborhoods. Vocational training would not be for all children. The socioeconomic status of a neighborhood would dictate the particular course of study to be followed in the neighborhood elementary school. Perhaps the earliest, certainly the most candid, explanation of the neighborhood basis for differentiation came in 1910 from William H. Elson, superintendent of schools of Cleveland. Superintendent Elson called for different courses of study for the elementary school, courses adapted to the needs of varying districts and of particular groups of children. Elson asserted:

> It is obvious that the educational needs of children in a district where the streets are well paved and clean, where the homes are spacious and surrounded by lawns and trees, where the language of the child's play-fellows is pure, and where life in general is permeated with the spirit and ideals of America—it is obvious that the educational needs of such a child are radically different from those of the child who lives in a foreign and tenement section....[50]

This neighborhood concept of education, with its implications of class education, came strangely from the lips of American educators.

WHO PROFITS? WHO LOSES?

Indeed much that was spawned by the industrial education movement was strange. It has not been generally realized how radical the whole notion of "differentiation" is, how subversive of old ideas, of traditional American principles. The contrast was usually drawn between the democratic education of America and the class education of Europe, of which Germany was usually singled out as the prime offender. In Europe, Americans like to say, a boy's career was fixed by his family's tradition and financial resources. In Europe, a boy entered an occupation similar to his father's. But in America, educational opportunity was divorced substantially from the individual family's capacity to pay and from its social position. In America

[50] Elson and Bachman, "Different Courses for Elementary Schools," pp. 357–59; and Elson and Bachman, "Need of Different Elementary School Courses," pp. 202–3. See also Ellwood P. Cubberley, *The Portland Survey: A Textbook on City School Administration Based on a Concrete Study* (New York: World Book Co., 1916), pp. 274–78; Paul H. Hanus, *School Efficiency, A Constructive Study Applied to New York City: Being a Summary and Report on the Educational Aspects of the School Inquiry* (New York: World Book Co., 1913), pp. 15 ff.

the public schools equalized the opportunities of rich and poor, gave all a fair start in life's race. This ideal of the availability of free, quality public education regardless of the social status of the prospective student, had been a vital part of American democracy. One of the proudest boasts of Americans had been that their public school system, with its "ladder" organization, came nearer the realization of the ideal of democratic education than any other country in the world. There was no cul-de-sac in American education. Each stage led to the one higher, from the kindergarten to the university. Furthermore, public education in America was characterized by its prolonging as long as possible the years of general education for all children, thus putting off as long as possible the time when students are distinguished according to their future calling in life. No one said it better than the venerable Charles W. Eliot who, in 1905, declared:

> In a democratic society the classification of pupils, according to their so-called probable destinations, should be postponed to the latest possible time of life. It is common in Europe to classify children very early into future peasants, mechanics, tradespeople, merchants, and professional people, and to adapt deliberately the education of children from a very early age to this decreed destination. In a democratic society like ours, these early determinations of the career should be avoided as long as possible, particularly in public schools. For example, the point in the program of the public high school at which pupils who are going to college diverges from the pupils who are not going to college should be placed as late as possible, not in the interest of the college, ... but in the interest of the pupils whose educational careers should not be too early determined.[51]

But now, towards the end of the first decade of the twentieth century, Americans were in a new mood. In 1907, a social settlement leader asserted:

> it used to be thought and still is thought by some that it is contrary to the genius of American principles of social equality that any young person should select his own calling, or that he should have it selected for him at an early age. Every boy and girl is a possible occupant of the White House. Such teaching is far more weirdly Utopian than that of our present day social dreamers.[52]

In 1909 a leading educator, Ellwood Cubberley, advised:

51 Charles W. Eliot, "The Fundamental Assumptions of the Report of the Committee of Ten," *Educational Review* 30 (November 1905): 330–31. Practically all European countries made provision for early differentiation; in Germany at about the age of ten, in England at eleven or twelve.

52 Woods, "Industrial Education from the Worker's Standpoint," p. 855.

Our city schools will soon be forced to give up the exceedingly democratic idea that all are equal, and that our society is devoid of classes, as a few cities have already in large part done, and to begin a specialization of educational effort along many lines in an attempt better to adapt the school to the needs of these many classes in the city life. . . . The new and extensive interest in industrial and vocational training is especially significant of the changing conception of the school and the classes in society which the school is in the future expected to serve.[53]

And by then, Eliot, like so many others, swept along by the force of the industrial education movement, was advocating the very doctrine he had so eloquently attacked just three years before. In 1908, in an address to the National Society for the Promotion of Industrial Education, Eliot advocated trade schools for children "who are unfortunately obliged to leave the regular public school system by the time they are fourteen, or even earlier." On this same occasion, Eliot called upon elementary school teachers to assume a new responsibility. They "ought to sort out the pupils and sort them out by their evident or probable destinies." A year later Eliot was describing American society as being divided into four "layers," each possessing "distinct characteristics and distinct educational needs."[54]

Not only was the American educational tradition now to be dismissed as "weirdly Utopian," but it was attacked as undemocratic. In an astonishing turnabout, differentiation in education was to be achieved in the name of "democracy." More and more in the literature of the industrial education movement, American public education is disparaged as "undemocratic," "class" education, really benefitting only a small proportion of the children in the schools, those preparing for college and the professions, and not providing equality of opportunity for the vast majority. The "educational publicist," said Eliot, "must keep in mind the interests of the 95 percent of the children, rather than those of the 5 percent. . . ."[55] The professional and managerial classes, the dean of Teachers College declared, are well provided for in the public schools. We must see to it that the "common man" is equally well provided for.[56] To Dewey, all education was voca-

[53] Ellwood P. Cubberley, *Changing Conceptions of Education* (Boston: Houghton Mifflin, 1908), pp. 53, 56–57.

[54] Charles W. Eliot, *Industrial Education as an Essential Factor in Our National Prosperity,* National Society For the Promotion of Industrial Education Bulletin no. 5 (1908): 9, 12–13; Eliot, "Educational Reform and the Social Order," *School Review* 17 (April 1909): 217–19.

[55] Charles W. Eliot, *Changes Needed In American Secondary Education,* Publications of the General Education Board Occasional Papers, no. 2 (New York, 1916), p. 18.

[56] James E. Russell, "The Trend In American Education," *Educational Review* 34 (November 1906): 30; Russell, "Democracy and Education: Equal Opportunity For All," pp. 155–58; Russell, "The School and Industrial Life," p. 450.

tional. The present system of education in America was undemocratic because it provided vocational training only for the future professional classes.[57] It was almost inevitable that one educationist, the Commissioner of Education of New York State, would exclaim, "Germany is educationally more democratic than the United States."[58] To be really democratic, American public schools had to offer the children of the masses the privilege of vocational education, and this as early as possible.

What really was involved here? Why the push and why at this specific time? · Why so aggressively? These questions are insistent. There was something more involved in the industrial education movement than America's race with England and Germany for industrial and commercial supremacy; something more than that the thousands of children in the public schools simply had to be wage earners at age fourteen or sooner; something more than the "new psychology." To get at what else was involved, it will be necessary to raise some questions different from those that are usually raised, questions like the following: Who were in the schools? Who was making policy for the schools? How did the schools' clientele affect the school reformer's work and attitudes?

It is certainly correct to say that no school system is created for children who aren't there. And it is also true that no school system is created for children about whom one doesn't have some preconceived notions as to their character, their capacity, and their proper place in life. Who were in the schools? At the turn of the century, the American public schools were attended in greater and greater numbers by foreign-born children, or the children of foreign-born parents. By late 1908, when the U. S. Immigration Commission made its massive study, 57.8 percent of the children in the public schools of 37 of America's largest cities were of foreign parentage. By 1908 there were half as many children of foreign parentage in the public high schools of the country as there were children of the native-born.[59] In effect, the American public school system was being transformed for the immigrants and their children. Who was making policy for the schools? Theodore Lowi, in his excellent study of ethnic politics in New York City, describes how the "Old Guard"—the native, white, Yankee Protestant—pushed roughly aside in city politics, still retained control of the Board of Education. The Board, said Professor Lowi, was one of the

---

57 John Dewey, "Learning How to Learn: The Place of Vocational Education in a Comprehensive Scheme of Public Education," *School and Society* 5 (March 1917), pp. 331–35.

58 Draper, *Our Children, Our Schools, and Our Industries,* pp. 7, 44; Draper, "The Adaptation of the Schools to Industry and Efficiency," p. 74.

59 U.S. Immigration Commission, *Reports of the Immigration Commission,* 41 vols., *The Children of Immigrants In The Schools,* vols. 29–33 (Washington D.C., 1911), 29: 14, 15, 23. In the public schools of Boston, 63.5% of the children were of foreign-parentage, in the public schools of Chicago, 67.3%, in those of New York City, 71.5%.

last enclaves of the "gentleman in public office."[60] To widen the focus from New York, American education in general in the pre-World War I period, at all levels, was the last enclave of gentlemen in public office. Native, white, rural or small-town-bred, Anglo-Saxon, and Protestant in origin and conviction, they dominated the highest echelons of the National Education Association, the U. S. Bureau of Education, the boards of education, the city and state school superintendencies, the schools of education and the teachers colleges, and the classrooms of the nation.[61]

How did the school's clientele affect the school reformer's attitude and activities? To ask this question is to ask the question, How did the new immigrants affect Americans in general? The decades 1880–1920 witnessed the greatest, and presumably the last, of the great waves of European immigration to the United States. Especially from the southern and eastern parts of Europe, myriads of the poor and ignorant flocked to America. These were the "new immigrants." For most, the city was their destination. In the city they encountered the old-stock, Yankee-Protestant American. The encounter was anything but friendly, culminating finally in the passage of restrictive legislation in the early 1920s. The phenomenon of nativism, thanks to the researches of John Higham, among others, is well known.[62] It affected the schools. Educators are men of their time, sharing the same attitudes, social philosophy, frame of reference, prejudices as their contemporaries. The pervasive anti-immigrant sentiment of the old-stock, Yankee-Protestant American was shared by the American educator, old-stock, Yankee-Protestant American as he overwhelmingly was. But at the same time as the "gentleman" held anti-immigrant sentiments, he also subscribed to the democratic doctrine which stressed equality of opportunity

---

[60] Theodore J. Lowi, *At the Pleasure of The Mayor: Patronage and Power In New York City, 1898–1958* (New York: Free Press, 1964), p. 30, *passim*.

[61] Available studies reveal that even as late as the early 1930s, 98.5% of the country's school superintendents were native-born, 90% were of Anglo-Saxon ancestry. The composite picture of the American school superintendent shows that: he is native, white, of long-established American ancestry; he was born, reared, and educated in a rural environment, by parents who were regular attendants at a Protestant Evangelical church. Studies done of school board members in the late twenties and early thirties reveal that school boards typically represented the professional and mercantile classes. About the regular classroom teachers, a 1911 study revealed that 91.3% of the men and 83.8% of the women were native-born, while 89.9% of the men and 85.5% of the women were of Anglo-Saxon lineage. The vast majority had been reared and educated on a farm or in a small hamlet. See Lotus Delta Coffman, *The Social Composition of The Teaching Population* (New York: Teachers College Publications, 1911), chap. 3; Frederick Haigh Bair, *The Social Understandings of the Superintendent of Schools* (New York: Teachers College Publications, 1934), sec. 3; Claude E. Arnett, *Social Beliefs and Understandings of School Board Members* (Emporia, Kan., 1932), *passim*. These studies are ably summarized in Jesse H. Newlon, *Educational Administration As Social Policy* (New York, 1934), chaps. 6–8.

[62] John Higham, *Strangers in the Land: Patterns of American Nativism, 1860–1925* (New Brunswick, N.J., 1955).

and free schooling. This ambivalence worked itself out in many ways. It served to pull the young of minority groups into the schoolhouse and provide them with all sorts of recreational and social facilities and medical and health services, at the same time attempting to provide these children with the sort of education which would keep them in their place.

A final note. There is more involved in the sharpening of discrimination in the first decade of the twentieth century than anti-immigrant sentiments. As Professor Higham suggests, it is necessary to widen the focus of nativism from anti-immigrant, antiradical, and racist sentiments to encompass the persistent social tensions woven into the fabric of our social organization, to encompass "status rivalries," the intense competition for status and position in a society featuring social mobility.[63] By the opening years of the twentieth century Americans were beginning to feel crowded. The frontier was losing its ability to keep hopes high; the historic census of 1890 officially declared the frontier—the open road westward and upward—closed. Old-stock Americans were becoming apprehensive about the decline of mobility and opportunity. At the same time they witnessed the spectacle of the "new immigrants" quitting the slums in conspicuous numbers, their children flocking into the elementary schools, crowding the high schools, pushing into college, and scrambling for jobs in the white collar world and the professions. As the immigrants climbed, obstacles were thrown across their paths. They were increasingly shut out of clubs, summer resorts, private schools. They found it increasingly difficult to enter college and college fraternities ad college faculties. Restrictive covenants began to appear in urban residential areas. Job opportunities began to contract. The public schools were also affected. American school reformers familiar with European education, realized that schools can promote or restrict social mobility, dampen ambition or cause ambition to soar. Industrial education became a defense against the swift upward thrust of the new immigrant.

In short, a growing apprehension that competition for position and prestige was becoming too keen is an important factor in the industrial education movement. The zeal with which progressives pursued industrial education into the lowest grades of the public school cannot be understood if this factor is overlooked. Still, the temper of the American public was more democratic than that of many of its erstwhile school leaders, in or outside of education. The Smith-Hughes Act of 1917 restricted federal aid to schools offering vocational training to persons over fourteen years of age and who had already laid the foundation of a general education in the elementary school. As one disappointed advocate of industrial training pointed out, the Act refused to recognize the junior high school as "the

63 John Higham, "Another Look at Nativism," *Catholic Historical Review* 44 (July 1953): 147–58.

vocational preparatory school of the future."[64] With passage of the Smith-Hughes Act, the steam went out of the industrial education movement. No doubt the movement resulted in more choice and flexibility in the school system. But it left another legacy, not so beneficent: the widespread conviction among American schoolmen that in a system of mass education, the academic side of school work was inappropriate for a majority of the nation's children.

NEEDS AND OPPORTUNITIES FOR STUDY

This essay has presented a point of view. It has raised questions and offered "answers." But it is not my answers that I am particularly concerned with impressing upon you; rather it is the questions. Regardless of whether the historian explicitly asks questions like those raised in this essay, let the reader himself judge the data and put the actors in the historical drama he is reading about in the witness chair and force them, by his astute questions, to testify. Then let the reader put the historian himself in the witness chair. On close inspection, the events of history turn out to be not hard and objective facts, but impalpable and subjective reflections of their time. The great historian, Leopold von Ranke, and his successors, taught us to rely on documents for our history; the documents, they were confident, would speak for themselves. Quite the contrary. They speak, rather, for us, and with a hundred different voices. The frequently expressed ideal that history be completely objective and dispassionate is an illusion. The history we read, after all, does not exist independently of the historian; it is something that comes to us filtered through the mind and the imagination of men. And bias is as human as error. Try as he may, the historian cannot shed his personality or his beliefs and prejudices. Historians are creatures—even prisoners—of their time, their place, their faith, their race, their social class, their country. Let the reader look sharply and read critically to detect the bias and "the frame of reference." Indeed, I wish that readers, interested students, apprentice historians would, as an exercise in historical research and writing, check for themselves the accuracy of my footnote citations, decide for themselves the validity of my interpretation of sources, then revise the above interpretation of the industrial education movement, or sections of it, according to their own understanding of what really happened.[65]

[64] Paul Kreuzpointner, "The Smith-Hughes Act From A Layman's Standpoint," *School and Society* 8 (27 July 1918): 103.

[65] This is a good exercise to employ on any work of history: verify the historian's footnotes as to accuracy and interpretation of sources. Before attempting this assignment, students should read Jacques Barzun and Henry Graff, *The Modern Researcher* (New York: Harcourt Brace Jovanovich, 1957), and Sherman Kent, *Writing History* (New York: Appleton-Century-Crofts, 1941), or Henry Steele

Again, it's the questions in which I'm interested. It's time to begin asking new, different, and tough-minded questions of the data of educational history—questions having to do with power, prizes, group interests. It's time to bring to our enterprise an awareness of the ethnic, religious, moral, and social conflict that have always characterized American life. And it's also time to ask questions having to do with the effect of educational institutions on individual growth and development. Are American schools as destructive of human personality and even, ironically, of human intelligence, as recent books and articles vigorously point out?[66] Finally, it is time to look at American education from the perspective of minority groups—Negro, Indian, Mexican-American, Puerto Rican. For example, today the Negro is no longer "the invisible man," yet we have hardly begun to unravel the history of Negro education. Although we have considerable knowledge of Southern Negro education, we know next to nothing about education in the black ghettos of the North.[67] One way to start is by reading the autobiographies of men like Malcolm X, Gordon Parks, Richard Wright, and Langston Hughes, who have revealed what it has been like to grow up black in white America.[68] We know even less about what it has been like to grow up as a Mexican-American and to go to school in America. The second largest minority in the Uuited States, the Mexican-Americans are still "forgotten Americans."[69] We know even less of the American Indians. What needs and opportunities await the historian of education is this field!

If we do what I have suggested above, if we ask the tough-minded questions; if we take flights from time to time into the unknown, use the

Commager, *The Nature and Study of History* (New York: Charles E. Merrill, 1965). The authors cover the theoretical aspects of research as well as provide manuals of style and technique for the researcher.

66 Herbert Kohl, *36 Children* (New York: New American Library, 1967); James Herndon, *The Way It Spozed to Be* (New York: Simon and Schuster, 1968); Jonathan Kozol, *Death at An Early Age* (Boston: Houghton Mifflin, 1967); Peter Schrag, *Village School Downtown* (Boston: Beacon Press, 1967); Nat Hentoff, *Our Children Are Dying* (New York: Viking, 1966); John Holt, *Why Children Fail* (New York: Pitman, 1964), Paul Goodman, *Compulsory Mis-Education and the Community of Scholars* (New York: Random House, 1966); Carl Nordstrom, Edgar Z. Friedenberg, Hilary A. Gold, *Society's Children: A Study of Resentment in the Secondary School* (New York: Random House, 1967).

67 Horace Mann Bond, *Education of the Negro in the American Social Order* (Englewood Cliffs, N.J.: Prentice-Hall, 1934); Louis Harlan, *Separate and Unequal* (New York: Atheneum, 1968); Henry A. Bullock, *A History of Negro Education in the South* (Cambridge: Harvard University Press, 1967).

68 Malcolm X, *The Autobiography of Malcolm X* (New York: Grove Press, 1964); Gordon Parks, *The Learning Tree* (New York: Harper & Row, 1963); Richard Wright, *Black Boy* (Cleveland: World Publishing Co., 1947): Langston Hughes, *The Big Sea* (New York: Knopf, 1940). But also see James M. McPherson, "White Liberals and Black Power in Negro Education, 1865–1915," *American Historical Review* 75 (June 1970): 1357–79.

69 Julian Samora, ed., *La Raza: Forgotten Americans* (Notre Dame, Ind.: University of Notre Dame Press, 1966).

concepts and findings of political science, and sociology, and psychology, and psychoanalysis; if, in other words, we approach Clio with soul, we will discover a new complexity and richness and usefulness in American educational history. There is a danger, the danger of tendentiousness, of entanglement in partisan commitments. But there is a worse danger. C. Vann Woodward has said that we have arrived at an age that demands a great deal of the historian. This has special meaning for us in history of education where today we have a great thirst for historical meaning and interpretation in the field of education. What is required are answers to the kind of questions posed above, or even more astringent questions. If historians of education evade such questions, people will turn elsewhere for answers, and modern historians will qualify for the definition that Tolstoi formulated for the academic historians of his own day. He called them deaf men replying to questions that nobody put to them. On the other hand, if historians do address themselves to the historical questions for which this new age demands answers, this period might become known in historiography as the "Age of Reinterpretation." [70]

[70] C. Vann Woodward, "The Age of Reinterpretation," *American Historical Review* 20 (Spring 1968): 95–110.

3

the school,
the society,
and the individual

Carl Weinberg

CARL WEINBERG. Perhaps I should have asked one of my colleagues to do this job for me, but I had the feeling that no one would. It is one thing to tie other people into my conception of humanism. It is another to ask somebody to place me into my own perspective. So I will attempt the task myself.

I have, for the most part, described my beliefs in the introduction, and communicated my stand on humanism as an intellectual, emotional, and social phenomenon. The stages of my own life reflect the development of my academic and personal attachment to humanistic learning. I began my career in the humanities, completing a masters degree in English literature and getting ready to begin on a Ph. D. in this area when it occurred to me that, in order to make this kind of commitment, I should like poetry. At the time I quite despised poetry because I was unable to make any social sense out of most of it, and my social and political commitments were quite strong. I don't say this defensively but descriptively: I simply wasn't able to get much out of poetry at the time. I thought it was a dying literary form (and quite well may be) and it should be left alone to go peacefully. I no longer believe this. At any rate, I then left off my academic career and went to teach English in a black ghetto school. At this juncture I discovered that none of my academic work was appropriate. I became interested in the students and, particularly in their deviant patterns. This led me into sociology with major interests in social problems and education. My version of humanism at this time was entirely social reconstruction: to change things so that the kinds of students I worked with in the ghetto would be able to climb the mythical ladder of opportunity to a position of equal attainment, or at least to have a choice of attainments.

In the next few years I found my interests shifting from an interest in the sociological aspects of education to the educational aspects of social living. I still teach the basic course in the sociology of education at my university, but I now teach it with a major commitment to the learning rather than to the discipline. That is, I don't consider that I am any longer an expert in what I teach. The way I lost my expert status was to dispel the myth that there is such a thing as important content in sociology. There are really only important ways of looking at the social world, and one of the ways that I find most significant is through the meaning that students can contribute from their own experience to the understanding of a perspective on society. Some of this, I hope, comes through in my chapter.

Essentially, this particular chapter deals with my interest in social reconstruction, although there are points where I push for humanistic understanding of important sociological concepts. In order to redesign a society, one needs to understand the foundation blocks of the one that he inhabits and, particularly, see how his personal agony and alienation is linked to certain conventional structures in the social order.

I will say more about myself and my views on humanism in the chapters on psychology, literature, and guidance. Each of these chapters represents another similar—yet different in important ways—perspective on humanism.

THE SOCIOLOGY OF EDUCATION

This chapter will be a humanistic view of the sociology of education. The sociology of education is simply the application of sociological tools—that is, concepts like role and status—to the study and analysis of school systems. To make this meaningful in terms of one's personal experience will be the task of the chapter.

Sociology is both knowledge and a system of finding and organizing that knowledge. It is, more than anything else, a large accumulation of empirical studies about persons in institutional life. The sociology of education mainly consists of a number of studies about persons in educational life, how they function, how they define their situation, how they succeed or fail, how they are motivated, etc. Some of these studies will be mentioned as we proceed, but only as they illustrate the relationship between a fact or idea and the routine activities and concerns of the sociologists. An example of this relationship would be the following kind of statement:

> James Colman, in a comprehensive study of the educational opportunities of American students,[1] found that, in many areas, advantages were usually associated with one's race and socioeconomic position. American sociologists are critically interested in the consequences of being black or poor in America, both because they wish to describe the different conditions of American social life, and because they wish to reveal regularities within the American social structure. That is, they wish to know more than the social reality that there are differences; they want to know what difference such differences make.

Usually, sociologists who study the educational system report their findings in terms of rates of difference. The following table is a good example:

TABLE 1. Going to college

IQ Quintile		(High) 5	Father's Occupation 4	3	2	1	All Boys of Given IQ Level
(High)	5	89	76	55	40	29	52
	4	82	53	29	22	14	30
	3	79	47	22	19	10	24
	2	72	36	20	15	6	17
(Low)	1	56	28	12	4	9	11
All boys of given occupational level		80	52	26	19	12	

J. A. Kahl, "Educational and Occupational Aspirations of 'Common Man' Boys," *Harvard Educational Review* 23 (Summer 1953): 185.

[1] James Colman, *Equality of Educational Opportunity,* U.S. Office of Education Report (Washington D.C., 1968).

This table tells us that there is a relationship between one's socioeconomic status and going to college, regardless of intelligence, or, if we might infer further, of ability. The sociologist in this case has differentiated all the boys according to their fathers' occupations (statuses), tested intelligence scores and college aspirations. Since clear patterns appear, we infer that being in different socioeconomic categories makes a difference in the way in which one looks at education. The patterns tell us that there is some utility in making socioeconomic distinctions. They do not tell us, however, how these rates occur, or how they are produced. This requires another kind of analysis, one we can intuit perhaps, but one that is far more difficult to demonstrate, largely because sociology has not developed its tools to tell us why as adequately as it is able to tell us *what* is happening.

A humanistic sociology of education would be one that considers explanations of how the regularities we discover occur. We want to know, for example, how persons who are black, poor, male, adolescent, etc. are affected by being these things. We want to know more than differential rates of school achievement. We want to know how, for example, it happens that black students don't do as well as white students.

The sociologist as a person

This is a difficult task that I have: to separate the man from his work and then to put them back together again and display him in his humanistic togetherness. While the task is difficult it cannot be avoided for the idea is central to a humanistic conception of sociology. That is, without understanding how the man who does the work is related to the work we cannot understand the way in which humanism fits into sociology.

Sociology is, in itself, only a perspective on the world. It is a perspective that sees society through its own conceptual glasses. This means that persons walking around in the world are viewed as members of some distinct category of persons, performing certain functions, in certain regular ways. The sociologist is a person who has learned to see through those glasses. It is as if one were learning to make out forms that are invisible, and then one day, with the right glasses, one sees a whole new world of shapes and moving forms. In this way the student of sociology learns to see status groups, and racial groups, and bureaucratic patterns where, before, there were only people.

Now, what about the sociologist's old glasses, the ones through which he saw the world before learning how to use the new ones? Or what about the ones he wears when he's not working? Doesn't he sometimes forget to change them when he goes about his work? It depends. It depends upon his belief in the scientific ethos. What this means is that he becomes committed, to a greater or lesser degree, to seeing the world objectively and reporting it that way.

Objectivity, as a professional commitment, requires the sociologist to refrain from allowing his own values to color what he sees. The whole posture of objectivity is derived from the sociologist's sense of himself as a scientist. As a scientist, he must be not only committed to objectivity, he must also be somewhat aloof from being concerned about the use to which his work will be put once he has finished it.

Now, our concern is whether a humanistic sociology, given this conception of the sociologist, is possible. I don't think so. I believe that, in order to see any humanistic possibilities in sociology, or in the sociological study of the school, we need to reject both the necessity, and the possibility, that the sociologist exist as a true scientist. We have to believe that the man cannot be separated from his values and perspective on the world, and we also have to believe that the scientific study of human beings, individually or in groups, is not really possible. It is not possible because human beings, unlike material objects studied by natural scientists, *experience* the world, as well as behave in it.

A humanistic sociology begins with this notation, for without understanding the importance of it, we cannot communicate our argument with the scientific approach to the study of persons. I would like to have you consider again the table interrelating IQ, socioeconomic status, and going to college. The two variables used to draw a relationship are IQ and socioeconomic status. Now, does a person experience his IQ and socioeconomic status, or can he possess these qualities without knowing of them, or are these qualities something we, as sociologists, have given him in order to study him?

There are no perfect relationships in sociology, and very few strong ones because we can never guarantee that the characteristics we attribute to persons mean anything to him at all. What does it mean to a person to be lower class, for instance? For some, it means frustrations; for others it means being the same as everyone else in the neighborhood; and for others it is the way it has always been.

Now it is possible to say, as many have, that the meaning of experience to the person is irrelevant to the study of behavior. Many behavioral scientists will argue that they are simply looking at behavioral patterns and describing regularities from these evidences. What persons experience is not pertinent from this perspective. Although these behaviorists are indeed acting like scientists, without dealing with experience they will never reach scientific precision, since what goes on in a person's head governs the way he acts in a given objective circumstance (e.g., low socioeconomic status).

On the other hand, is it possible to really be objective about the human condition? Most of the sociological research on schools deals with the question of inequality, with certain biases operating in the selection of the problem. And what about the meaning of data? Most sociologists are content to let a phenomenon be defined by a symbol of itself, called an indicator.

Again, let us examine the indicators on Table 1: IQ is a score on a test; "economic status" is father's occupation; and "aspiration" is going to college. Now this is fine, except that, in the extrapolation, we are told that a relationship exists among intelligence, status, and aspiration. Do the indicators really mean what they are supposed to mean, independent of any verification as to what they mean to the person who is supplying the researcher with his data? And what about the issue of the data itself? Do the results we get on questionnaires accurately tell us about the person? We really believe that the results on an attitude questionnaire reflect the real attitude of the respondent. He could be lying, he might not know, he might be in the process of changing. It all seems so damn uncertain that you would think that sociologists would declare a moratorium on their labors and consider doing something else, perhaps in another way.

It does appear, short of a moratorium, that many sociologists are willing to admit to their biases and want to attack the structures that they once wished to "analyse." They have set out, empirically and analytically, to uncover the dysfunctions or disjointedness within a society that appears to be running down. In this light, then, a humanistic sociology of education is possible, because a "person" rather than a "scientist" is emerging to do the job.

A sociology of education, in this humanistic respect, must be an applied sociology. The choice of problem and the kind of data we, as sociologists, use must reflect a concern with the human condition. There was once a time, and not very long ago, when the sociologist-scientist shied away from applied research and from work associated with education, since education was, by definition, an applied field. What we are now looking for is the kind of school that is able to overcome the traditional tendency to allow social differences to invidiously affect those who experience those differences. And what we are looking for is a sociology that is able to expose the meaning of those differences to the people who experience them.

A conceptual framework for understanding education

Education is a very general concept. It can refer to learning, to a system of transmitting the culture, to a quality of an individual reflecting his status as well as his ability, to a formal organization where students attend classes from 9:00 to 3:00, to a graduate or undergraduate school where teachers are trained, to a means of social mobility. The sociology of education, as an academic discipline or subdiscipline, is, among other things, a way of looking at this phenomenon. It is a way of revealing, describing, and managing it; it provides us with a specific framework, which helps us to look at the whole by analysing the components. Sociology, as a general discipline, has evolved a number of working concepts. These concepts can be, conveniently, applied to all aspects of societal life. We can, for example, use the· concept of role to aid our analyses of schools as well as political systems, religious organizations, and families. What we will attempt to evolve in this section is a sociological description of educational systems, utilizing both formal and real-life conceptualizations, as well as experiential qualities of the concepts. Our goal is to make the social structure of schools come alive.

Social structure

A social structure is the pattern of relationships and interactions that characterize a specific unit of social life, a system, at one point in time. In order to be a structure, these patterns, by definition, are relatively stable. This stability is maintained by a system of norms, values, and roles, which we will discuss subsequently. In a school, as in other social institutions, we cannot see a social structure. We can only see benches, persons, materials. But the way these are used, the way persons move, the things they do, insofar as we can say these uses and movements are guided, tell us that a social structure exists. If children sit quietly, stiffly, and answer the teacher politely, these are patterns. If teachers direct the activities of the class, this is a pattern. If, when a student speaks out of turn, he is punished, this is a pattern. The way in which teachers talk to their principals, the kinds of assignments they give to students, the cost to students of not doing them, are all patterns. The social structure of the school consists of the set of activities, utilization of facilities, and ways that people traditionally use to communicate with each other; in other words, the evidences that tell us we are, without question—even with our eyes closed—in a schoolroom.

We know we are there because of the configuration of individual structures, or components, not because of the existence of any single one. Adults and children, books and papers, even chalk, desks, and blackboards, can be found almost anywhere. But when desks are lined up one behind the other, children seated orderly, an adult standing, books and papers passed around and on the desk, we have a school. If, in the interests of bringing education up-to-date, or to correct some deficiencies in the school's functioning, we change these patterns, we still have a school. Insofar as the new modes become stable through time, we evolve a new social structure. When a college student begins to notice that he does a number of things differently on the campus than he does on the beach, he begins to take account of the social structure. His experience with the social structure can be described more specifically with reference to several concepts which are the foundation blocks of that structure: the norms, values, and roles.

Norms

The formal concept of a norm—an ideal pattern of behavior—suggests that there are certain things that persons are expected or obliged to do. These expectations are usually tied to one's position; that is, a student may not be obliged to do some things that a teacher is obliged to do, and vice versa. Norms often refer to the limits of acceptable behavior that apply to everyone regardless of his position in the institution. For example, neither students, teachers, nor administrators are expected to disrobe in the classroom. Often these regulatory norms are formalized as rules, and these rules help persons to know the kind of behavior approved or disapproved by the school.

Most norms are internalized; that is, they are inside of us. If we behave in a certain way, it is because we expect it of ourselves, not because there is somebody watching. In this way, institutions effectively control the behavior of its members. In institutions, such as prisons, where most of the members do not believe in its institutional norms, more manifest controls are necessary.

In the classroom, we have both forms of social control: internalized expectations and enforcement. We do not talk back to our teacher; we do not criticize him even if we suspect he is depriving us of an education. We may no longer be aware of our responding to such social controls. If asked, we might attribute our restraint to a specific concern about punishment. Usually, however, we restrain ourselves because we are all participants in the normative system, and to violate some norm requires more psychological exertion than we are often able to handle. The anxiety and nervousness we feel when we consider going against the norm demonstrate its power over us.

Educational systems represent the normative order more than other institutions. In order to socialize students from different backgrounds in common ways, schools have had to stand as examples of the normative system which orders the total society. As Waller described the school many years ago, it operates as an institution which represents the Protestant morality to a degree that most real human beings would not presume to imitate.[2]

Values

A value is a standard against which things are approved or disapproved relative to each other. We have standards of quality and standards of excellence, standards of beauty and standards of performance. In schools, we have standards of academic performance, ethical standards, standards of popularity and standards of interpersonal relations. These are the standards that most students try to achieve, and in terms of which many are crucified for failing to achieve.

The values that operate to structure school behavior are those which are reflected in the general culture, based on our American traditions. We

---

2 Willard Waller, *The Sociology of Teaching* (New York: Science Editions, 1965).

value industriousness, success, cleanliness, cooperation, respect for authority and order. We devalue laziness, failure, messiness, physical aggression, and lack of restraint.

Students are constantly maneuvering to attain the values that are important in their lives. Consider what we have all done and continue to do in order to achieve the goals that we have been socialized to desire. We work hard even when we hate what we are doing, we memorize things we will never remember. We compete with each other, feeling badly when we lose and often guilty when we win. When we cannot attain our goal, we often pull down others to prevent them from succeeding. This behavior in the classroom is poignantly represented by the following example from Henry's observation of elementary school students:

> Boris had trouble reducing $^{12}\!/_{16}$ to the lowest terms and could only get as far as $^6\!/_8$. The teacher asked him quietly if that was as far as he could reduce it. She suggested that he should "think." Much heaving up and down and waving of the hands by the other children, all frantic to correct him. Boris pretty unhappy, probably mentally paralyzed. The teacher quiet, patient, ignores the others and concentrates with look and voice on Boris. After a minute or two, she turns to the class and says, "Well, who can tell Boris what the number is?" A forest of hands appears, and the teacher calls Peggy. Peggy says that four may be divided into the numerator and denominator. . . . Boris's failure has made it possible for Peggy to succeed; his misery is the occasion for her rejoicing. This is a standard condition of the contemporary American elementary school. To a Zuñi, Hopi, or Dakota Indian, Peggy's performance would seem cruel beyond belief, for competition, the wringing of success from somebody's failure, is a form of torture foreign to these non-competitive cultures.[3]

Because we value stability, we become uncomfortable when confronted with the possibility of instability in our educational life. When we are permitted a great deal of flexibility in the way we learn, we often become anxious and ask for structure. We want an outline of what we are supposed to know. The one thing in education that we do not seem to value very much is learning. There is very little time to learn when we have to get good grades, which we seem to value much more.

Roles

Roles are expectations for behavior for those who occupy a specific position in a social system. Roles are often conceived as actual enactments and linked to the expectation concept by the fact that what people do is ordinarily an indication of what they are expected to do.

[3] Jules Henry, *Culture Against Man* (New York: Random House, 1963), p. 27.

Schools, like other formal organizations, are bureaucratically organized. That is, there are a number of positions that are arranged in a hierarchy of status, each carrying more authority than the position below. Being a student is a role, usually at the bottom of the hierarchy. Students want to become nonstudents, just as children want to become adults, in order to gain a degree of freedom they do not have in their present role.

What is a student's role? When we ask about roles, we ask both about what a social type does and what he is expected to do. Persons experience their roles personally. We feel expectations. We feel the pressure of conforming to them and we almost always accede to this pressure. A student asks for information, for grades, for permission to leave the room, for the opportunity to impress the teacher and others. What he does not expect is also descriptive of his role. He does not expect freedom to control his own educational life, nor does he expect to be treated like a responsible human being. He expects to be distrusted and therefore does not object when his exams are monitored or when his teacher asks him to bring a note from his parents explaining his absences.

> Individuals quickly learn the expectations of their specific roles, particularly when such roles are traditional, like son, student, brother, friend, teacher, etc. The pressure of conforming to these expectations is great but one is not required to behave congruent with that conception. When he perceives the expectations and acts accordingly we say that he is "role playing". When he has internalized these expectations such that he is acting in terms of his own set of beliefs about how he should act, we say that he is "role taking".[4]

When the expectations of behavior for a particular role conflict with a person's self-conception—that is, the way he feels he is and must be as an individual—then he experiences the kind of role conflict that we call self-estrangement.[5] Most persons, at one time or another, experience this feeling of being called upon to play a part personally uncomfortable to them. Many individuals throughout the country now suspect that this feeling is especially common to the student role. If persons have a sense of how they, as individuals, learn best, and this cannot be accomplished in the traditional student role, then a role strain appears. To reduce this strain, many students either drop out of school if they are old enough, or attempt to declare their independence in any way they can. Much of the current conflict on college campuses is a result of this process.

[4] R. Turner, "Role Taking, Role Standpoint, and Reference Group Behavior," *American Journal of Sociology* 61 (January 1956): 316.

[5] See M. Seeman, "On the Meaning of Alienation," *American Sociological Review* 18 (December 1953): 373–80.

Sanctions

Sanctions are forms of controlling the behavior of members of a social group. They are both general to society at large and specific to institutions or subunits within the society. Having a language and a number of symbols in common, most members of the society quickly recognize a sanction.

In the classroom, students are sensitive to all the forms of reward and punishment. A smile from the teacher, a nod that an answer is correct, a commendation, an election victory, an appointment to a responsible job, a good grade on a test or report card, are all positive educational sanctions, and students work to attain them. They structure their behavior in terms of them. They work for sanctions rather than knowledge.

A poor grade, a detention, extra homework, being sent to the principal are also sanctions. Most students do their best to avoid them. As we are socialized according to the expectations of specific roles in society, we are also conditioned to be sensitive to the consequences of violating them. In the school, the approval of our teachers and peers are the goals for which we strive. Up to the point where we find that everything we do brings us disapproval, the quest for this approval keeps us controlled or motivated. In this way, a social institution protects its values and norms and maintains the stability of traditional roles.

Sometimes time-honored sanctions become weak because those persons who are controlled by their wish to receive positive sanctions and avoid negative ones begin to stop caring about certain rewards and punishments. It is at this evolutionary stage of a particular society that change is most possible and most likely. When college students refuse to be threatened by dismissal from school or a court record, then the university has lost its most significant formal means of control. At this point, either manifest enforcement or structural changes must occur. We have witnessed both trends in recent days.

Status

Status is the evaluation of a role. In American, most positions in the social structure are ranked. They are ranked in terms of the qualities or goals that we value. What we seem to value most is wealth, and persons achieve status to the degree that they secure wealth.

Each institution has its related status values. School status requires the student to attain good grades, access to higher education, and to be popular among his peers. Grades and access to higher education, however, are indirectly linked to economic values.

Status in everyday educational life, on the primary and secondary level, is a good report card, the favor of the teacher, having many friends in the classroom, moving up through the grades. On the campus status accrues from being an athlete, a member of a good fraternity or sorority, or a student body officer. There is a status difference between a student and a teacher, and between an assistant professor and a full professor.

Status is esteem. We like others to look up to us, to respect and applaud our attainments. To court such esteem often means that we must sacrifice our basic interests, shift away from our best skills. This means, for example, that we may need to abandon our artistic skills and interests in order to attain occupational success. Teachers do not have as much status as engineers, lawyers or doctors. In some cases, this explains why many persons who might have led successful and exciting lives as schoolteachers are leading dull ones as engineers, lawyers, and doctors. Status differences also explain why some high school students drop out of school when they are enrolled in other than academic curricula. School systems have never been able to discover a way of improving the status of vocational courses such as industrial arts. School administrators, having the same values as the rest of society, do not esteem the vocations as much as the professions.

There are several ways to achieve status in most social systems. Status is usually a combination of one's success in a number of areas. One's occupation, income, family lineage, education, all contribute to one's combined status. This is also the case with schools. Gordon's study of a high school described three structural patterns, or systems, by which students attained status:[6] (1) the formal system in which status was involved in the process of making grades; (2) the semiformal system which involved student participation in extracurricular activities, through which these students achieved status from being popular; and (3) the informal system which accounted for the status conferred by membership in a particular friendship group, or clique. In universities, for instance, membership in certain fraternities is more prestigious than in others.

Status is an important concept in sociology; it explains the basic patterns of social mobility, rates of deviance, and the various adaptations to cultural goals. Society is organized around status values and the struggle to attain them. In the classroom, this structure of status values is the most efficient structure by which school control is maintained. When one achieves status in our society, one gains a sense of power and well-being, a feeling that one has successfully met life's challenges and achieved personal victory over others.

External and internal systems

When education takes place in a formal organization, such as a school, it becomes useful to distinguish some of the components of that organization. Homans distinguished between the external dimension of a social system

---

6 C. Wayne Gordon, *The Social System of the High School* (New York: Free Press, 1957).

and the internal dimension.[7] The external system is all the activities which take place that directly justify the system's existence. Regarding the school, we are talking about activities, interactions among students and faculty, and sentiments that evolve in order to move students through the various grades to prepare them for adult life in the society. The use of books, discussions, lectures, instruction; the organization of curricula, the formal interactions according to role types, the giving and grading of exams; reports to parents, referrals to the counselor; the note to the vice-principal about the gum-chewing, the suspension for holding hands in the hall, are all examples of how the external system operates in the schools.

Personal interactions, communications, and emotional responses among the members constitute the internal dimension of an organization. When persons revise their activities, rearrange their patterns of interaction, and change their feelings about what they are doing, the internal system is operating and is reacting upon the demands of the external system.

If you have ever observed a teacher lessen the homework assignment because students moan, then you have observed the operations of the internal system. When students reduce their drive according to the informal rule of "don't be a rate buster," the internal system is at work. When universities begin to drastically revise their curricula of their policies towards minority groups, then we see the effect of the internal system operating to change the external system.

Even second graders can perceive the existence of an internal system, although they would not use those words. They know how to convince each other of the mutual necessity of getting the teacher to change an activity or a rule, of the kinds of strategies which will accomplish this. As one child, interviewed by the author, responded, "If the teacher keeps on giving us all that work, I'll just stay home, and get my friends to do it too."[8]

Manifest and latent functions

We have, particularly in recent days, heard a good deal about the notion of "working within the system." Most students are not revolutionaries by nature nor by ideology. Everybody seems to willingly admit that there are always problems, and most people are convinced that these can be solved without destroying our traditional institutions. If we agree with the goals and activities established to achieve these goals—the manifest function of institutions—then we find it most reasonable to assume that we can and should work within the system. The problem often is that our perspective of "the system" is incomplete, because we have only looked at its manifest functions. Many institutions fulfill important latent functions

7 G. Homans, *The Human Group* (New York: Harcourt Brace Jovanovich, 1950), pp. 90–110.

8 See B. Joyce and C. Weinberg, "Using the Strategies of Sociology in Social Education," in *The Social Studies: Structure Models and Strategies,* ed. Martin Feldman and Eli Seisman (Englewood Cliffs, N.J.: Prentice-Hall, 1969), pp. 456–62.

and they are supported by society more often on the basis of these latent functions rather than on manifest ones.

The manifest function of universities is to develop the minds of students, to help them think about and solve problems. But when students begin to challenge the basic assumptions of the whole society, the college budget is cut with public support. This happens not because the school failed to fulfil its manifest function—it perhaps accomplished that too well —but because it failed to fulfill an important latent function, which is to produce social conformists who do not threaten the status quo.

A latent function is a useful sociological concept. It helps us to describe the structural basis for the existence of many social forms. It can help tell us why some traits exist in society even when there seems to be no useful purpose for them. Many Indian tribes persist in their ritual rain dance. Although the manifest function (to make it rain) is no longer believed by the members, the latent function (to cohere members of a social group) is necessary to the viability of that group. We can ask ourselves about the function of many of our traditions, and by utilizing the notion of a latent function, understand a great deal about the social structure. The importance to sociology of analyzing latent functions is that it both clarifies seemingly irrational social patterns, like rain dances and wedding rituals, as well as directs our evaluation of the success of an activity away from its "supposed" function to its real function. That is, we don't evaluate rain dances on the grounds of the amount of rainfall produced.

This last value of looking at the latent function of institutions or social patterns is critical to our concern about understanding the system or working within the system. Since moral judgments, and hence social action, seem to arise from the way the public perceives the manifest functions of an institution, analyzing latent consequences may reveal beneficial social aspects that had previously not been considered. It is possible, for example, that both the church and state in Catholic countries were able to maintain family stability by permitting prostitution to flourish. With restrictive divorce codes, the accessibility of other sexual outlets helps to prevent movements that may threaten to change the traditional patterns. Prostitution, in this evaluation, is a spin-off or siphon for energy that might otherwise become political to attain similar ends.

In education, some student activities are being judged by the larger society as disrespectful of many traditional values such as law and order, respect for authority, and bureaucratic efficiency. It is possible, however, that such activities are promoting the kinds of change that will make education congruent with the changing culture outside of the school. The more static that schools remain in the face of shifting cultural standards, the more likely that the school will cease to be an important socializing agency. As many students and teachers increasingly consider the school obsolete and irrelevant, university and school administrators will increasingly reassess the function of the school in a quickly changing society.

The structure of competition: function and dysfunction

Students are required to compete with one another for a variety of educational rewards. They compete in terms of standards of achievement established by the school in line with traditional performance expectations. The manifest function of competition is motivation. Persons are motivated to achieve their goals in terms of these standards. The latent function of competition operates to control the behavior of students by keeping them rigorously committed to the goals they seek. It maintains their conformity, since deviance diminishes the qualities they need to compete for the rewards of the school. We have come to believe that worth is determined by the number of people competing for something. It makes A's and B's worth something by the sheer act of forcing people to compete for them. In the final analysis, competition clouds our vision of worth in learning. We come to believe that what is worth something is whatever you get by competing for it, rather than what you want to achieve.

A dysfunction is a consequence of seeking certain manifest or latent goals which adversely affect some members of society. There are several dysfunctional consequences of competition. Let us consider these in the context of our educational system. First of all, we need to find out who is adversely affected. Although probably everyone is, the most seriously affected by the dysfunction of competition are the school dropouts, the "losers," who enter the adult world without vocational training or the possibility of access to higher education.

There are two other groups ·in the competition, however: the "survivors" and the "winners." The survivors are those who barely make it through high school. They usually have the credentials to enter a junior college, but seldom a four-year school. While they are at the junior college, they are "cooled out,"[9] a term used by Clark to designate the process of sidetracking or modifying aspirations so that a student seeks a career as a medical technician rather than a doctor. What is the human dilemma for this person? What does it mean to him to have his aspirations raised only to have them sent crashing as he realizes that his real status in society is only a second-rate position? For this person, it is sometimes easier to fail in the system and then develop his own structure for facing life rather than be coopted to seek high status and then be relegated to an inferior position.

The "winner" can be described in terms of his academic achievement, his popularity among his peers, and his easy transition from high school to college. But what has his victory cost him? Let's first look at female winners.

The educated woman in America has competed with males academically for at least sixteen years. In the process, she has been encouraged to think of herself as intelligent, curious, knowledgeable, cultured. As a

---

9 B. Clark, "The 'Cooling-out' Function in Higher Education," *The American Journal of Sociology* 65 (May 1960): 569–76.

housewife, she lives in a world of people one to three feet tall, shifting her dialogue from, "That's an interesting point to consider," to "That's a good baby." The millions of tranquilizers consumed in suburbia by the trapped housewife speak of the strain such women experience from the difference between their expectations and their rewards. If success through competition is an internalized social habit, what happens to the fulfillment drive when women become mothers and housewives? It may seep into the marriage, and we note that divorces are common today, or it may require rechanneling, whereby these women pay psychiatrists billions of dollars yearly to help them accept their new roles.

The "successful" man in America drinks three martinis before he is able to take a bite of food. He has ulcers, is overweight, has chronic anxieties, fights with his wife and children, goes into depressions, and sometimes commits suicide when his career flounders or goes sour. He is the organization man, the dysfunctioning product of American competitiveness, who, like a prizefighter, keeps swinging long after he has lost the fight.

What we have done in judging the function or dysfunction of competition can be usefully repeated in judging the functions of differentiation within the classroom, extracurricular activities, bureaucratic organization, achievement and intelligence tests, and so on. Most educational structures exist because they serve some function, and an astute educator should be capable of analyzing the manifest and latent consequences of these functions and assess how well they operate.

THE SCHOOL AND OTHER SOCIAL UNITS

The sociology of education is a field concerned with the interaction of the school with other institutions, such as the family and church, and other social units, such as adolescent peer groups. We can discuss briefly the kinds of interactions which are studied and written about in the literature.

Education and the economic system

Here we are interested in the way a person's income, his education level, his social status within the community, and his occupation relate to the kind of education his children receive. One of the early important studies in the field was conducted by A. B. Hollingshead, in which he demonstrated that a student's educational behavior was related to his parents' social position in a small midwestern community.[10] He did this by developing measures of economic standing, some of which were based on reputation and others upon objective indicators, such as occupation and income. According to these measures, he then divided the community into five social classes. The next step was to look at the academic performance of the students from

[10] A. B. Hollingshead, *Elmtown's Youth* (New York: John Wiley, 1947).

each class level. He found, as he expected, that students from the upper classes enrolled more frequently in college preparation courses, developed cliques only within their own class, had higher professional aspirations, dropped out of school less frequently, and received better evaluations from school personnel.

In a small community, where everyone attends the same school, a study of economic advantage such as this one can reveal dramatic differences. Today, most schools are homogeneously grouped as to the economic standing of pupils' families. Nonetheless, most of the studies of a child's economic position show a distinct relationship to his educational attainment or aspirations. As one's social position increases, so do one's successes.[11]

Race

When we speak of race as an American sociological category, we ordinarily mean to differentiate between white majority and nonwhite minority groups. The most prominent minority group in the literature of sociology is the Negro. In education, the dominant focus has been upon the black man's position in the opportunity structure. It is well-known that he, like Mexican-Americans and Puerto Ricans, is underrepresented, in proportion to his numbers, in institutions of higher learning. His graduation rates from high school are lower than for Caucasians. His position within the school is inferior; that is, that schools, through many channels and activities, favor Caucasians.[12]

Educational sociologists are concerned about the discrepancy in educational opportunities. They, like the Kerner Commission on Civil Disorders, are interested in the structure of racism, how these inequalities occur, and how they are produced.[13] Several ideas are relevant to this kind of analysis:

1. *Differential Socialization:* This simply means that the social habits learned in the homes of Negro students are not conducive to educational success. The aspiration level of black students, in terms of making it through the school system and on to higher education, is low. A black person's commitment to delayed gratification is not quite the same as that of a Caucasian. His language is often less than "perfect" English. He has not internalized the value of passivity in social interaction. He approaches others physically, often with aggression.

2. *Middle Class Standards:* This notion is similar to the first, ap-

---

11 Natalie Rogoff, in a study of 35,000 high school seniors, demonstrated that even when scholastic ability was held constant, the economic status of the family influenced college aspirations markedly. In B. Clark, *Educating the Expert Society* (San Francisco: Chandler, 1962), p. 61.

12 James Coleman, *Equality of Educational Opportunity* (Washington, D.C.: National Center for Educational Statistics, 1966).

13 See *Report of the National Advisory Committee on Civil Disorders* (Washington, D.C.: U.S. Government Printing Office, 1968).

plying here to the school rather than to the student. The middle standards of the school are universally and often rigidly applied. They are established according to the achievement performances of students who have accepted and internalized the ethic of hard work and educational success. Standards for moral behavior and standards for academic achievement are equally important in the evaluation of the student. This means that persons who are industrious, respectful of authority, clean, physically unaggressive, well-groomed, and use standard language form, are rewarded with educational prizes such as grades and honors.

3. *Unequal Distribution of Human and Material Resources:* Anyone who has visited a typical ghetto school recognizes that the environment is different from that of a typical suburban school. The rooms and buildings are older and usually in need of repair; the audio-visual equipment is either nonexistent or badly used; the teachers are more hostile; the work that students perform is either routine or repressive. Kozol and Cole have vividly described the educational conditions in such schools. Although these are individual and not really sociological observations, the data from the Coleman report and elsewhere substantiate the picture.[14]

4. *Segregation vs. Compensatory Education:* Here we are faced with the assessment of a real ongoing problem. Social and educational reformers are trying to break down the structure of racism. We know that improving the facilities and instruction for lower-class black students helps, but this does not meet the demand for integration. "Separate but equal" is a myth. Evidence suggests that black children in integrated schools improve faster than their peers in the all-black schools.

5. *Home Rule:* The decentralization of educational authority and control is a popular theme in the socioeducational literature. Black leaders believe that segregated schools have value only if black personnel make the major decisions in these schools. This issue has created strange bedfellows. In California and elsewhere, both political conservatives and black radicals are interested in decentralizing schools, although, we suspect, for very different reasons. While the black leaders hope to provide a better education and stronger and more positive black identity in community schools, conservatives appear to like the idea of self-help and self-determination. At the same time, private enterprise is viewed as a possible form of school management. This means, in one sense, a profit and loss business for Negro entrepreneurs in the ghetto who contribute services to the community-owned school.

The family

Literature that relates family life to education usually focuses on the economic theme. The socialization, or child-rearing, activities of families

---

[14] Coleman, *Equality of Educational Opportunity.*

have usually been studied in relation to social class differences. Other kinds of topics in this area would be:

1. the working mother and her effect on the educational success of the child
2. children of large and small families
3. broken homes
4. family geographic mobility.

The interaction of family and schools has not been viewed in any particularly new or productive way. That poor people's children become poor people, and that children of migrant farmers experience educational barriers are obvious conclusions. Often, however, these data help make a case for policy decisions, if politicians are interested in bringing about some changes. A more challenging and currently relevant consideration is one which would analyze the way in which family beliefs and patterns can help explain deviant phenomena such as college dropouts, drug-taking among schoolchildren, and political radicalism on the campus. The question of whether or not adolescent and college-age "deviants" are going through a rebellious stage, or have found a genuine ideological commitment, is unclear. How can we explain the fact that students whose parents have lived a life of middle-class conformity are rebelling? What notions will help explain the disaffection of middle-class children from the educational aspirations of their parents? The struggle of disenfranchised whites and blacks to change the system may only be possible with the support of persons within the system—students who are educationally successful and who want to change that system.

The peer group

Along with the family, the peer group represents, particularly for adolescents, a significant influence. Often, when expectations of family and peer group clash, the child conforms to the peer group. Sometimes the same confrontation occurs between the adolescent peer group and the school.

The youth group constitutes a distinct entity, what Coleman has called an "adolescent society."[15] He has shown how the character of adolescents and their value system has influenced the organization of the schools they attend. If they like football, the school will have an athletic emphasis. If they are eager to study and get into college, the school will take on an academic posture.

Students who work together for common purposes have been shown to influence not only the way each other thinks but also the degree of commit-

15 J. Coleman, *The Adolescent Society* (New York: Free Press, 1961).

ment and involvement that each will assume. The society of "young radicals" who have been making an impact upon the college scene are stimulated less by their successes than by their association with others in a common purpose.[16] Much of the research and writing emphasis of the near future will be upon such students. They exist on the college campus and in the high schools. They also exist in ghetto elementary schools and they are starting to organize very young. Their impact upon the system of education is an interesting and important question.

THE SCHOOL AS A SOCIAL SYSTEM

Many sociologists have attempted to view the school as a microcosm of the larger society, as an organization with functions, roles, and bureaucratic relationships. We have talked about this somewhat in the first part of this chapter. C. Wayne Gordon, whom we discussed earlier, has usefully broken the school down into three systems and attempted to explain how students achieve overall status through their participation in each system.[17] This analysis allows us to observe a graphic relationship among all three positions. Persons in similar status positions are shown to choose each other as friends, and the tendency for good students to be popular students is revealed.

From another perspective, we see the way the system allocates persons to the occupational world. Parsons analyzes the selection and evaluation of persons based upon achievement and the way students develop capacities and commitments to function in adult roles. Students are categorized according to their cognitive and ethical performance; that is, they are judged by the school grades and their "respect" for the teacher. Once these categories are established, students are allocated along channels of success or failure commensurate with these definitions.[18]

Students are ordinarily defined early in their school career by their performance and personal style, from which their status can be predicted. This status label is one that they usually carry, or one that carries them, through their entire academic career. One of the consequences of this definition is that students almost never become free to act in opposition to it.

For example, when a student who has been defined as a high achiever fails a test, we normalize this unpredictable happening by saying that he had a bad day. If a student who has been defined as a low cognitive achiever does well, we say he cheated. If a high moral achiever violates a rule, we

16 K. Keniston, *The Young Radicals* (New York: Harcourt Brace Jovanovich, 1968).

17 Gordon, *The Social System of the High School.*

18 T. Parsons, "The School Class as a Social System," *Harvard Educational Review* 20 (Fall 1959): 297–318.

look for the source of his being upset. If a low moral achiever spends a week conforming to all the rules, we suspect ulterior moitves.

SCHOOLS AND SOCIAL CHANGE

The school has always mirrored, if not exaggerated, trends and patterns in the larger society. When our society shifted to a more scientific mode, after the Russians sent the first satellite aloft, schools mobilized their science facilities and shifted their emphasis accordingly. The history of the relationship between social changes and educational changes is a parallel history. In order to understand the interaction between school and society, we can trace certain historical shifts in our cultural patterns.

Urbanization

In rural society, interaction was personalized. This means that we identified the mailman and shopkeeper by name rather than by uniform. Students in school were linked to their families in several ways. Teachers would deal with children in terms of the skills that were needed in the home, or discipline children commensurate with the status of their families. Urban society demanded another set of school-home relationships, since the family no longer serviced all the needs of its members. Living in the city required a different set of behaviors for family members, and families required a different set of services from the schools. Since occupational succession (sons following in the footsteps of the father) was no longer the pattern, children had to be educated to find their own occupations in industrial society. As the function of the schools changed, so did the patterns of interaction. Since community schools were homogeneous, and since most students were enrolled for vocational training, students needed to be differentiated. This was also necessary for the management of large groups. To facilitate these new requirements, the schools had to develop ways of grouping, advising, and training students that were different from the past. In the same manner that urban persons would define others, usually in terms of occupational labels, schools evolved their own form of labeling. Students became labeled in terms of achievement, moral behavior, and later, in terms of vocational choice and curriculum. College preparatory students, for instance, were expected to be high academic achievers and vocational-course students were expected to achieve less. That may be why we get less.

Social mobility

By 1945, at the close of World War II, the United States was becoming an affluent society. The efforts of labor unions, combined with the general prosperity produced by a war economy, raised the mass of society upwards on the socioeconomic ladder. But status within the prestige structure could not be based on income alone. A large segment of the society looked towards education to preserve and increase their status. The children of the working class were sent off to college to ensure a better and easier life than that enjoyed by their parents. Education seemed the major path to social and economic success. Public schools came to be viewed more as selecting agencies than training ones. The competition for the rewards of the educational system, linked closely to occupational opportunities, began early. You who are reading this book are familiar with the process, and can understand how competition for grades, honors, popularity, and college entrance replaces much of what we think of, in the pure sense, as learning.

Mass social mobility led to other conditions which seriously affected the educational quality of the school. Those who were not included in the race for success became clearly discernible as members of educationally disenfranchised minority groups. The economic success of some and the failure of others led to ecological migration in a pattern we have called de facto segregation. These success patterns began to evolve into a process of increasing specialization, requiring greater amounts of formal education. All persons caught in the whirl of intensified striving for social rewards were in some way mutilated, separated from their fellow humans. Segregation and specialization have this common potential: social and personal alienation.

The prosperity of the 1950s and 60s led to redistribution of humans into ecological arrangements called slums and suburbs. The organization of the schools has become patterned in terms of different educational goals, for those who have and those who have not. Discrepancies of personnel and facilities become obvious to any observer. Teachers in the suburbs are better trained, better experienced, better paid, better supported by specialists and facilities, than their counterparts in the slums. But one changing pattern has become apparent, and that is in the way the poor have discovered their political and social influence. A political maneuver, a parents' strike, or a riot, can influence school administrators to become responsive to the needs of ghetto communities, and can influence government agencies to set up programs to encourage equality of opportunities. Between the forces of conscience and politics, the poor are beginning to have a chance for the same kind of education offered to the middle classes. Those of us who have been through the system and succeeded might respond that there doesn't appear to be any good reason for them to want it, but this too may be another effect of affluence. When persons are struggling to climb a mountain, it seems selfish and patronizing of those at the top to yell down, "Don't bother, it's a gravel pit up here." The point is not that we are witnessing a cycle of succession-rejection, but that frustrated peoples are separated by opposite motivations. The poor want "up" and "in"; the middle-class dissenters or dropouts want "down" and "out." This is why a coalition of blacks and students, for example, is unlikely.

Institutional interaction

Society is made up of a number of institutions with a separate, yet interdependent, institutional life; that is, what happens in the home is affected by economic, political, religious, and educational patterns. Changes in one sector affect changes in others. The shift from a farming to an industrial economy, for instance, brought about decreased fertility rates, since children were no longer needed as workers. As the pattern of children succeeding to their fathers' occupations became outmoded, schools began to expand their educational function. As the role of women in the family changed, schools had to accommodate a whole new set of feminine aspirations.

The school today has, despite the complaints of many, evolved into an educational structure for the common man, requiring that any child old enough to attend must go to school. Child labor in the factory has become obsolete with developments in child labor laws, and with the increased application of the democratic ethic. A democratic nation requires an enlightened electorate, and with universal suffrage, all citizens need to be educated. Unfortunately, the only aspect of fulfilling this requirement has been compulsory attendance.

In recent days we have observed a growing concern on the part of many administrators and students that politics has become part of university life. In Washington D.C., as well as in many state capitals, legislators are introducing bills to control the behavior of students. Many politicians are capitalizing upon the fears of many conservative citizens that college students are a threat to the kind of life that their generation has created and in which they hold a comfortable and vested interest.

Another social unit, although not an institution in the sociological sense of the word, has seriously influenced educational life: the peer group. As a force controlling values and behavior, the strength of loyalties between age mates has never been greater than it is today. We can speculate on the reasons for this. The increased solidarity of the peer group appears to be linked to the phenomenon of decreased family dependency. The family, like the formal organization, has become a group of specialists, each member being involved in activities not shared with anyone else. What we have come to call the generation gap is a product of this evolution. Lacking any set of common values, young people turn to each other for support in these values. Rapidly-changing social experiences have made it difficult for members of one generation to teach their children what to expect of the world they are facing on a daily basis. The peer group has had to assume this socialization responsibility. Male-female relationships, for example, seem to change dramatically every ten or so years, and an adolescent taking his cues from his parents is apt to find himself socially incompetent.

The interaction of formal educational structures with the peer society has developed a pattern which sometimes creates dramatic confrontations. On a routine basis, the school has, for some time, been responsive to student interests. In high schools and colleges, a whole network of student interest activities (sometimes called extracurricular) has been established. Often teachers will use educational materials that will reflect the interests of certain student groups, such as the car, sports, surfing and dress and music fads. Rules of deportment have changed in many places as a result of student values. Some schools and school districts have made what they consider to be concessions to student values towards dress and personal grooming. The length of skirts and hair, informal dress, hair tinting, and similar issues have provided school administrators with an ongoing experience of confrontation with the adolescent society. In more recent days, on both high school and college campuses, the issues are more significant. Essentially, students appear to want to be treated as whole human beings with a sense of responsibility and some legitimate claim to participating in decisions which affect their lives. Special interest groups, such as organized minority students, have pressed their claim beyond the standard university structures into the larger community, asking that the school feel some responsibility for the life in the ghetto. This can be done, they argue, in several ways, the most important being improving the educational opportunities of members of the nonwhite communities through more permissive admission standards and through financial support for qualified as well as special students.

Social life today is highly interdependent, as we have seen. For those who do not wish to experience social change, either by ignoring the whole social scene in hopes that it will go away, or by resisting it politically, the future appears very threatening. The future for those who are just beginning to sense that they can play a part in making it, appears very exciting. Classrooms and campuses are currently charged with this kind of excitement, and even though the forces of repression, trying to dam up human striving and potential, may have their day, it is too late. Too many on the campus have experienced a taste of educational freedom, of experiencing power and some control over their educational life. This will never be relinquished.

The scientific revolution

Social change has come about, in part as a response to scientific developments. Science, in our society, has always been linked to technological efficiency which in turn is linked to industrial profits. Americans, since the turn of the century and for some years before, have grown up with the understanding that many people were engaged in the task of finding better ways of doing almost everything. We believe that, through science, we can eventually achieve every task. Today's generation does not find it surprising that we have landed men on the moon. Change is inherent in the process of discovering "better" ways—change in our daily routines, our entertainment and our world of work. We, as individuals, are always keeping up with and adapting to changes produced by scientific innovation. Furthermore, we are confident that in the hands of scientific technology we are well cared for. We undergo strange medical treatments of which we are ignorant, cross continents in machines that we don't understand, comply with computerized estimates of our bills and bank balances, and subject our best china and furniture to mechanical cleaning processes. We trust science. We must, because our lives are based upon it.

This attitude towards science has carried over into the school. Citizens come to expect that their children will be taught with the most modern techniques and facilities available. Parents from one community will protest vigorously the fact that another community has employed teaching machines while theirs has not. We do not appear to care much about the irrelevance of what we are taught; we are only annoyed if we are not taught in new ways. It is not science itself which has worked for or against a better education. In some important ways, it is our attitude about it. Politicians, for example, can allocate billions of dollars for space exploration and the public does not object since, one fine morning on color TV, we can all watch the blast-off and landing. But if allocations for education become too high, politicians will fight each other regularly. The products of this money are hidden, the results are not obvious, cannot be viewed on the TV. Most citizens, like most educators, cannot differentiate between a good educational product and a bad one. The student in his black robe receiving a piece of white paper looks the same whether he has received a good education or a bad one. For this reason, educational changes do not occur as rapidly as changes in other segments of our lives.

Technological changes, however, have forced the patterns of educational life to undergo some revision. New technology has created new jobs and made others obsolete. Specialized training had to accompany the development of new specialties, and specialists in education had to emerge to teach and guide students towards these new specialties.

The most profound effect of the scientific ethos upon education, however, came not from the development of new machines, but from the discovery of more "scientific" theories about how people learn. We took from psychiatry and psychology many ideas about learning and motivation, and in a relatively short period of time, began to base our classroom organization and related activities upon it. Students were grouped in certain ways, tested frequently for intelligence, interest, aptitude, and personality, counseled for personality problems, and managed interpersonally as if he (the child) might fall apart at any moment. In many classrooms, the shift was from complete nonconcern about the emotional component of the learner to an oversensitivity by which the child's personal strengths were in doubt and his mind was ignored.

Technology has, in some ways, been utilized as an educational tool. The teaching machine, based upon a set of ideas about how rewards can be programed into the learning activity such that learning occurs, is gaining wider acceptance. Perhaps other, more sophisticated technology will follow in the years to come, until one day we can all just take a pill and have immediate knowledge of the laws of physics. We continue to rely upon science to patch up the holes that we discover in the educational process, and to provide us with new discoveries, new inventions, new techniques. The amazing thing about educators, and those citizens who are concerned about solving the problems of education with some brilliant new discovery, is that they are unable to associate the problems that our society is currently experiencing with this attitude in the first place. Where has all our social and personal alienation, disruption, and disorganization come from if not explicitly from those forces which have made us a specialized, technological, and impersonal society?

Social movements

Some of the most dramatic changes in educational structures have come about as a result of large groups of persons banding together to demand change of our major social institutions. When black people began to challenge their treatment by whites on a mass basis, dramatically signaled by the bus boycotts in Birmingham, Alabama, the civil rights movement took on a dynamic posture. The Supreme Court decision to desegregate the schools in 1954 followed, and the demand of black people and many supporting whites made it necessary for educators, as well as politicians, to begin to think about policy. Integration and compensatory educational programs, such as Headstart, began and large sums of government money for bringing dropouts back into the school and for training teachers for the ghetto were allocated.

Minorities of Latin American descent, in the Northeast and Southwest, have taken their cue from the black movement, and are demanding a better American experience. The school appears to bear the brunt of challenge since these groups, like other Americans, recognize the function of education as a social equalizer. The civil rights movement itself has passed the stage of calling for integration, since this seems to be the most superficial aspect of what nonwhites view as American racism. Racism, as a concept, involves more than individual prejudice and discrimination. It involves the notion of a total institutional structure organized to provide rewards differently, depending on one's race. The call for decentralization of the schools, for community control, is the next stage of confrontation with the educational establishment. This kind of arrangement would put not only teacher selection and recruitment in the hands of citizens of the community, but would also call for a radical restructuring of the school curriculum in which white middle-class values and ideas would not be the central values and ideas stressed in the classroom.

Minority students have made some of their most vigorous protests on the campuses of American colleges and universities. They have called for an increase in the number of minority students, ethnic studies programs, better integration of faculties, and the support of nonwhite students financially and through a system of tutorials.

The face of the civil rights movement has grown angry and hard in the last few years, and the demands are becoming more difficult to satisfy all the time, since educators look futilely for some specific change that they can provide to assuage the anger. "What can we do for you?" they ask. They, for the most part, have not learned that the white educator must understand the structure of racism in all its manifestations and put an end to it wherever he finds it. It is his system, he has made it in his image, and he alone knows how it works. He must provide leadership in restructuring the school, for eradicating those patterns which dehumanize the relationship between persons and perpetuate invidious consequences of being nonwhite in America or in American schools.

The humanistic movement

The most serious threat to the core structure of American society as we know it is a movement as yet unnamed and in whose success lies a new conception of the value and function of education. It cuts across ages, sexes, races, statuses, religions, and nationalities. It involves all those who wish to see a society in which isolation, deprivation, and anxiety is not the price of everyday living. The force was born out of our present stage of depersonalized institutional living. It is nourished by our industrial progress, our meaningless affluence, our job conditions where men are only roles, and our schools, where students are regarded as products.

The symptoms of this kind of living can be discovered in persons running everywhere seeking for affiliation. They seek organizations which will take them in and care for them, like Alcoholics Anonymous, Synanon, and a host of religious cults. They seek therapy by the droves, sensitivity training, group dynamics. They seek happiness in drugs, drinking, or sexual orgies. Or they seek relief of the condition itself, and for themselves by affiliating with others who want to bring about change. They become change agents.

Many in this latter category are college students. In them the spirit of protest is most vital. Students are demanding educational reform, in the direction of a more humanistic education where there is freedom for the individual to explore the limits of his own potential.

The college has not been unresponsive to this mood. There is more flexibility in curriculum choice, more innovative experimental courses, experimentations with new forms of evaluation of student performance. It is becoming more difficult to dismiss faculty members of whom the students approve, and students are gaining access to many important committees involved in curriculum planning, policies related to student life, and the recruitment of faculty.

The spirit is being felt in the public schools also. High school students are pressing their own demands and winning the right to be more themselves. In the elementary grades, many teachers are experimenting with new ways to involve students in their own experience. There is pressure emanating from a growing force for more personalized living, to make schools human places, to return students to their life as children, to allow them to believe that it is worthwhile, perhaps even special, to be a child and not to be an ongoing performer seeking institutional rewards.

Society is at a juncture where the forces of technological efficiency and institutional regularity are in a life-and-death struggle with those persons who are victimized and who know it. Education and educators can play a passive role, as they have always done, and accommodate to traditional social expectations and lead us further down the path towards total deper-sonalization, or they can serve as an active agency of social change. They can do this by making the school the kind of therapeutic environment that is required for persons to grow as individuals in productive affiliation with others, and to be total human beings.

4

humanistic
educational
psychology

Carl Weinberg
and
Philip Reidford

PHILIP REIDFORD and CARL WEINBERG. Since I have written about us both separately, I will suggest here only what we have to do with each other. We are personal friends because we are academically compatible. I don't really think it is possible to keep a friend, at least not a good friend, for very long if you each have different versions about how to live your life whether at home or on the job. We both see the academic environment as highly impoverished, particularly as it is reflected by the work and personalities of our colleagues. We both have a very great belief in something called wisdom, which, like poetry, may be a dying conception of man's possibilities for intellectual and/or emotional contribution to the college environment.

Our contribution here was intended to reflect one way of bringing education from knowledge to wisdom, at least in the area of educational psychology. We believe that if it is done the humanistic way wisdom is possible. If it is done in the conventional way, the best that is possible is knowledge. Knowledge, as I believe I have suggested in another place, is to wisdom as flesh and bones are to life. One can have many bones and much flesh, but without the capacity to reflect on one's existence we do not have human life.

This chapter should be understood as our attempt to present conventional ideas from education and psychology and to apply these ideas to the kinds of humanistic purposes they might serve. Then we go on to describe the principles and assumptions from humanistic psychology which we think are directly linked to an understanding of how one learns humanistically. The last part of this chapter is a humanistic approach to humanistic learning. In other words, it provides an example of what we are talking about that, in itself, carries the message about how people learn.

In the days when an idea could be silenced by showing that it was contrary to religion, theology was the greatest single source of fallacies. Today, when any human thought can be discredited by branding it as unscientific, the power previously exercised by theology has passed over to science; hence science has become in its turn the greatest single source of error.

Polanyi[1]

Although science, in this way, may have become the greatest single source of human error, it also has become one of man's greatest assets. Our leisure environment reflects the technological advantages which are the by-products of science—automobiles transport us on land, airplanes transport us in the air, medicine cures us, television informs us, fertilizers feed us, and teaching machines instruct us. Yet, at the same time that these marvels make life physically easier and materially more secure, they create problems with which science and the men who use them cannot or will not deal. The pollution of our environment is widespread—fish die from chemical and thermal pollution of rivers and oceans; the air of our nation is contaminated with poisons; the chemically treated foods we eat cause widespread physiological side effects; the noise of cars, planes, electronic music, pneumatic hammers deafens us; and the goal-oriented education provided by teaching machines and instructional objectives prevents us from developing our inner strengths and from molding our development to response patterns which are relative to our minds and hearts. Hence, the extrinsic products of our advanced society give rise to excessive environmental problems. Although we advance scientifically and technologically at an increasingly accelerated rate, we run a fairly high risk of self-destruction by not developing humanely.

As McLuhan has pointed out, the medium is the message. That is to say, the medium conveys to us how we should live, how we should respond, and what is important. Currently our environment, the medium, conveys two primary messages: (1) strive for profit, live for the day, enjoy the flashy extrinsic, because destruction is imminent; and (2) technological advancement without human advancement spells doom, and what is valu-

1 M. Polanyi, "Scientific Outlook: Its Sickness and Cure," *Science* 125 (1957): 480–84.

able is knowing ourselves, not consuming. Consider what man is or what could man be: a machine or an art form? A substantial factor in the determination of the societal life style is contributed by the emphases of our formal education. The influence which educational psychology has on the development of school curricula contributes to the direction which educators follow in nurturing intellectual and attitudinal norms of the population. The emphases of school programs are partly determined by the theories and the outcomes of experiments of educational psychology. Such theories and experimental outcomes are frequently considered by those people who design educational programs. Since the design of educational programs can be determined by the kinds of educational psychology which the curriculum writer prefers, it is important to understand the advantages and limitations of the various schools of educational psychology which the curriculum writer can choose from.

EDUCATIONAL PSYCHOLOGY

The conventional definition of educational psychology is the application of psychological principles to the practice of education. The sense of this definition for many educational psychologists, then, is that education is the technology and psychology is the pure science.

To traditional educational psychologists, psychology is an empirical science. Empirical science operates something like this: The scientist makes observations about certain phenomena. From these observations he generally acquaints himself with the theories and research that have been reported about the problem area. Based on the scientist's observations and the information which he has gleaned from reading work relating to the problem, he is able to formulate a hypothesis or hypotheses. Once the hypothesis has been stated in a way in which it can be tested scientifically, the scientist runs an experiment. The results of the experiment are then subjected to statistical tests. The outcome of these tests indicates to the scientist the probability of the results occurring in the experiment at an above chance level. What this means simply is that, if one looks at the results of an experiment, one can see if they were in the predicted direction. Then in order to refine one's judgment about the probability of the occurrence of the results found in x times out of one hundred, one subjects the data obtained to statistical tests.

Hence, the scientist, in this case the educational psychologist, obtains a probability statement about the outcome of his experiment. Providing the probability of obtaining the results in said experiment is low, the educational psychologist can make some tentative generalizations. Unfortunately, a probability statement is not a truth; it is simply a refined guess or conjecture. Many educational psychologists take the position that empirical testing is the most objective way to proceed in order to develop educational programs; however, this is not really the case. One can grant that it is more precise to test an idea (hypothesis) empirically rather than just make a conjecture or guess. There are, however, two important problems inherent in the empirical approach to finding answers for education. The first is that in order to run a controlled experiment, one must specify what variables or factors are operating to effect the desired changes. In a classroom this is virtually impossible, for too many things are happening both within and without the classroom that cannot be controlled by the experimenter. For example, the experimenter can't take into consideration the psychological state of the teacher and her pupils. If the teacher has a headache on the morning of a critical experimental procedure, the effects of the procedure may be entirely different than if the teacher had just become engaged the night before. Similar psychological states caused by an infinite number of home and school circumstances will also affect the receptivity and motivation of the pupil. The second problem of the empirical approach of discovering effective educational programs is the moral implication of an educational psychologist or a curriculum planner specifying what a learner should learn. Why, for example, will it be more useful in the future for a student to learn a language than psychology? Why must pupils achieve a specified performance level in arithmetic, reading, or social studies? Who among us knows what the world will look like in ten years? It is our contention that students need to be provided with opportunities to learn to think, to adapt, to perceive. Inasmuch as the rate of social, scientific, and technological change accelerates each year, we cannot possibly know the job and life skills that will be necessary in the future. We do know that, in order to be able to understand, appreciate, and participate in the changes, each student will need to have some basic process skills. The development of these skills is not independent of content, but the specific content itself is, for the most part, irrelevant to the life needs of the pupils.

VALUES AND SCIENCE

When a decision is made about what and how children are to be taught in schools, a value judgment has been made. Determining what people should learn and how they should learn it, is a way of specifying what you want humas beings to be. If, for example, children are taught arithmetic by programmed instruction, then they are being taught more than arithmetic. They are being taught that there is a right answer and a right way to arrive at that answer. It is our contention that the only moral way to teach children is to equip them with the means to evaluate information. Moreover, children can be, and should be, instructed in sharpening their perceptions, both intellectual and sensory. If the aim of education were to provide every child with the tools to evaluate himself and his world, then the moral and value question would be left open to each individual and not to the state.

There is, however, a well-established myth in science that the scientist's findings are independent of the moral considerations of these uses. This viewpoint has been debated intensely since the use of the atomic bomb. Nonetheless, the use of scientific psychological principles is often advocated independent of the moral and ethical implications of such use. When examining the following psychological principles, moral considerations should be kept in mind.

PSYCHOLOGICAL PRINCIPLES

Three well-known psychological principles are *distributive versus mass practice, reinforcement* and *contiguity*. These were discovered by the behaviorists and their use was demonstrated in the classical and operant conditioning models.

Distributive practice

Distributive practice refers to the timing of a learning endeavor. It has been found that if one learns a body of material at several different sittings rather than at one sitting, he will remember the ideas better. The applicability of this principle to a learning situation presents difficulties, however. To begin with, the optimum interval has never been specified. One doesn't know whether it is better to learn chunks of material for fifteen minutes every three hours or to learn chunks of material for a half-hour every eight hours. Moreover, the research which has been done indicates that there may be differences in learning rote material as opposed to learning meaningful material.[2] Rote learning tasks are essentially non-meaningful. For example, in a typical rote learning task, one learns series of numbers such as 4782, 9365, 7487; or nonsense syllables; such as *bok, hec, sib.* If there is a difference, then the distribution of the distributive practice may well be different for meaningful material than it is for rote material.

Contiguity

A second well-known principle of learning, that of contiguity, presents other problems for the educator who wishes to use the principle to design educational programs. Contiguity is the time interval between the onset of a stimulus and the elicitation of a response. An optimal time interval—contiguity—has been found to be .5 second. When the contiguity interval

---

2 J. Glaze, "The Association Value of Nonsense Syllables," *Journal of Genetic Psychology* 35 (1928): 255–67; D. Lyon, "The Relation of Length of Material to Time Taken for Learning and Optimum Distribution of Time," *Journal of Educational Psychology* 5 (1914): 1–9, *passim;* H. Reed, "Meaning as a Factor in Learning," *Journal of Educational Psychology* 29 (1938): 419–30.

is .5 second, the optimal amount of learning is said to occur. This principle was discovered by stimulus–response psychologists who were interested in a classical conditioning approach to learning. In Pavlov's most famous experiment, a dog was given food powder which caused him to salivate. The administration of the food powder was paired with the sound of a bell. After a number of such pairings, the sound of the bell alone elicited the saliva. In this case the contiguity interval that was considered was the interval between the onset of the food powder and the onset of the bell. The optimal interval here was also found to be .5 second. Just how such a psychological principle is applicable to a school setting is questionable. First the teacher has to determine what the stimulus and response is. In the teaching and learning of multiplication tables this is not difficult to ascertain. However, what is the stimulus and what is the response of a history lesson, a geography lesson, a citizenship lesson, a reading lesson, a language lesson? If the stimulus and response conditions of a learning situation are this difficult to ascertain, then how does one ascertain when contiguity is at the optimum interval?

Reinforcement

One theory of learning states that learning occurs when there is a stimulus, a response, and then a reinforcement. Stimulus refers to some phenomenon which indicates to the learner that a response is appropriate. An example might be a teacher saying, "Johnny, what does 2 × 2 equal?" In this case the correct response to the stimulus is 4. However, if Johnny had responded "7," then 7 would be considered the response, albeit an incorrect one. A reinforcement is the stimulus provided after a response has been made. A reinforcement can be either positive or negative. Examples of positive reinforcement range from food pellets for rats to verbal approval for humans. The learning theory developed by Hull, and since elaborated upon by others, states that a positive reinforcement increased the habit strength of a response and hence, after repeated occurrences of the correct response followed by positive reinforcement, learning occurred.[3]

This learning theory was primarily developed through experimentation with animals or with humans in rote learning tasks. It is questionable whether laws of learning extrapolated from studies on animals or with humans on rote learning tasks can be generalized to verbal learning tasks. Ausubel, reviewing experiments on rote versus meaningful learning reported that differences were found in the rate of learning and degree of remembering between rote and verbal learning.[4] In a well-known article by

[3] Clark Hull, *Essentials of Behavior* (New Haven, Conn.: Yale University Press, 1951), pp. 29–40.

[4] D. Ausubel, *Educational Psychology* (New York: Holt, Rinehart & Winston, 1968).

Gagné, the role of repetition and reinforcement are shown to be relatively insignificant when one deals with a complicated learning task that demands learning a sequence of events.[5]

Gagné's learning model[6]

In an elaboration of the use of simple psychological principles in the promotion of learning, Gagné proposes that the kind of learning that is desired will, in part, determine the program to foster the teaching-learning process. He suggests that there are eight kinds of learning: signal learning, stimulus-response learning, chaining, verbal association, discrimination learning, concept learning, rule learning and problem solving. Each type of learning is unique in two ways. The prerequisite skills of experience that a learner must have in order to handle each type is unique to that type of learning. In addition, each type of learning differs in terms of the learning outcomes. Gagné states that the eight kinds of learning are hierarchical; that is, signal learning is the simplest kind of learning, whereas problem-solving is the most complicated, and there is a progression from least to most complicated.

The transfer value of Gagné's learning paradigm is striking. *Transfer* refers to the generalization of process or content variables from one learning task to another. Since one type of learning is seen as prerequisite to another, the assumption is that previously learned skills (mainly process skills) will transfer to a new learning task and thereby facilitate the learning of the new task.

The objection that humanists have with a learning model of this kind is that it presupposes that the educational psychologists, the curriculum planner, or the teacher knows what it is that the child should learn. In order to be able to design educational programs which utilize part or all of Gagné's learning model, one must know the subject matter to be taught, the state of the learner, and then design an instructional sequence which is congruent both with the state of the learner and the learning model. As already pointed out, however, there is little reason to believe that we can presently predict what subject matter will be relevant for life; we take the position that knowing how to think analytically and to perceive deeply should be the focuses of education. This is not to say that some bodies of facts which are not of utilitarian value now might well be of value for the future. If educational planners would take the trouble to identify these, then we undoubtedly would want to use a learning paradigm, such as Gagné's, with which to teach. The point is that such bodies of fact, although important

---

[5] Robert Gagné, "Military Training and the Principles of Learning," *American Psychologist* 17 (1962): 83–91.

[6] Robert Gagné, *The Conditions of Learning* (New York: Holt, Rinehart & Winston, 1965).

for day to day learning, are, in our opinion, ancillary to what should be the main concern of education—the development of imaginative critical thinkers.

PROGRAMMED INSTRUCTION AND BEHAVIORAL OBJECTIVES

Two alternatives to teaching as an art are programmed instruction and behavioral objectives. Both methods rely upon empirical confirmation of a program's effectiveness by testing the learner's success or failure to learn both the subtasks and the final task. Moreover, programmed instruction and behavioral objectives both use well-known psychological principles, such as repetition, reinforcement, shaping, contiguity, and distributive practice that are built into the instructional sequences.

For example, linear programmed instruction as described by B. F. Skinner starts with the task to be learned.[7] The task is then fully described and analyzed by the programmer. The purpose of this step is to allow the programmer to be fully conversant with all the essential parts of the task, so that when he designs a program he will include every essential part. Moreover, the assumption is that the learning of some parts of the tasks depends upon learning earlier parts; therefore, a careful study of the tasks should be done in order to sequence the learning steps in a way which will ensure optimal learning. Programmed instruction may utilize a teaching machine or it may be in book form. No matter what its format, all linear programs involve several basic psychological principles. The task to be learned is broken down into a sequence of small steps with the learning of later steps dependent upon the learning of earlier ones. The step learning procedure is based upon the principle of successive approximations. This was developed by B. F. Skinner who used pigeons in his early experimental work.[8] An example of this principle would be teaching a pigeon to peck a metal disk. A hungry pigeon is put into a small metal box about $1\frac{1}{2}$-by-$1\frac{1}{2}$ feet. On one wall of the box is a metal disk which, when pecked, will activate a mechanism which will drop some food into a cup and simultaneously make a loud click sound. In order to get the pigeon to peck the metal disk, the experimenter gives reinforcement (activates the mechanism which drops food into a cup and makes a loud click sound) for a movement that the pigeon makes that brings him into the general direction of the disk. Each subsequent reinforcement is given for behavior which goes in the desired direction (toward the metal disk) and is an advance over the pre-

---

[7] B. F. Skinner, *Cumulative Record* (New York: Appleton-Century-Crofts, 1959), pp. 145–82.

[8] B. F. Skinner, *The Behavior of Organisms* (New York: Appleton-Century-Crofts, 1938).

viously reinforced behavior. As the pigeon comes closer and closer to the disk he is successively reinforced for his behavior that is in the desired direction, until he finally pecks the disk.

Another important principle utilized in programmed instruction is positive reinforcement. When the learner demonstrates that he has learned a step, he is given positive reinforcement immediately (contiguously) after his demonstration of new learning. Such reinforcement ranges from M & M candies to social reinforcement, such as the word "correct."

In order to ensure a low rate of failure on instructional programs, the programs are usually tested on a sample of individuals for whom they were intended, previous to widespread distribution. Such testing reveals which items are being failed by too many students. Such failure might indicate that the item in question needs to be broken down into more than one step.

One of the great educational contributions of programmed instruction is that it has made many educators aware of all of the skills involved in any one task, and that, by careful planning, these skills can be taught. For example, it has become increasingly evident that children from diverse environmental and cultural backgrounds come to school with different skills, and that it is only by recognizing these different skills that a teacher can hope to be successful in teaching her pupils a certain body of knowledge.

Behavioral objectives in the instructional process is a method of organizing instructional material and teaching in order to increase the likelihood of learning. Historically, the development of behavioral objectives owes a debt to programmed instruction, cybernetics, and task analysis. The two major functions of behavioral objectives are: (1) to make specific the goals of any instructional program so that the outcomes of instruction can be evaluated in terms of student behavior—this function demands that the educator specify exactly what his instructional objectives are and how they will be accomplished; and (2) to communicate the goals of instruction to teachers, students, and curriculum planners. Just as programmed instruction and cybernetics furnish knowledge of results, so do behavioral objectives. Some of the important features of a well-constructed behavioral objective are knowledge of results, opportunities to practice, guidance from the teacher, opportunity for active response, motivation, provision for students to proceed at a pace congruent with their abilities, description of the end goal of the instructional sequence, and sequenced material (as in programmed instruction, the material is usually sequenced from simple to complex, with later steps dependent upon earlier ones).

Both behavioral objectives and programmed instruction are efficient methods for teaching children subject matter that is straightforward and necessary; for example, multiplication. A limitation of both methods is that the instruction must be designed in such a way that its behavioral effects can be measured. Unfortunately, there are many behaviors which we are not yet able to measure accurately. Does this mean that we shouldn't attempt to teach them? Another limitation is that no provision is made for measuring the long-term effects of an instructional procedure such as behavioral objectives. It may well be that the long-term effects of teaching children using the behavioral objective method will make such children dependent upon knowing specifiable outcomes in order to learn. But if it is the goal of education to teach children to be able to deal with change in imaginative constructive ways, then it may be more profitable to provide open-ended experiences that do not have specifiable behavioral outcomes.

DEVELOPMENTAL PSYCHOLOGY

Educational psychologists generally attempt to determine not only the principles of learning and their applicability to education, but also to decide the state of the learner when he comes to the learning situation.

There are two main schools of developmental psychology. One explains the intellectual development of the child in terms of qualitative stages. This school is best represented by the work of Jean Piaget. Another school explains development in terms of learning. That is to say, a child develops intellectually and emotionally because of the effects of experiences and the learning that has accrued because of these experiences.

STAGE DEVELOPMENT

Piaget states that there is qualitatively different intellectual functioning between an adult and a child. These differences in intellectual functioning account for the differences in the ability of a child and an adult to learn certain material. Piaget describes the development of a child from birth to adolescence in terms of three stages. Each stage has certain characteristics which indicate to the educator what the child is able to learn within that particular stage. For example, as Piaget describes development,[9] there are three stages: the preoperational stage, 0 to 7 years old; the concrete operational stage, 7 to 11 years old; and the stage of formal operations, 11 years old onward. The preoperational stage is broken up into several substages. Inasmuch as the concern of this chapter is primarily with formal education only, the stages and substage descriptions of the child between the ages of 4 and 12 years will be dealt with.

The final substage of the preoperational stage is the substage of intuitive thought. This substage usually begins at about four years of age and ends at about seven years, when the concrete operational stage begins. A

[9] Jean Piaget, *Psychology of Intelligence* (Paterson, N.J.: Littlefield, Adams, 1963), p. 123.

child in the intuitive substage of preoperational thought is limited in his ability to function intellectually. For example, when presented with a typical conservation program—two identical glasses are both filled with the same number of beads; the contents of one of these glasses of beads is poured into a taller thinner glass, and the child maintains that there is a different amount of beads in the tall thin glass—the child centers on one dimension of the problem, in this case either the height or width of the glass, and seems to be unable to consider both pertinent variables simultaneouesly. This inability to conserve beads—and the same outcome would take place if one conducted the same experiment with water—is taken to mean that the child is unable to reason deductively. In addition, problems of ordination and seriation are too complex for the child in the intuitive substage. For example, a child may be able to repeat the months of the year in an ordered series, but not be able to consider the twelve months and their relation to each other without going through the whole series. A child in the substage of intuitive thought would not be able to solve the following problem: If April is the month following March, what is the month following September?

If, as an educator, you accept Piaget's stage theory, then the limitations on what you can teach a child in the intuitive substage immediately become evident. Analysis of the conservation problem reveals that its solution depends upon the operation of reversibility. What this simply means is that, in order to know that pouring beads from one shaped container to another does not change the amount of beads, you must be able to reverse the pouring operation mentally, and visualize the beads in their original container. The operation of reversibility is often necessary in arithmetic, grammar, and logic. Therefore, if you wish to teach a child between the ages of four and six something that demands the operation of reversibility, do you teach him something else and wait until he becomes concrete-operational, approximately seven to eleven years, or do you just try harder?

At approximately seven years of age, a child becomes concrete-operational; that is, he enters the stage of concrete operational thought. The move from the intuitive substage of preoperational thought represents a qualitative advance in the child's ability to think. The evidence for this qualitative change is exemplified by the child's ability to solve the conservation problem. This solution indicates that he now possesses the operation of reversibility. Moreover, problems of seriation are within the child's ability to solve. The limitations of this stage of intellectual development reside in the concrete approach that the child uses to solve problems. Although language serves to identify the salient aspects of a problem, language alone is not a sufficient condition for the child's solution of the problem in this stage. Any problem presented to a child or any teaching situation should have concrete examples. The child in this stage is not able to deal with abstract concepts, but must have concrete objects that he can handle in order to work out solutions.

The final stage of intellectual development as delineated by Piaget is the stage of formal operations. This stage occurs at approximately eleven years of age. The qualitative difference between the stage of formal operations and the concrete operational stage is that in the former the child is able to reason abstractly. In the latter, this is not the case; the child needs concrete examples of the concept.

Another explanation of intellectual development is offered by learning psychologists such as Gagné. For example, Gagné has hypothesized that as long as the learner has the necessary prerequisite skills, he can learn anything. This is as much as saying that new learning depends on prior learning and experience that are appropriate to the new learning task.

These two developmental approaches do not represent all the positions of developmental theory; however, they do represent two of the more prominent. The problem with Piaget's theory is that when it is tested experimentally with children, many of the conditions do not always hold true. For example, one often finds that children who are in the concrete-operational stage are able to handle some abstract problems on an abstract level. Piaget's experiments, as well as those of his supporters, are only probability statements of development. Hence, the exceptions, such as the example given, lower the probability and certainty of his statements. For example, the concept of *conservation* is a benchmark measure of the onset of Piaget's stage of *concrete operations*. This concept is supposed to occur developmentally; that is, without direct learning experience. In fact, Piaget explicitly states that conservation of substance cannot be learned, for if it could, one could advance a child's developmental level by instruction. Unfortunately for Piaget's theory, several experimenters have taught children the concept of *conservation of substance*.[10]

The limiting factor in Gagné's idea is that one must determine the prerequisites for a learning task in question, and then determine which of these prerequisites a particular learner has. In order to be able to do this, the teacher must know specifically what he wants to teach the learner. This raises a major issue about the differences between traditional educational psychology and humanistic educational psychology. The former specified how to use psychological principles, but more how to use psychological principles to teach specific learning tasks. Developmental stage theory has the same limiting function. Although developmental stage theory does not attempt to specify what to teach, it attempts in a general way to specify

---

[10] D. Brison, "Acquisition of Conservation of Substance in a Group Situation," (Doctoral dissertation, University of Illinois, 1965); D. Brison and C. Bereiter, "Acquisition of Conservation of Substance in Normal, Retarded, and Gifted Children," in *Recent Research on the Acquisition of Conservation of Substance,* ed. D. Brison and E. Sullivan (Toronto: Ontario Institute for Studies in Education, 1967), pp. 53–72: S. Engelmann, "Cognitive Structure Related to the Principle of Conservation," in ibid., pp. 35–51; E. Sullivan, "Acquisition of Conservation of Substance Through Film Modeling Techniques," in ibid., pp. 11–23.

what cannot be taught. In the first case, the teacher assumes that he knows what the child should know. In our public schools children are taught reading, writing, arithmetic, and social studies. In many introductory texts on the cultural foundations of education, the purpose of education is stated as the transmission of our cultural heritage to succeeding generations. It is our contention, however, that in an age when the world is changing at a fantastic rate socially and technologically, none of us can know what the world will look like fifteen years from now. Hence, the content which we presently value may be inappropriate for the man of 1980. Moreover, it does not appear that what we teach children at the present time is very useful in dealing with his life and life's problems.

PSYCHOLOGICAL LEARNING

As we move from traditional psychology to humanistic psychology we can contrast the two on several important dimensions which have already been implied in the work so far.

First, traditional psychology uses probability statements as truth or laws. Humanistic psychology does not use the tools by which statements of probability are meaningful. Humanistic learning is knowing as certainty, not probability, and this can only make sense within the head of the learner, for only he can know for sure that he knows something. For the humanist this, at least for the present, is adequate as a test of learning. We realize that this kind of statement can get us into trouble. If taken to the limits of what it might mean it suggests that anything can be a test of learning as well as the basis for education. We do have a philosophical version of the purpose of education which has to do with human betterment, and we do have a vision of man that sees him as integrated. Our assumptions bear very heavily upon this perspective. But as to the notion that learning cannot be objectified, all we mean to suggest here is that we need to shy away from evaluation and rely upon our faith in people who, when left alone and not intimidated, will learn good things in a good way. This is an article of faith. All versions of education and learning must seek their legitimacy on the same basis.

Second, traditional psychology, as this is applied to learning, makes the assumption that learning can only be defined in terms of a product which is measurable. The work on programmed instruction and behavioral objectives illustrates how the stuff to be learned, in the program or inherent in the objectives, exists independent of the learner. This suggests, further, that learning is what students do with the material that has been identified for them, and that their progress is only what can be measured from questions on that material.

Humanistic psychology, as applied to learning, makes a very different kind of assumption. It assumes that learning is more than what we can measure, and that often, by specifying in advance what is to be learned, the student may be diverted from real progress that could occur as he chooses his own learning goals.

Thirdly, traditional learning psychology treats the person as an object, as if he can be manipulated much as an element in an experiment in physics. By using or approximating the methods of science, the behavioral scientist assumes that he is able to devise laws for students much as the geologist devises laws for the erosion of rocks. He does this by applying the rigid criteria of scientific control, again assuming that persons can be controlled as physical objects can.

Humanistic psychology distrusts this definition of the person, and shies away from experiments which involve treating qualities of persons as so many numbers. Humanistic learning cannot be put in a numbers bag.

Finally, at least for now, the contrast between traditional and humanistic approaches to learning can be sensed in the different styles of the two parts of this chapter. In this first section on traditional educational psychology, we are retarded by the necessity to use abstract technical concepts. Traditional psychology is as much jargon as anything else. But you can't really communicate about it without these terms, since they represent so much of the tradition of the discipline. Behaviorism, reinforcement, conditioning, operant, cognition, motivation are terms which all have special meaning within the field, and talking about such notions without applying the accepted terminology is practically impossible.

As we move on to our notions of humanistic psychology, we will begin to broaden our base of communication.

HUMANISTIC PSYCHOLOGY

Humanistic educational psychology is the application of principles of humanistic psychology to education. These principles will be stated, described, and examined with respect to the role they might play in improving classroom learning.

Many of the principles of humanistic psychology have to do with learning as a condition for, rather than as a direct correlate of, the learning experience. In other words, it is necessary to create an environment for, and an openness to, the learning stimulus on the part of the learner. For the most part, the applications of traditional psychology did not focus upon conditions but upon the learning act itself. The point here is that the most stimulating lecture ever delivered produces no learning whatsoever if the learner is asleep at the time it occurs. Many of the principles of humanistic psychology have to do with figuratively awakening the learner so that he will be able to attend to the learning stimulus that is simultaneously in the outer world and the inner world.

The principles of humanistic psychology, as they are applied to the learning process, conceive of learning itself as a different phenomenon from the conception put forth by traditional psychology. Traditional psychology views learning as an outcome of some experience involving some specific kind of change in the learner, and evaluated by some concrete product. Humanistic learning is specifically the kind of learning that occurs when we *feel* the truth of something as well as understand it in our head. The key word is, of course, "feel." This notion is not very popular in the scientific disciplines, but we have already dealt with the issue of science. Scientists, who in education we call empiricists, think of feeling as a kind of intuition, and consequently having nothing to do with universals, which are their concern. The truth may be quite the opposite, that is, intuitive truth being more universal than scientific truth.

Humanistic learning is indicated by a before-after sequence, as is the case with the traditional view of learning. It is concerned with change; but the kind of change that humanists talk about is not always observable in the same way that "scientific" learning is observable. In other words, it is not always possible to demonstrate that this change has taken place, except to take the word of the person, and he may not always know.

Let us describe a learning event, one that we all know and have felt. Persons grow comfortable in their environment to the degree that they trust others in their environment. In primitive tribes, parents help children come to this trust by introducing strangers as relatives, cousins, or uncles. In race relations we know that prejudice decreases to the extent that persons come to trust members of other races. Continued exposure becomes the vehicle by which this occurs.[11] In the American soldier studies, black units were integrated with white units. This led to decreased prejudice of whites towards blacks. The whites learned something in their experience and this led to decreased prejudice. They did not learn about prejudice, however. They learned something about trust, which is related to prejudice. Now is this a humanistic learning experience? Yes, but incomplete. Although numerical descriptions are not quite accurate, we might say it is only half a humanistic learning experience. A full humanistic learning experience is one where something happens to a person and he understands in his head what has happened and why. The soldiers in our examples were changed, but they didn't know why.

We are trying to teach about this trust. We give definitions of the concept, we talk about conditions under which one comes to trust, and we might talk about conditions under which persons do not trust. We give our students a test and they give back to us the definitions, the conditions producing trust, and the conditions hindering it; all clearly thought out. Has the student learned about trust? Not in humanistic terms. But suppose we take the student to a new environment, a room with many people, where

11 S. Staufer et al., *The American Soldier: Adjustment during Army Life* (Princeton, N.J.: Princeton University Press, 1949).

he knows no one (we have all been to parties like that; can you remember your first feelings?), where he does not know what to expect, what will be asked of him, what he should do. He does not trust the environment. If we ask him to think about what he is feeling, since this is an intense moment for him, he should be able to get in touch with his feelings. Suppose, then, asking him to keep his present feeling in mind, we take him by the hand and lead him about the room, introduce him to the people, have them speak to him about what they do and what they are there for, give him a role to play, a job to do that fits in with what the others are talking about. He is now more comfortable, he is coming to trust his environment, and he can relate this trust to his experience. Now, should he put this feeling together with his definitions and his knowledge of conditions, he has learned about trust in the humanistic sense. Should he care to look at the prejudice studies or the research on culture shock or read about some of the habits of primitives, his understandings will go much deeper than if it was all, so to speak, "in the head."

We will now attempt to show how the principles of humanistic psychology, as these relate to learning, can be applied to education. Please keep in mind that the word "learn," as we use it in the following principles, refers to *humanistic* learning.

PRINCIPLES OF HUMANISTIC PSYCHOLOGY

1. Persons learn in a free environment

One can learn almost anything under any circumstances, if we mean learn in the traditional sense. Rats can learn to deal with a maze in a cage, and this example can apply to children in school. However, one cannot learn humanistically in a cage. One must have freedom to learn, and one learns best in a free environment. When Carl Rogers speaks of "freedom," he speaks mainly of an internal freedom, where a person who is free within himself, who is open to his experience, who has a sense of his own freedom and responsible choice, is not nearly so likely to be controlled by his environment as is the person who lacks these qualities.[12]

If we can produce this kind of person, the likelihood is that he will not tolerate an external environment that reduces his personal freedom. Training persons to know the value of freedom is, in a sense, training a society that will never submit to totalitarian control. It is a way of guaranteeing revolutionary activity, should environments become unfree or repressive.

The kind of environment that is free allows the person full exposure to his human potentiality. One needs this human potential to learn human-

---

[12] Carl Rogers, *Freedom to Learn* (Columbus, Ohio: Charles E. Merrill, 1969), p. 270.

istically. Without it, one is literally prevented from learning in the way we have described. If, in any way, the school prevents the free utilization of feelings, then children cannot use these to learn, and if they cannot use these to learn, they simply cannot learn. The point is that feelings are necessary.

Applied to the classroom, this notion requires that a teacher not only permit a great deal of individual initiative in determining one's learning experience, but the experience of using one's full capacities. In other words, the classroom environment should not only permit self-determination and self-expression, it should encourage it.

Freedom in the classroom is retarded by preconceiving the outcomes of the learning experience. When we say that a student must know this or that, we are really saying, if our curriculum is linked to our outcomes, that the child is not free to learn what he wants in the way that he wants to learn it. Any resistance at all on the part of the learner to the objectives or tasks of the classroom forces him to shut off his human potential. If he is resentful, his feelings are not free to participate in the learning activity. Traditionally, that has not bothered many teachers, since teachers have not been able to see how feelings were specifically pertinent to the learning task except, of course, that it is easier to learn something if you like it. Unfortunately, educators seldom recognize that if a principle is valid it is fully valid and worth more than limited attention.

Now, of course, we are faced with an ethical question. Should the child determine what he should learn or should we, as experts, determine what it is that he should learn? If we incline toward the latter position, we have taken upon ourselves the role as conservative keepers of the status quo, and guaranteed the child, unless he can recover from the harm we have done him, a mediocre life. Mediocrity, in humanistic terms, is only being able to use a small portion of your capacity to learn and grow.

The psychological principle that anxiety interferes with problem-solving ability is an instance of the larger issue of freedom to learn. Freedom means that one need not attend to issues unrelated to the knowing act itself. When we attend to the consequence of learning something and not the process of learning, then we are simply not free to learn. If you think about the conditions under which you have always learned, you will recognize the problems most students in most schools have to face in every learning act. Think also about the learning tasks you have had to rush in order to "get it in on time," or about the language you have tried to use in order to sound good. What most of you have learned then from these learning tasks is how to succeed. If that is your only goal, then the value of education becomes highly questionable. But this opens a Pandora's box of ethical and philosophical issues that would take a whole book to describe. Suffice it to say here that humanistic learning is unconcerned with social success or failure, only with the quality of human learning which is so importantly tied to human health and well-being.

With respect to one issue that should be bothering you, the question of how young children can direct their own learning, we need to express this: that there are principles of learning that are universal, many of which are embodied in this paper, and these principles must be known and applied by a teacher. These principles have nothing to do with what a child should learn but how he will be best able to learn it. For example, we feel there is a qualitative difference between telling somebody a fact and helping him phrase a question. Directing one's own learning experience simply means that a child or adult may be free to inquire about anything in any way they wish, using the teacher as a resource for providing materials, providing experiences that will help students know what they would like to know about, and arranging ways to get the best kind of help available. The school, in this way, needs to be viewed as one vast resource to help children get in touch with the world and with themselves. Part of providing experiences to help children seek answers is helping them to learn how to read and write and figure, but as a means, not as an end in itself.

Finally, freedom in an academic environment, from nursery school to graduate school, means that the student must make his own choices about doing and being. In this way he will not only learn well, he will learn rapidly. We can build forever better and better instruments of instruction and train experts in the uses of these devices, and in one elementary or secondary school career the child will not learn half as well as if he were left to discover for himself without being evaluated, scheduled, manipulated, timed, and predetermined what there is to be learned.

We do not have the evidence to substantiate this empirically, largely because humanistic experiments in education are rare, and evaluative tools are not available. But we do infer the truth of such a notion from the simple example that it is a far more difficult task to teach a child the notion of "hot" and "cold" with books, tapes, and demonstrations, than it is to put his hand in hot water or stick it in a bowl of ice. When this occurs, the child learns not only what hot and cold are, he also learns what it means to be cautious around objects that produce similar sensations. The child, then, must be free to discover his own experiences or at least his own way of relating to the experiences and opportunities that we provide for him. And he must, most particularly, be free to do with those experiences anything he wishes, including rejecting them until he is ready to use them.

2. The child learns by relating the world to his own experiences

We are talking here about a very old principle of educational psychology, but not one that has found acceptance in the establishment of the field. This is, more or less, John Dewey's notion of learning by doing, with the added directive that the experience of doing must be selected by the learner in line with his own theory of what he needs to do. When we say theory, we mean some implicit, probably intuitive, assumption that a particular act will reveal something to me that I want revealed. The importance of emphasizing the child's choice of experience has to do with the idea so well described in *Teaching as a Subversive Activity,* that not only do we learn what we do, we learn what we are made to do.[13] If we are encouraged to *do* memorizing, we learn memorizing; if we are encouraged to learn to think, we learn to think, if we learn at all. If left to his own devices, the child will never decide to *do* memorizing; he will never decide to read about things that have no meaning for him; he will never decide to add up a column of meaningless numbers. The child's basic interests in this matter is our key to understanding what we have to offer him. If he chooses to play with blocks, then we must think about offering him some block-playing experience that might relate to our concerns for his learning about his world.

Learning by relating the world to one's experience is a psychological principal having to do with the relationship between learning and the application of all our senses to the problem of knowing.

Experiencing an event brings into play one's sense of sight, sound, smell, touch, and sometimes taste. Consider a unit on Brazil. We are about to move down the Amazon. We might see a film about it, but here we only see, although that is somewhat better than only reading about it. Suppose, on the other hand, that we could have a tropical experience, see the dark green, the thickness of the growth, feel the moisture in every pore, hear the buzzing of the insects and the squeals of the jungle birds, smell the heavy sweetness of blossoms and the rotting of vegetation and animal meat, taste the berries and the beans. Create your own experience, your own event, and then decide how to best simulate the experience. Is there anything we described that we could not experience separately? Could we not, using our imagination, experience the sights, sounds, smells, tastes, and feel of the jungle? And in doing so—creating a jungle and experiencing it—we come to know it.

We can only know the world in any real sense through our experience with it. If we must rely heavily upon our imagination, we may construct a monstrous distortion of the reality. This, in fact, is what has happened to most of us. We develop stereotypes which lead to significant acts of violence upon others; that is, we act in terms of a rigid perspective of what a person is or is not, thereby closing off the possibilities for understanding and cooperation. Currently our nation is divided over many issues of differences. Persons are prevented from honest experiences with others who are different from themselves. In the classroom we mainly see others who are like ourselves. If there are differences, we do not experience them. Around issues of

[13] N. Postman and C. Weingartner, *Teaching as a Subversive Activity* (New York: Delacorte Press, 1969).

race, age, sex, income, and religion, we construct our personal images and arrange our patterns of interaction based upon these constructions. Because our constructions are so often erroneous, blacks do not relate well to whites, youths to adults, men to women, poor to rich, workers to students, and so on. This should point out, if nothing else, the necessity for building accurate, experiential images, rather than merely academic ones.

3. Persons learn cooperatively

By "cooperatively" we do not necessarily mean in a group. This would imply learning collectively, which is a slightly different issue. The notion of learning cooperatively refers to relying upon others to support the learning experience rather than retard it. We require feedback from others in order to know where we are with respect to where we think we are and where we want to be. Feedback is a crucial dynamic in humanistic group work. It is used in sensitivity training, encounters, human relations seminars and similar activities. It refers to the process of being helped to evaluate what one is saying, doing, being. This evaluation, if the learning environment is cooperative rather than competitive, will always be intended constructively. If the person knows that the environment is cooperative, then he will heed the feedback. If he conceives of the environment as competitive, or that it consists of a number of isolates each doing his own thing, the feedback will be treated hostilely or ignored. In order to contribute to the humanistic learning experience, feedback must be defined as constructive. In order to accomplish constructive feedback in the classroom, and to create a cooperative learning environment, we must rid the environment of all those forces which cause interpersonal relations to be noncooperative. What are these forces? The first force is that which requires persons to compete against each other for the rewards of the system. It is a system of unidimensional standards used to differentiate students and classify them according to their accomplishments. These standards are invidious. They set in motion a network of defenses and antagonisms that undermine any possibility of cooperative education.

A second force is one which prevents persons from determining what they do with their time and denies them any power to influence the decisions which affect their own lives. In this way the educational environment is composed of persons who hold different degrees of power. Whenever this is true, the environment is divisive. Those who do not have the power resent those who do. And those who do, become defensive when they are accused of wielding power against the interest of those whom they control.

A third force which inhibits the formation of a cooperative learning experience is the pervasiveness of moralistic judgments in the school and classroom. The school conceives its function as producing moral citizens; "moral," in this case, refers to a commitment to behave in ways prescribed by tradition. Persons in the classroom act as protectors of that moral tradition in a way that restrains deviation. With everybody proving his own moral fiber by watching that of everybody else, the possibilities for a cooperative educational environment diminish. The only way to balance individual ways of viewing the world with a unidimensional moralism is to somehow create an atmosphere in which relative values are not only understood but relished. Part of the cultural revolution hinges on this belief in relativism, that there are no rights or wrongs in most aspects of social living but only different preferences. When persons can respect the other's need to do his own thing in his own way, then the foundation for cooperative efforts is laid. We do not, of course, expect that the destruction of the life or freedom of others will be included in that relativism. Freedom, in this sense, is not only doing your own thing, it is protecting the right of others to live and work in their own way without being manipulated by anyone else. The beginnings of a cooperative environment rest upon the collective assumption that my freedom depends upon freedom guaranteed to everyone else. And if you, as students, can understand this one point, you can understand why millions of persons in this country and others protest the involvement of American military forces in other lands. Freedom to determine one's own political structure is a universal principal which must be protected for others as well as ourselves.

4. Persons learn from the inside out

Persons learn by constructing a sense of something from within themselves, not by being given labels for that outside world.

We are about to learn about Italy during the Renaissance. Let us take a hypothetical lesson on this subject:

> The "Renaissance" is a period in history when Europe was awakening from its lethargy of the Middle Ages. Persons began to create artistically, to explore new worlds, to invent, to attempt new political adventures. It was the age of Leonardo da Vinci (remember the *Mona Lisa?*); of Michaelangelo (remember David and Moses?); of Galileo; of the Borgia popes and the mad Savanarola, of Machiavelli, and Dante. Here is Rome and there is Florence, the artistic center of the Renaissance. Below Rome is Naples and to the northeast of Florence is Venice, where gondolas carry persons along the canals to their various destinations.

When history is taught as a world of labels, of imposed meanings—if any meanings at all—and geography becomes the names of places and rivers and mountains and directions, does all this have anything to do with learning? *Not in itself.* Learning is making things meaningful for a purpose. If the child does any learning, it is for himself; he must have a purpose or he would not have learned. If we construct the learning for him, we have given him our meaning, our understanding, our relevance. He then really learns only labels and other people's meanings.

We give the child a language that we think he needs, but we never communicate to him that things in themselves are not necessarily what we call them; that is, a thing is more than a name. A thing has functions, bears relationships, has intrinsic qualities that may not at all be captured by its label. The best example in educational life is our labeling of the quality "intelligence." We don't know a great deal about intelligence despite the fact that it is one of our most popular educational psychological concepts. Intelligence is something that educators, as well as students, talk about all the time; it is a notion we use to differentiate, evaluate, and to allocate students to particular groups. But few educators understand intelligence. The problem with intelligence, like most concepts, is that we destroy its real existence by imposing one of our own. We don't acknowledge that the qualities of human beings are always in process whereas "things" are always fixed. The utility of anything is the meaning it has for us and by imposing meaning we impose utility. That is, by labeling something we give it a meaning and impose that label and meaning on everybody else. Persons are hampered in their learning to the degree that the meaning and utility of a notion or thing or concept are imposed from outside. With physical objects, certain laws have been discovered, and these laws can be translated into language that persons understand and have communicated. It is a physical law that water runs downhill. "Runs downhill" is a concept that children can understand. But if they have never seen water run downhill, if they have never tried to get water to run uphill, they have learned from the outside in. Through linguistic symbols, through fixed definitions, they have caught an idea. But they *learn* it without any words at all. When they see that fluid go in a direction that they can sense because they have sense perception of space and direction, when they witness that process, they construct meaning from it. They have understood events from observing them. This is learning from the inside out, giving things meaning because, and only because, we sense that meaning. This is humanistic learning.

5. Persons learn in relation to their human qualities

We are not here concerned with our senses, since we discussed this notion in the section on experience. What we mean here is that a person, as part of being human in a social world, takes on certain irreducible qualities. These are his basic qualities, upon which all other qualities are elaborations. These qualities lie in the fact that he is (a) unique; (b) a child or an adolescent; (c) a sentient being; (d) part of the human experience; (e) a social being; (f) a political being. Let us elaborate.

The Student is Unique: The student must ask himself the question "How am I different from others?" What is it that distinguishes each person from others and what do these differences mean? It is here that we must begin to familiarize persons with themselves by asking what it means to be different, and what difference being different makes. We may well want to examine the way in which being different from others influences the motivation and adaptation of persons to different roles. Why is it, for example, that black men are disproportionately represented on athletic teams? Why is it that men and not women hold all the political power? The kinds of questions that can be raised from focusing on differences are many and varied and should be emphasized in the curriculum.

The Student is a Child (or Adolescent): This category differs from the first insofar as it does not focus upon differences, but upon similarities, specifically on age similarities. Most schools are age-graded. One doesn't usually have adults, adolescents, and children in the same class. But suppose they are together in the learning environment. We can still talk about what it is like to be where we are on the age ladder. That is, we can try to communicate to others what it is like to be 10, or 20, or 50 from the standpoint of the number and kind of our experiences. Our major focus is upon the child as child. That is, we want to emphasize the educational importance of constructing experiences to permit the child to know what he is. Traditionally, educational systems have attempted to make children into little adults from the first grade on, to communicate to them what it takes to be a worthwhile adult and then shove them on the conveyor belt. That is, we begin to socialize them to adult citizenship roles and deprive them of their childhood while in school.

Children have a special construction of the world; they have a marvelous way of exposing themselves to the strange and mysterious, until we as adults tell them how it really is, because that is the way we want it to be. In their heads and hands children can transpose objects into weapons or wands, magical creatures, or sources of energy. If we have ever believed in encouraging creativity in children, then we should have been outraged at the way the school denies children the right, as well as the opportunity, to be creative; because, in effect, they begin school prepared to utilize their imagination, their curiosity, their wealth of free-flowing emotion. They can speak to one another freely, write and draw spontaneously, and interact with others in the classroom as themselves. Then we tell them how to speak, what to speak about, and when it is appropriate to speak. All children need in the beginning are the skills for communication of themselves. By the time we provide them with the skills, they no longer have the personal qualities required for the creative act. We teach our children guardedly, even tentatively. We don't give them skills unless they prove they deserve them, which is to act mature—not like the free spirits they are.

The Student is a Feeling Person: Feelings, as we have discussed earlier, help student learn. Some feelings, however, that we produce in children inhibit them from learning. We have to communicate to the students both processes of feeling and learning. How, for example, does fear of failure get in the way of what we learn, and how we learn?

We have the responsibility, if we believe in the humanistic purposes of education, not only to permit students to feel, but to develop that capacity that is at the heart of the creative process. Later on, in the section on strategies, we will be talking about ways to promote our capacities to feel. It is important here that we theoretically understand the idea that feelings are critical to the complete learning experience.

The Student is Part of the Human Experience: There are certain physiological processes that human beings experience in common, such as birth, growth, sex, and death. Children are ordinarily protected from these experiences: birth is considered too private, growth too complex, sex too personal and immoral (except under conditions that children wouldn't completely understand), and death too frightening. If education intends to familiarize persons with the nature of their world, it cannot ignore such fundamental processes as these.

The Child as a Social Being: What does it mean to be a social being? How are we social, how are we not social? These questions begin to get at some of the areas that need to be explored to reveal to students their relationship to their environment. There are many social circumstances in which students find themselves. How does one learn about these in such a way as to develop a learning strategy for understanding social life, rather than just knowing some facts about what we call social institutions?

We need to direct the curriculum in this area to focus upon the function of social arrangements. Before we teach about the structure of American government, for instance, students should understand the function of government itself. In order to approach this subject, however, we need to raise the issue of what it means to interact with others. How do we use others? How do we react to others? Why?

The student must come to know society humanistically in order to participate in its processes. Currently a segment of our society has been called the "silent majority" (which, incidentally, was originally intended to refer, in ancient Anglo-Saxon mythology, to the world of the dead). If society is to be vital in the lives of all of us and if education is to improve our ability to live socially, then we must not become members of the silent majority, the world of the dead. For those persons, education has been a monumental failure; that is, unless we define the end products of education according to material values. In this case, any kind of an education, except a humanistic one, will do.

HUMANISTIC STRATEGIES AND EDUCATION

Having discussed the principles upon which the theory of humanistic psychology is based, we can turn to the strategies of applying these principles. Principles, or assumptions of the sort that we have discussed, guide our choice of strategies in the following way: If we decide, according to the principles of general psychology, that persons learn from reinforcement, then our strategy becomes one of choosing appropriate reinforcements. If we decide that persons learn by experiencing the world, we choose strategies to help them gain that experience.

All the different strategies in humanistic psychology add up to the same thing—humanistic learning. For convenience, we will talk about these humanistic strategies in three areas: a) learning about the world; b) improving your capacity to experience; and c) relating to others.

Learning about the world

Strategies related to this area have to do with providing experiences to help people know or understand concepts, things or ideas that describe the universe about them. We have emphasized that persons need to construct their understanding from their private worlds of sense and memory. That is, they have to not only understand things intellectually, but emotionally as well. This notion should begin to make more sense as we talk about specific strategies.

1. Role Play: Most role-play techniques are intended to help persons understand a social situation by having them represent types in an everyday drama. Let us take a dramatic example. We want high school students to think about racism. We structure a situation: Mr. Jones is a white school principal, Mr. Smith is the white drama teacher, Dick is a black student, Mary is a white student, Mrs. Porter is the white president of the PTA. Dick and Mary were chosen as the two best performers in the class. The play calls for a romantic scene between the two. The situation is complicated by the fact that several parents have protested and Mrs. Porter has asked the principal to either change the leads or change the play. The principal invites all parties to attend a meeting in his office. Only the principal and Mrs. Porter know in advance why the others are being asked to the principal's office. Now we choose five students and play out the drama. As persons begin to apply stereotypes of the role of each of the persons, they begin to see the basis of conflict in racial questions, the way issues are avoided, the rationale people use for racist decisions. For example, the student who portrays the PTA president will attempt to communicate her objection, using typical rationalizations, like "It might upset too many people," or "Why create conflict when things are going well?" Later, in examining her choice of arguments, she will look upon the assumptions that she and others made about race (i.e., a problem, conflict, etc.).

2. Gestalt Learning: Gestalt learning evolves from the Gestalt psychology of Fritz Perls, in which persons come to understand their relation to the world by taking the role of others in relation to themselves. George has a feeling about a career as a military officer. To act this out, we may say, "All right, George, be the military officer and talk to George the student, then be yourself and talk to the officer." This is an example of another form of role play, different from the first in that Gestalt learning always includes the real person in the acted-out sequence. Gestalt learning is a way of asking students to act out the role of other persons or persons of the same type as oneself. It's a way of getting one's stereotypes played out in the open and, at the same time, an opportunity to express one's feelings about those stereotypes.

Be-the-thing game

This is a technique for helping persons understand function. That is, in seeking ways to pretend you are a thing, one always pretends either the form or the function of a thing, and the main importance of this exercise is to feel the difference. Suppose we are going to act out an Indian tepee. We could quickly get ourselves into a position where we look like one. But now suppose we are asked to be the tepee without showing its form, showing, instead, that it houses, warms, provides space for decorating, or forces a person to sit in a certain way.

A variation of this game is to be a part of speech or an abstract concept. To be a part of speech, you again must demonstrate its function, which is important for understanding, since there is no way to represent its form. Choose six students, tell them each to be a part of speech and to act out, nonverbally, their relation to each other. Together the group is a sentence. Do you begin to see the possibilities?

The rules discomfort technique

We have students talk about things that make them uncomfortable. They will normally come up with such notions as "calling a girl," "taking a test," "coming home late," "being dirty," "not knowing what to wear for a party or being dressed differently from others," or "speaking in front of people."

What we attempt to do here is to get persons to act out a situation in which they are personally uncomfortable. This gets us to develop a set of rules about how persons are expected to behave, which, in turn, adds up to our social contract. Students are encouraged to examine their social contract as a way of seeing the social structure, particularly in its relationship to them.

These are a few strategies for getting persons to look into their relation to society, to begin to feel the meaning of their social experience. Now let us turn to a consideration of other kinds of strategies.

Learning about yourself

Persons have a number of feelings which they never explore. They have, in particular, feelings about their body image, their sounds, their coordination. In order to understand, we have to learn how to see with all of our senses. Most people rely upon the most superficial utilization of their senses. Strategies intending to advance one's capacities to know the world are those which focus upon the development of the senses. How many of us, for example, know how to observe? We see, but there is much we do not see. Industrial society has succeeded in turning people off to anything but the grossest sensations. That is why the grossest forms of entertainment, the most obvious, are the most successful. The following are a number of sample techniques to improve one's ability to experience the world.

Sensory awareness

Sensory awareness deals with feeling your body, knowing something about your capacity to project your mind inward to an awareness of yourself. It is a training mechanism, intended to help people differentiate between feeling and thinking. Modern, as well as classical dance, in which persons feel and then express a mood or an idea through body motions, provides this kind of experience.

Other activities associated with sensory awareness would be exercises involving rhythm, coordination, and self-exploration through touching and being touched. The "sculpture game," where persons shape each other into various forms as if they were works of clay, is one example of a touch-and-being-touched activity.

The hand exercise

Let us live through our hands. Two persons come together, close their eyes and hold hands. Then they are instructed, each in turn, to show feelings through their hands, and to attempt to pick up the feelings that the other person is communicating in his hands. Feelings of anger, fantasy and flight, caring, affection, concern, and so forth can be transmitted this way. And those who experience the exercise begin to learn how much a part of our emotions can be transmitted, as well as picked up from others, if we "tune in."

Silence strategies

These techniques are used mainly to demonstrate to persons how much they depend upon language. Persons sitting around in a small group, asked to communicate to each other without sounds, begin to feel the frustration from being unable to rely upon language. Once persons are able to diminish their anxiety about speaking, they are then able to pay attention to their feelings. This demonstrates how we use language to avoid dealing directly with our feelings. Most people speak "off the top of their heads," which is to say they do not link what they are feeling with what they are actually saying. They have not seriously considered or thought through how they really feel. It is very difficult to look at a person without talking to him, so we start talking before we engage our feelings about the other person. Silence strategies, if nothing else, force us to concentrate on others, rather than deal with them verbally in a quick, convenient, easy, and often trivial manner.

Risk-taking exercises

In order to know oneself, one needs to know what things or conditions are required for us to act comfortably. In other words, we have to know our dependencies. Risk-taking is a way of revealing those dependencies and fighting our way through them. Persons are asked to talk about social conditions that they avoid and to begin to analyse why they avoid them. Such a condition as being alone is common. If persons have difficulty being alone, they depend on others for their comfort. A risk then, is to be alone for a period of time beyond that which we would normally tolerate being alone. In conquering aloneness, others are relieved of the burden of being depended on, and the person himself is able to choose friends and be with them for more constructive reasons than dependency needs.

There is much that we can learn about ourselves and the world if only we are able to take risks. We are trying here to represent the need to deal with certain personal conditions to open doors to learning. This is simply the notion of sharpening the pencil in order to write.

STRATEGIES FOR RELATING

The idea of developing a strategy for improving interpersonal communication involves a process of clearing the wave lengths. Persons have been talking for some time now about increasing specialization and the way in which this produces a society of experts who cannot talk to each other. The fact of the matter is that even close friends cannot talk to each other, cannot talk to the points of critical issue because of an insensitivity to those issues, in ourselves and others.

Many people who are not at all sensitive consider themselves very sensitive. By this they mean they are very sensitive to what affects them. Relating to others depends on sensitivity to others, and this requires getting over the egocentrism of worrying at all times about how things affect me. Relating to others is a matter of discovering not only what it is to be me, but what it is to be not me. Techniques or strategies that require us to experience parts of ourselves that we have never known get at the me-not-me problem. For example, to understand what it means to be affluent is to experience being poor. What it means not to be a member of the majority is to become a member of a minority and experience what it is like. This not only illuminates what being me is, it reveals the feelings associated with being not me. One female student of ours, in order to understand this notion, went one evening to an all-male gym class.

Now with the notion of experiencing ourselves through experiencing others before us, we can approach the subject of strategies for relating. We must always be aware that strategies in themselves are simulations of what must happen in everyday life. Since persons are so untrained in seeing others, these stategies should become part of the educational task.

Be something you are not

Being something we are not contributes to our capacity to relate better to others by:

1. forcing persons to take a risk, which is a chance we all have to take to know another person.
2. illuminating what we are in a way that shows us how we are viewed from perspectives other than our own.
3. telling us something about how those in the positions we have assumed feel about being in that position.

Black people in American society, particularly those who attend our institutions of higher learning, are forced to behave as members of a minority. What does this mean? It means that you are highly visible, it means that you must always be on your best behavior, it means that you are constantly sensitive to stereotypes that members of the majority group apply to you.

Persons who are in the majority don't have to think about any of these things. In order to demonstrate how others experience being members of a minority, it becomes necessary to put yourself in such a position. White high school students can spend a few days in a black school. Adults can spend a few days, or even one evening would suffice, with a society of adolescents. Teachers should become students in order to understand how students feel. We need to look around us at the characteristics of persons that constitute our social world, and try to simulate what it means to have those characteristics.

The circumstance strategy

In every social group there are persons who play certain roles or who are forced to experience adverse conditions of group participation. Improving social relations requires that we build a group structure which negates the adverse effects of group life. Sensitivity to others requires that we know when a person is being excluded, pushed too hard, rejected, or denied the opportunity to do what he does best.

We need to simulate circumstances such that each person in a group is able to experience what it feels like to be self-estranged, rejected, powerless, or excluded. Once we become sensitive to what it feels like and how this feeling is produced, we will be able to prevent this from happening. A cooperative environment, as we have argued earlier, is a better learning environment than one that ensures all the adverse conditions we have just mentioned.

An example to demonstrate one of these conditions is to have three persons talking, with two persons instructed to gradually exclude the third one from the conversation. Once the person realizes he is excluded from the conversation he can begin to think about how it feels and what his reactions might be. Then, along with other members of the group, he can discuss the phenomenon and develop ways to prevent this from happening.

The encounter

We will conclude with a brief discussion of the encounter. This is a process of forcing persons to confront how they appear to others, and how they inhibit their own human potentialities. The encounter is, in some ways, the cooperative arena for learning. It is where persons come for help when they have trouble experiencing an idea, and it is the place where they begin to formulate for themselves what they want to know about the world, because it is important to them as persons.

An encounter is a confrontation, a dealing with, a revealing or showing yourself as you are to others. It is an experience of seeing "how it goes" when we do confront or show. This means that persons come to strengthen their capacities for open and honest communication by practicing it with others who have the same desires.

All learning that is humanistic requires encountering, coming out to meet a notion or to know a thing or an idea. Nonencountering, whether from lack of awareness or fear that keeps us from experiencing life, closes our access to humanistic learning. Encountering is a way to open those channels. Hopefully, if the political and social struggles of the present do not destroy education entirely, the encounter will succeed the nonencounter as the educational mode.

5

education
and
literature

Carl Weinberg

The particular version of humanism that I had in mind as I wrote this chapter on literature was undoubtedly my most precious, the one most important to me, and so, obviously, most difficult to talk about without using the tools of literature. Perhaps this is not obvious. Try to talk about your most sensitive and exquisite feelings, or your deepest understanding. You will almost always end up using simile and metaphor, and saying something like, "It's like . . . " or "It seems as if . . . " or "It feels like . . . " Think of the ways persons describe love; it is always a matter of comparing it to some-thing we might be able to relate to, like a spring morning full of sunlight and the fresh odor of morning grass, or like an uncontrollable inner giggle. (Well, make your own descriptions if you don't like mine. I am only trying to make a point.) The perspective of humanism that is so important to me in this chapter is the one that deals with understanding—that is, understanding through one's poetic senses—which is, ulti-mately, the only way we really come to understand anything very important about how one lives one's life.

The Buddha raises his hand and displays the perfect flower and his disciples nod in understanding. Siddhartha and all the other major religious figures in world history taught in parables and in poetry and in song. When we began to learn from sources that appeal only to our rational faculties, we began to lose the capacity to understand the important human messages, and this capacity has gone downhill ever since. These messages that can be derived from literature have to do with understanding and with understanding what one needs to understand. These are messages about how to live, how to confront experience; about freedom and beauty; about how to face death or imprisonment. They are messages about personal meaning and why this is important. These are the messages of humanistic education. They may also be the messages of philosophy, religion, and art; but these are not my thing. I hope my chapter advances the possibility that humanistic understanding can be retrieved in your education.

My interest in including a chapter on literature in a foundations of education book begins with my habit of using works of fiction in my own foundations courses, and by my belief that creative writers have more to say about human experience than anybody else. And they say it more interestingly.

There is also a practical consideration. I believe that rather than convince you that you should read for instruction rather than pleasure, it would be easier to use for instruction what you read for pleasure. You probably read more fiction now than you read texts or journal articles. After you graduate and become teachers the chances are slight that you will keep up with the academic writings. Perhaps you will read social and psychological journals now and then as these help to explain educational behavior, although this is not very predictable. More likely, you will probably continue to read works of fiction throughout your life. I hope to be able to provide certain guidelines which will help you use this reading to improve your understanding of educational life, and thereby your capacity as a teacher.

As I think about the teacher I realize that I have a certain version of him in mind. I do not think about a person stuffing knowledge into the heads of little people. I think of a person helping children to understand the world they live in, either in general or through the perspective of their special disciplines. I am thinking particularly of the kind of world which today's teacher needs to make sense out of in order to impart that sense to his students. And I am thinking of today's student, with the decisions he has to make about the kind of life that he must choose for himself, the kind of strength and understanding that he will need in order to come to grips with the freedom that he is beginning to demand.

The student today cannot avoid some kind of confrontation with the demands and crosscurrents of the outside world. As he sits in his classroom, his society is in turmoil. In all likelihood, he will become part of that turmoil. His goal will be personal stability, meaning, purpose. He will want to be a productive human being within a context that he deems conducive to and supportive of that productivity. His teacher will have to help him find his way on the difficult road he will choose. To this end his teacher will have to help him understand the contemporary world and his relationship to it. The teacher that I am thinking about in this chapter is one who cannot accept his functions as skill training alone. Why learn to read, to figure, to reason? Today's teacher is in the business of changing the world, even if he does not realize it. He will be remembered by his students as having advanced or retarded them in their capacity to advance those changes or adapt to them. Not many years ago, almost all access to culturally defined goals was through education. A teacher had the students' life success or failure hanging on his evaluation. Today education is even more important. We are not only talking about success or failure in economic terms. We are talking about freedom or imprisonment in personal terms. Children will either learn to value freedom or surrender to authority.

Now, concretely, how do I see the teacher's role? I see the teacher assuming that the child has the capacity to understand the world around him. I see him working to bring those capacities to an operational level. I see him presenting the child with ideas and facts which convey the diversity of social life. I see him requiring the child to think for himself, about himself and his personal relationship to the world of ideas. I see the teacher asking the child to get in touch with his feelings and examine how his feelings influence his thinking. And I see, perhaps most emphatically of all, the teacher helping the child overcome the barriers that stand in the way of his learning and understanding.

Assuming that you see the teacher's role in somewhat the same terms as I do, we can go on together to consider the use to which we can put the work of the creative writer in accomplishing this educational task.

HARD AND SOFT KNOWLEDGE

My emphasis on literature revolves around several themes, one of which has to do with the kind of knowledge we like to give prospective teachers. I think it is important to have you begin thinking about the knowledge that you do receive in your classes, particularly those classes which relate to your teaching career. It is, in general, knowledge about how people learn, how they change, how they react to specific techniques, how they are motivated. Some of this knowledge comes in the form of theories based upon the intuition of so-called experts. Other knowledge comes to you in the form of empirical evidence, called research. Most of our scientific knowledge, or so-called scientific knowledge, about education is based upon studies that you will have more than your fill of before you graduate. These studies are based upon observable behavior or upon data accumulated by asking persons, often students, questions and recording their responses. These responses are then transferred to IBM cards, fed into a giant computer, and out come the results that tell us how it really is. But IBM cards aren't flesh and blood, nor do they represent flesh and blood. They usually represent only what people say, which may not be what people mean nor what they feel. If we are looking only at behavior, in one short space and time, we really know very little about the whole person, but we confidently spew forth interpretations and theories as if we knew the whole story. There are many reasons why we do not know the whole story, and there are many cautions which should be noted, even if we do treat our data as reliable and accurate. First of all, we assume that the instruments we use, called tests, questionnaires, or interview schedules, are measuring something real. We call IQ scores "measures of intelligence," but we don't really know what intelligence is. We call responses to attitude surveys "attitudes" when they are really no more than what persons feel like telling us, or think we want them to tell us. We think interest profiles get at something called student interests when it is often a matter of preferring one form of drudgery over another. And what do we do with all these scores? We assume they are meaningful and we use them. We make assumptions like, "if students have higher achievement scores using technique A rather than B we should use technique A." This assumes that technique A produced more or better learning when all we know is that kinds did better on an achievement test as a result of technique A. I can think of many important learning goals, such as appreciation or insights into oneself, which will not show up on an achievement test.

For the most part we do not know what has happened to produce the results we see. We don't know why the results turned out that way.

Now the behavioral scientists will argue that it isn't necessarily their function to reveal why, only what and how things are at the moment of their inquiries. We can accept this. We can acknowledge that a number of studies have revealed that persons improved their reading skills significantly by using method A or B rather than C or D. And we can see by looking at the evidence that rich kids achieve better than poor kids. On and on through the psychological and socioeducational literature we go, looking for something to tell us about the human beings that are affected in some predictable ways by forces outside of them, but we find little. And, by the way, these predictable patterns are seldom more than slight tendencies, hardly laws and almost never explanations. The result is that we feed these studies to our students, to you, and believe that we are giving you something that helps you understand kids and how they function in educational contexts. And we are serious. Really, the best we have done is communicate to you the kinds of things that educational scholars do, and maybe a bit of how they do it. Would you like to join the corps? Let me go on a bit further and attempt to integrate my concern about literature into the discussion.

Hard knowledge as we use it in education and the behavioral sciences refers to behavior that we can observe and in some way record. Because it is observable, to us and to others who may also wish to look, we consider it to be reliable.

Soft knowledge is a set of facts about human behavior which we cannot observe or record. They are ideas or descriptions about the human animal that persons either speculate about or record out of their own subjective experience. Novels are the most common representations of this approach. But, in the language of the behavioral scientist, they are not reliable. They present soft facts and are not respectable in the world of education because they have no legitimate claim to accuracy. They appear to only represent the perspective of the author. Reliable knowledge is supposed to represent a whole class of persons similar to the subjects of a study.

My belief happens to be that the evidence provided by the creative writer is, to the degree that we evaluate his writing as good, as reliable as any that we derive from the kind of scientific investigations we conduct. In many ways, with a different vocabulary, literary critics are talking about a kind of reliability when they assess the worth of an author. What kind of reliability is this?

In some ways it is the same kind of reliability the behavioral scientist talks about: observable and able to be replicated. The reliability of novelistic descriptions of contexts for example, are observable: life on a farm, in the ghetto, in the executive suites of the world, in the court of kings, on the beach in Cannes, or on the streets of New York, Paris, or London. The question for literary evaluation becomes a consideration of how well these contexts are revealed to the reader. We don't really want to know if they are accurately described; we almost take that for granted. Are we able to feel the context, smell it, see it, touch it? If the author has led us to the point where we feel we know the place he is describing, then he has communicated his knowledge to us and we accept it as being reliable. We believe that if we were there, we would know it as he does.

A further test of literary reliability is the way in which an author develops his theme. We must believe in his integration of events and human responses. That is, we look for an explanation, which he makes us accept as reasonable, for the behavior of his characters, for their responses to the universal forces which confront them. Out of this interplay of forces and human lives will emerge an adaptation which we may judge as being consistent or inconsistent with the characters. In this consistency lies much of our criteria for reliability. That is, out of a wide range of possible responses to universal forces such as love, poverty, hatred, or desire for wealth, the character's response must be consistent with our understanding of him as he has been revealed to us. If it is, then the action or behavior can be said to be reliable.

We do not want to get bogged down over the use of the term "reliability." The question we are dealing with concerns the worth of literature, which I want to designate as a kind of soft knowledge, for the purpose of understanding the world. The value we must ultimately pursue is not so much reliability but insight and understanding. And this leads us to the question of what we really know as a result of hard and soft approaches to knowing.

With hard knowledge we learn about specific, statistically-verifiable patterns of human experience. We come to know something about the rates of educational progress of nonwhite Americans, family organization of school dropouts, and drinking habits of American college students. We learn that students can memorize more English words than nonsense syllables, that teachers prefer children who are clean to those who are dirty. We have a whole encyclopedia of educational facts.

With soft knowledge we know something about how it feels to be black, poor, a child, a teacher, or alienated. We experience—if the writer has created an experience—conflict, joy, fear, anger, struggle, success, and failure. What we know is how human beings exist in various situations, not only how they behave.

We can illustrate these differences in relation to some hard and soft facts on the subject of being black in America. First, let me give you some hard facts.

Some hard facts[1]

1. Over 90 percent of Negroes who live in the north live in cities, usually in areas of high population density.

2. Approximately 18 percent of Negro workers are considered white collar workers. About 48 percent of white workers are white collar. About 35 percent of Negroes in the work force are service workers, such as maids or hospital attendants. White service workers number about 10 percent.

3. Negro unemployment rates are usually three times that of white workers.

4. Life expectancy for the American Negro is about seven years shorter than for his white counterpart.

5. In 1961 better than 60 percent of Negro families had incomes under $4000 per year. Twenty-seven percent of white families had incomes under $4000 per year.

6. Negroes comprise 17 percent of the total population but 70 percent of the public housing population, 75 percent of those on relief and 65 percent of those in jail.

Soft knowledge

...I combed not only the bright-light areas, but Harlem's residential areas from best to worst, from Sugar Hill up near the Polo Grounds, where many famous celebrities lived, down to the slum blocks of old rat-trap apartment houses, just crawling with everything you could mention that was illegal and immoral. Dirt, garbage cans overflowing or kicked over; drunks, dope addicts, beggars. Sleazy bars, storefront churches with gospels being shouted inside, "bargain" stores, hockshops, undertaking parlors. Greasy "home-cooking" restaurants, beauty shops smoky inside from Negro women's hair getting fried, barbershops advertising conk experts. Cadillacs, secondhand and new, conspicuous among the cars on the streets.

All of it was Lansing's West Side or Roxbury's South End magnified a thousand times. Little basement dance halls with "For Rent" signs on them. People offering you little cards advertising "rent-raising parties."

---

[1] Facts taken from R.W. Mack, "Race Relations" in *Social Problems,* ed. H. Backer (New York: John Wiley, 1966).

I went to one of these—thirty or forty Negroes sweating, eating, drinking, dancing, and gambling in a jammed, beat-up apartment, the record player going full blast, the fried chicken or chitlins with potato salad and collard greens for a dollar a plate, and cans of beer or shots of liquor for fifty cents. Negro and white canvassers sidled up alongside you, talking fast as they tried to get you to buy a copy of the *Daily Worker:* "This paper's trying to keep your rent controlled...Make that greedy landlord kill them rats in your apartment..."[2]

In 1966 the percent of white families who had an income of $7000 or more per year was 55. The percent of Negro families earning over $7000 per year was 28.

Approximately 8 percent of white families (1966) live in housing classified as substandard. Almost 30 percent of Negroes live in substandard housing.

The unemployment rate for whites is 3.3 percent, for blacks the figure is 7.3 percent.

New York, Chicago, Los Angeles, Detroit, Philadelphia, Washington D.C., St. Louis, Baltimore, Cleveland, Houston, and New Orleans all have Negro communities of between 200,000 and one million people. These are called ghettoes where black people are overcrowded, overcharged for rent and food, riddled by crime and drug addiction, prone to illness and a high infant death rate. There are numerous bars, rundown schools and rat-infested housing.[3]

WAYS OF KNOWING

As one can observe from the examples on black life in America, we come to know not only different kinds of things from the two approaches to knowledge, but we come to know them in a different way. It is these different ways of knowing that distinguishes the two approaches most significantly, for how we know has a great deal to do with *how well* we know. We know objective or hard knowledge with our heads; subjective or soft knowledge we come to know with our whole being. Understanding concepts like being black in America or being a student through objective facts only indicate for us some of the empirical referents for those conditions. That is, persons are described in terms of things that happen to them in the outside world: that they learn at certain rates, have specific mobility patterns, earn so much money, have court records, participate in so many organizations and clubs, and so forth. But the notion of being black, or

[2] From Malcolm X, *The Autobiography of Malcolm X* (New York: Grove Press, 1964), pp. 75–76. Reprinted by permission of Grove Press, Inc. © 1964 by Alex Haley and Malcolm X; © 1965 by Alex Haley and Betty Shabazz.

[3] G. Lenward, ed., *The Negro in the City* (New York: Washington Square Press, 1968), pp. 19, 46–48.

being a child in an adult-dominated world, cannot be completely known through empirical descriptions. In order to know these notions we must find some path into the experiential world of our subject. Soft knowledge provides that access. But is it wise to use this knowledge, when is it only one man's interpretation? The question is answered by considering how this knowledge contributes to our insight and understanding. The value of this insight and understanding from soft knowledge can only be assessed by each person in terms of how he uses them.

We are interested, in this book, in describing a humanistic education, as well as a humanistic way of knowing the world of education. Experiencing the world through the viewpoint of another is not only a more complete way of knowing that world, it is developing one's capacity to know with one's whole being the world in which one must live. It is this quality of being able to experience that produces the teacher who is sensitive and responsive to the child's world in the classroom. Humanistic education must be accomplished if we are to permit persons to leave our colleges and assume responsibility for the many lives that it will be their task to educate.

I do not want to close this section on hard and soft knowledge and leave you with the feeling that all the textbooks should be burned and all the studies ignored. I would agree that many should. But the important thing to bear in mind is that for many purposes, the accumulation of objective facts in education is critical to the development of the field. There is a methodological or technical component to classroom teaching as well as an interpersonal component. So far, our scientific inquiries have told us very little about the latter, but they can be important to us in several ways, as long as we do not confuse facts with the experiences which produced them. Sooner or later (probably later) the behavioral scientist will question how the facts are produced. He will begin to ask about the experiential bases for behaviors or attitudes. We know a good deal about what we call conditions associated with attitudes, such as social class, religion, age, and sex, but we know very little about why persons under certain conditions or with certain qualities develop their particular attitudes.

Until we discover an empirical basis for knowing how these come about, we may have to base the greater part of our insights on creative intuition and subjective knowledge, both our own and that which others describe.

After all, from where do we get our ideas to do the kind of research we do? For the most part, we look to verify patterns which we sense to be inherent in human behavior. There are very few scientifically-verified truths of social living that we did not intuitively know anyhow. The creative writer is usually one whose senses about universal truths were highly acute. Furthermore, he can make principles of human struggle and adaptation come to life before us, thereby making the principles meaningful.

THE CREATIVE WRITER

I want to talk about the writer of fiction, and for the most part, ordinary fiction. This does not exclude the greats, but rather includes the legions of writers that the average person or teacher reads. I will talk mainly about novels, since that too is the common experience. And finally, I am interested here in a form of communication, independent of quality, not an evaluation of the enduring qualities of one writer's attempt versus the transitoriness of another. This discussion should be read as remarks about the utilization of subjective writing in our practical experiences, not as an attempt to get you to be able to differentiate good literature from bad.

The creative writer provides his reader with an experience. Since he would like to be read, he usually chooses an experience that he believes the reader will understand and relate to. For this reason his topics are often current. But because he wants to be read beyond his own historical time, he attempts to embody in his work some permanent values or principles about the human condition. Literature has evolved a set of conventions that loosely bind the writer to express himself according to certain literary forms. These conventions help to ensure a communication bridge between the writer and the reader. Since the writer wants to communicate, he usually chooses a form that readers can understand, an experience to which they can relate, and a problem that they consider important.

For the most part the writer deals with universal themes: love, growing up, discovering meaning in life, the effects of war, the consequences of being alienated from society, struggling against forces beyond one's control, and facing human conditions such as responsibility, sickness, and death.

Having chosen a topic he employs his skill, which consists not only of having new, fresh insights into the course of human experience, but communicating these in a stylistically-significant way. Through time the best attempts survive and come to be classified among our great works of Literature, with a capital "l." I am more concerned, however, with literature as a way of communicating experience, although many of my examples will come from the works of literature (with a capital "l") since these are easily accessible to all of us.

The good writer is able to evoke emotional responses that allow the reader to combine feelings with his understanding of what is being communicated. It is this capacity that is the writer's unique contribution to our educational goals.

Let me attempt to illustrate this special capacity with reference to the understanding of a universal theme—the kind of theme which might well provide the teacher with some guidelines for helping students understand life and living: on growing up—

The reader may remember, that Mr. Allworthy gave Tom Jones a little horse, as a kind of smart money for the punishment, which he imagined he had suffered innocently.

This horse Tom kept above half a year, and then rode him to a neighbouring fair, and sold him.

At his return, being questioned by Thwackum, what he had done with the money for which the horse was sold, he frankly declared he would not tell him.

"Oho!" says Thwackum, "you will not! then I will have it out of your br——h;" that being the place to which he always applied for information on every doubtful occasion.

Tom was now mounted on the back of a footman, and everything prepared for the execution, when Mr Allworthy entering the room, gave the criminal a reprieve, and took him with him into another apartment; where Mr Allworthy being only present with Tom, he put the same question to him which Thwackum had before asked him.

Tom answered, he could in duty refuse him nothing; but as for that tyrannical rascal, he would never make him any other answer than with a cudgel, with which he hoped soon to be able to pay him for all his barbarities.

Mr. Allworthy very severly reprimanded the lad, for his indecent and disrespectful expressions concerning his master; but much more for his avowing an intention of revenge. He threatened him with the entire loss of his favour, if he ever heard such another word from his mouth; for he said, he would never support or befriend a reprobate. By these and the like declarations, he extorted some compunction from Tom, in which that youth was not over sincere: for he really meditated some return for all the smarting favours he had received at the hands of the pedagogue. He was, however, brought by Mr. Allworthy to express a concern for his resentment against Thwackum; and then the good man, after some wholesome admonition, permitted him to proceed, which he did, as follows.

"Indeed, my dear sir, I love and honour you more than all the world: I know the great obligations I have to you, and should detest myself, if I thought my heart was capable of ingratitude. Could the little horse you gave me speak, I am sure he could tell you how fond I was of your present: for I had more pleasure in feeding him, than in riding him. Indeed, sir, it went to my heart to part with him: nor would I have sold him upon any other account in the world than what I did. You yourself, for none ever so sensibly felt the misfortunes of others. What would you feel, dear sir, if you thought yourself the occasion of them?—Indeed, sir, there never was any misery like theirs." "Like whose, child?" says Allworthy, "what do you mean?" "Oh, sir," answered Tom "your poor gamekeeper, with all his large family, ever since your discarding him, have been perishing with all the miseries of cold and hunger. I could not bear to see those poor wretches naked and starving, and at the same time know myself to have been the occasion of all their sufferings.—I could not bear it, sir, upon my soul, I could not." (Here the tears ran down his cheeks, and he thus proceeded) "It was to save them from absolute destruction, I parted with your dear present, notwithstanding all the value I had for it.—I sold the horse for them, and they have every farthing of the money."4

I chose this little episode in the life of Henry Fielding's Tom Jones for several reasons: [1] to show that good writing is enjoyable reading (which teachers might keep in mind when making assignments; [2] to juxtapose universal forces against each other (Tom Jones is struggling to maintain the integrity of childhood innocence in the face of a distrusting, suspicious adult world) ; [3] to emphasize the power of concern for others; and [4] to illustrate a very simple educational principle: that a teacher (master) does not secure loyalty and trust from a student with threats of punishment.

I am not suggesting that any of these notions are new to you. But there is a difference between intellectually understanding a concept and experiencing its significance. The truths which creative writers try to communicate are secondary to the way in which they do it. Can you feel the necessity to maintain integrity which Tom Jones feels, to reach out and embrace others less fortunate than himself because that is the way one must live his life? It means little to say that we should help the disadvantaged. They will never really be helped by the wishes of well-wishers. Persons, to do anything really significant for themselves and others, must put their whole selves, not only their heads, into the experience. The teacher's responsibility is to deal with the whole child. To do so effectively he must know what being a whole person is. He must understand more than lectures or philosophies or social or psychological studies can tell him. He must feel what it is all about. This is what the creative writer can offer him.

Tom Jones is a growing-up experience, as are the *Education of Henry Adams, Tom Sawyer* and *Huckleberry Finn, Oliver Twist, Studs Lonigan, The Catcher in the Rye* and *Portnoy's Complaint*. Really, can this experience be communicated with all our texts on developmental psychology?

I sometimes feel uneasy about offering you small sections of a work of fiction because, obviously, the total work conveys the experience, and no segment can really have much meaning by itself. Those of you who have read Claude Brown's important book on growing up black in a white world, *Manchild in the Promised Land,* can relate to this. You can't dip in here and there and come up with any segment that represents the experience. But when you have finished the book, you know what the black experience is.

Nonetheless, I do wish to represent, as best I can, the contemporary dilemma of finding personal meaning in an impersonal world. It seems, from most literature of the past several hundred years, that the issue is universal. The problem today appears to be more critical because our major

4 Henry Fielding, *Tom Jones* (Baltimore, Md.: Penguin English Library, Penguin Books, 1966), pp. 142–43.

institutions have become more and more bureaucratic. If you wish to experience the human effects of this kind of living you can go to New York
and work in an advertising firm, or read Sloane Wilson's *The Man in the
Grey Flannel Suit*. Or you may feel that the experience is not only horrible
but common to almost every form of contemporary adult functioning, that it
is a personal "sellout," and you decide to get out of the race. What are the
possibilities, at best? Let me take you briefly to an imaginary world, the
apotheosis of the life away from the contemporary struggle. It is the world
of Hermann Hesse's Nobel Prize-winning book, *Magister Ludi*. The main
character, Joseph Knecht, has been raised to join, eventually to lead, an
intellectual institution whose main task is to develop and maintain the highest form of self-contained intellectual and cultural life, called the Bead
Game. Knecht is not running away, he *is* away from the outside world in
every sense, except some feeling that gnaws at him. It is expressed at times
in a great desire to teach the very young of his order, but he is restrained
from doing this by the requirements of his high station in the order. He
recognizes that his life contains the highest serenity possible to man. His
thoughts are always on the beautiful intricacy of knowledge and thought,
and the relationship of all forms of knowledge to each other.

> To achieve this cheerful serenity is to me, and to many others, the finest
> and highest of goals.... Such cheerfulness is neither frivolity nor com-
> placency; it is supreme insight and love, affirmation of all reality, alert-
> ness ton the brink of all depths and abysses; it is a virtue of saints and
> knights; it is indestructible and only increases with age and nearness
> to death. It is the secret of beauty and the real substance of all art.

But the time comes, which we are led to accept as right and necessary,
when Knecht decides to leave this serenity, his noble and isolated world.
On his journey to the outside world he stops to explain his decision to leave
to a fellow Magister of his order:

> The trouble was that during my apprenticeship under Father Jacobus
> I had made the discovery that I was not only a Castalian but also a
> man; that the world, the whole world, concerned me, and exerted certain
> claims upon me. Needs, wishes, demands, and obligations arose out of
> this discovery, but I was in no position to meet any of them. The life
> in the world as the Castalian sees it is something backwards and inferior,
> a life of disorder and crudity, of passions and distractions devoid of all
> that is beautiful or desirable. The world and its life was in fact infinitely
> vaster and richer than the notions a Castalian has of it. It was full of
> change, history, struggles, and eternally new beginnings. It might be
> chaotic, but it was the home and native soil of all destinies, all exalta-
> tions, all arts, all humanity; it had produced languages, peoples, govern-
> ments, cultures; it had also produced us and our Castalia and would see

all these things perish again, and yet survive. My teacher Jacobus had kindled in me a love for this world which was forever growing and seeking nourishment. But in Castalia there was nothing much to nourish it. Here we were outside of the world; we ourselves were a small perfect world, but one no longer changing, no longer growing.[5]

And so Knecht leaves his sanctuary convinced that serenity lies not in a place, or a position, or a status, or in a condition, but in a man, and that the road to this serenity is always unfolding with each new.beginning, each new challenge. This is a theme which Hesse wrote of so beautifully in *Siddhartha* and consummately in *Magister Ludi*. It is also the theme of Thomas Wolfe's *You Can't Go Home Again*. It is the theme of Hemingway's life revealed in the totality of his work. We encounter this quest in contemporary existential writers like Beckett, Sartre, and Camus, who are exerting a widespread influence upon young intellectuals both in Europe and America. It is the living, breathing message that there are no answers to life, only questions and questioning, of going on without a sign, of struggling without a hope, of living without a reason.

What can a teacher give his students in these terms? Without understanding himself he can give little, but what if he understands that a meaningful life does not exist in comfort or physical security? Then of what use are reading, and figuring? Of what use is a secure job. And aren't these the goals of education today? We give students what we think they will need to protect them from any kind of struggle or social anxiety. We teach them in terms of rewards that are, in fact, protections against growth.

If the creative writer gives us anything of value, it is perspective on values, a view of what is worthy in life and living. With this perspective the teacher can avoid the error of assuming that what takes place in the classroom is an end in itself. He will be aware that protecting the sanctity of classroom rules may cost the child the individuality he needs to find meaning, and the kind of internal consistency which Hesse calls serenity. Our responsibility as teachers is to encourage individuality, so the child can, in the end, achieve serenity.

LITERATURE AND VALUES

The school bears the kind of relationship to children that parents do: it communicates a set of values that our society considers worth maintaining. It does this through a system of rewards and punishments that guarantees

[5] Quotations taken from Hermann Hesse, The *Glass Bead Game,* trans. Clara and Richard Winston (New York: Holt, Rinehart and Winston, 1969). Copyright © 1969 by Holt, Rinehart and Winston, Inc., and Jonathan Cape Ltd.; reprinted by permission of the publishers.

that if people do not respect our codes they will at least recognize that there are consequences to violating them. Fortunately the process is never fully successful. Persons never seem to be able to accept a set of rules which violates them as human beings. When Mark Twain sent Huck Finn off on his adventures down the Mississippi, we were able to admire the experience, even if we were unable to violate our training and do something similar. Huck was revolting against the smothering confinement of formalized living and formalized education. Most of us couldn't really go with him, except in our fantasies, but part of us went. It was a safe way to protest our own restricted living, even though it was soon forgotten, except in spirit. Through *Huckleberry Finn* we were transported into the experience of freedom. For many of us the need to be ourselves has been smothered under layers of security-bound acts and rationalizations. It is restored now and again as we retreat to a fictional world which expresses our need for freedom, and allows us to vicariously experience it.

The creative writer has a way of instructing us in values that is educationally superior to the lectures of pedagogues, sermons of clergy, and the manipulating strategies of parents and teachers. How much richer, for example, is Fielding's portrayal of honesty in the young Tom Jones, who is able to be a rascal of a boy at the same time he lives a genuine, concerned honest life, than the partriotic tales of Washington and the cherry tree, or Lincoln returning the few pennies! The teacher needs to consider his role in maintaining the culture through implanting traditional values. Even if he believes in these values how should he communicate them? Most students view teachers as symbols of an almost ludicrous virtue. Their utterings are seen as hollow slogans: "Be good;" "Work hard;" "Tell the truth;" "Have noble (this means not dirty) thoughts." How convincing is this kind of teacher? Think back upon your own teachers and answer this for yourself.

I am talking again about the difference between an idea and an experience. The creative writer represents his values in the experience he provides. If he wants to talk about the antihuman elements in everyday living he does not tell us what he thinks about them. He throws a flesh-and-blood character into that world and portrays the effects such living has upon him. One of the best contemporary examples of this type of portrayal is Salinger's *Catcher in the Rye,* where the young Holden Caulfield feels brutalized, frustrated, and disappointed by people he meets. He concludes that the world is made up of phonies and prostitutes, and if we succeed to project ourselves into his experience we come up with the same assessment.

As I said, I am not talking about vicarious living, I am really talking about gaining some appreciation of the value of being true to yourself, of fighting for the freedom to be that.

It is difficult to know how to develop a set of principles that are meaningful as a basis to live one's life. Many authors have shown that this attempt can destroy a human being, but many convince us that turning away from this inevitable choice would be a worse fate. It is similar to the difference between pathos and tragedy.

PATHOS AND TRAGEDY

Pathos is a condition, very common in contemporary literature, where a person is victimized by the forces of everyday living to the point where he is ultimately destroyed. Willie Loman, the major character in Miller's *Death of a Salesman,* is a case in point. Willie tries to hang on and survive in a world of commerce that has passed him by. His self-image is strongly dependent upon his success or failure as a salesman. When he fails at this, he fails as a man. Many of the novels of the 1930s portrayed this kind of pathos: Drieser's *American Tragedy,* Wharton's *The Age of Innoncence,* John Dos Passos's *U.S.A.* An excellent example of the contemporary failure of man to come to grips with himself or his world ending in pathos is Fitzgerald's Dick Diver in *Tender is the Night.* Diver, the auto-biographical hero, is destroyed essentially because he does not know what to do with his feelings. He cannot come to grips with some kind of purpose. He sits back in his affluence in the midst of an exciting world of expatriates in Europe and withers away trying to make his social life his reason for living.

Tragedy, however, is a different concept in literature and life. Many great figures of literature are tragic characters, not pathetic ones. They fail, often they die, but they do so meeting the challenges they know they must face, rather than avoiding them and retreating to a world of security.

Hamlet is forced to make a choice: "To be or not to be?" Should he be tragic or pathetic? Should he move against a "sea of troubles" or take the way out that most bureaucrats and mothers suggest: "don't get involved"? He takes the chance of losing everything—his mother, his kingdom, his woman, his life. But what would they have been worth to him had he chosen to violate his life principle in order to retain them? This, then, is the important issue of the play, the important moral issue to come to us across the ages. Who would have preferred that Hamlet live with his knowledge of evil in order to live happily with wine, sporting, and Ophelia? No one who understands the value—indeed the necessity of living congruently—of doing what your best moral principles require you to do.

This is also the message of other tragic figures in literature and life. Whom else would you suggest made the same decision, the same moral choice, to chance death courageously in the face of immorality, evil, or social injustice rather than to play it safe? Recall Ulysses, Hector, Romeo and Juliet, Joan of Arc, Captain Ahab. The choice of characters in fiction, for this inspiring moral quality, have been paralleled in real life and are recorded in biographies and autobiographies. I suggest the following list to which you can add your own favorites: Christ, Michaelangelo, Van Gogh, Gandhi, Malcolm X, Martin Luther King, George Gordon, and Lord Byron.

This is the dilemma of modern man. He has the choice in his everyday life. He can stay within the padded tunnel and stifle on his stuffed pillows of living, or he can come out and take the chance of getting his head knocked off. It is not an easy choice. Most children are taught at home and in school to play it safe. Don't take chances. What then, do we value? What should our children value? How are you, their teachers, going to communicate a set of values about life and living? Remember, they will get from you what you believe, and they will get it from what you do, not from what you say. Are you about to stand up for what you believe, for the kind of classroom that you want to conduct? And where will you get your values? Have they all been implanted beyond your doing anything about them? Perhaps you will get them from what you read. Perhaps insights into how to live your life can be derived from the way characters whom you admire have lived their life, or a part of it. I said in the beginning that I would attempt to offer some suggestions about ways of approaching your reading that might help improve your understanding of life in the classroom. Let me try to do this.

LITERATURE AND PERSONAL CHANGE

I want to begin my assessment of what literature can do for you as a person and a prospective teacher by making known one of my biases, one which you can either corroborate or reject out of your own experience. Literature as a course, or a program of courses, in the American university (perhaps elsewhere also) is designated as one of the humanities. My feeling is that the humanities may provide the least humanistic orientation to learning that we have. One is usually introduced to his college literature experience in large impersonal classes presided over by removed, often detached, instructors who lecture monotonously about the virtues of the masters. You are told about literature. You do not discover it, do not experience it, do not use it; only study it, dissect it, and take tests on it. In this process students usually make very inappropriate use and interpretations of what they read. For example, we learn (if one wishes to call it that) an author's view of the world. We look at Steinbeck's *The Grapes of Wrath*, for example, as an attitude towards American industrialization. We sympathize with the migrant fruit pickers, regret their sorry living conditions, and add it all up as a commentary on the life styles of a segment of American society in a particular place at a particular time in American social history. But do we see the heroism of the Joad family, the power of the mother, and the development of a commitment in the son? What is this commitment made of, how does it come about, why is it important in universal language rather than as a comment on the times? The real question is, do we discover a bit of our own strength and commitment in the *Grapes of Wrath,* or do we simply understand how it all was? How many of your literature instructors led you to personal meaning, commitment, strength, self understanding, as he took you through the readings?

I hope that your instruction in literature was not as sorry as I expect it was. I hope, at least, that you have some sense of what is good writing and what is not. I think it is important to have standards, to require of the author certain accomplishments, such as clear and consistent character delineation, a reasonable relationship between events and their consequences, the choice of a meaningful and perhaps significant universal subject, and interesting writing. You shouldn't think, as some students do, that if a writer is very dull that he must be profound. I do not wish to talk further about the evaluation of literature, but only about a few themes which might guide your reading so that you will develop the kind of understanding that will produce the kind of teacher who is sensitive to the world around him.

1. The way attitudes are produced

I mentioned earlier that hard data offer us facts. We are shown how people are and what they think. We are almost never given evidence which describes how these people came to be the way they are, how their version of the world was produced. Literature frequently does this for us, gives us a set of reasonable explanations telling why persons develop as they do. It is through an understanding of these forces that we can avoid duplicating many of them, or, looking at results more positively, gain insights into the kinds of experiences that students need to be provided in order to develop in certain ways.

Let me use the example of Holden Caulfield once again, since I expect that most of you have read *Catcher in the Rye.* Why does Holden hold such a jaundiced view of American life, particularly educational life? Who gives him a sense of meaningful commitment so that he is willing to link his life to others and to traditional patterns of social life and occupational aspiration?

His teachers operate entirely outside of him, his parents have set him adrift, his brother is off to Hollywood on an ego trip of his own, strangers in the big city offend and exploit him. Only his sister has meaning for him; she is, to him, the only real human being in his world. And when he sees "Fuck you" inscribed on the bathroom wall at her school, he wants to protect her from this universal definition of interpersonal relations. Perhaps the world is not made up exclusively of phonies and prostitutes. Salinger is not saying that it is. He is only saying that here is one boy's experience and such must be his conclusion.

William Faulkner once said that should a band of black and white civil rights workers come marching down his Mississippi street bent on overthrowing the Southern order as he knows it, he would have to fight them. Some words from a Nobel Prize winner! Do we reject this view of the world out of hand or do we really understand the Southern mind? If you have read Faulkner, who recreates this world for us, you can understand the torment of the Southern mind, the way it has become encapsulated in its history, its tradition, and you can understand the need for a man, bereft of all else, to hang onto that tradition which defines him as a person. It is curious that we seem to understand the willingness of men to die for love or country, but not to resist to the last forces that would undermine his whole identity. We need not accept this attitude, but we can at least understand it.

Look at the child who does not want to learn, the inveterate classroom failure. Why does he resist what we believe is good for him, an education? Speculate about the way he developed an image of himself as a failure. One important principle about human adaptation is that persons fight for stability, and much of this stability resides in one's conception of himself. A teacher must understand this notion, must approach students with an understanding of what they are doing when they resist our efforts. Literature provides us with a legion of insights into this phenomenon.

Sometimes the writer portrays a man who achieves that elusive state we call happiness. We are convinced, although we are usually skeptical about a happy man, that this character has really made it. What, then, was there in his experience that caused this happiness? There are not too many books which carry this theme. Authors usually describe reality, and reality does not offer us many examples of persons who are contented as cows grazing on a meadow. For most authors, reality is a razor cutting away at every illusion and few persons escape its ravages. Sometimes, however, not in spite of but because of the savagery of everyday living persons not only survive but prevail. Maugham's hero in the *Razor's Edge* escapes from the contentment of affluence, plunges himself into a spiritual existence for a time and returns to the horrors of the real world only to grow more with each painful experience, concluding his career as a cab driver seeking a fuller relationship with humanity. Stephen Daedalus in Joyce's *Portrait of the Artist as a Young Man* and later in *Ulysses,* wanders through the painful life of a young man confronted but not beaten by everyday traumas of unfullfilling education, work, family, angry men, and pathetic seductive women, to a state of commitment to a search for his soul, the uncreated conscience of his race." Then there is Hesse's beautiful *Siddhartha* whose hero learns that he must surrender everything to gain the world. There is pain in loss of family, friends, loved ones. Siddhartha learns that he must surrender his son, as he did his loving woman, so that his own serenity is not dependent on others but upon himself.

From books like these, I as a teacher have learned that my job is not to protect my students but to equip them. To deny them the "slings and arrows of outrageous fortune" is to deny them the soil wherein men grow and become strong in themselves. In this way children also grow and become strong and confident. There is an important message here, not only for teachers but for parents. It is the message that security breeds complacence and stagnation, and insecurity breeds inner strength.

> God does not send us despair in order to kill us, but to awaken new life in us. (Herman Hesse, *Magister Ludi*)

We need to understand not only how specific attitudes are produced, but, more importantly, we need to know how a meaningful life can be produced. We have to begin to build a set of beliefs about the experiences which are necessary to produce the kind of attitude which maintains us in our efforts to live congruently with a sense of order and purpose.

2. The consequence of beliefs

Another way of structuring one's reading is to look for some understanding of the emotional price persons pay in order to be the way they are, to believe what they believe, or not to have any beliefs at all. The desperation of those who are trapped in their own conventions is dramatically symbolized in Sherwood Anderson's *Winesburg, Ohio* by the woman who, restrained by her sexual inhibitions all her life, disrobes one fine day and runs naked through the streets. Hemingway, in *The Sun Also Rises,* portrays human life without commitment, where the only cause for living is sensual pleasure.

Through Budd Schulberg's *What Makes Sammy Run* we experience the price one pays for unbridled ambition. We see this theme unfold again and again, from Lucifer in Milton's *Paradise Lost* to Jason Cord in Harold Robbins's *The Carpetbaggers.* For some insights into the consequences of settling for security we can look to Shakespeare's Polonius, Sinclair Lewis's Babbitt, or more dramatically to the present in such popular books as Jacqueline Susann's *Valley of the Dolls* and John Updike's *Couples.*

We, as teachers who recognize our influence over others, must understand not only how persons become who they are, but also what the costs are for becoming that way. A good portion of the books you will select at random will provide some insight into the consequences of seeking one particular goal over another, be it power, wealth, wisdom, comfort, or security. For the most part, there appears to be some agreement among most writers that almost all roads lead to some form of personal alienation. We must understand that if this is true, it is only true in certain ways. That is, not everyone need be victimized by his beliefs. It is only when these beliefs center upon goals that are outside oneself, or means that are incongruent with one's sense of self that alienation is assured. Ultimately we want to ensure, as best we can, a belief in the dignity and the worth of life, regardless of pain, frustration, anxiety, or personal loss. We do ourselves and our students a disservice by attempting to attach our belief in the dignity of life to a set of material goals or social positions. We must attach beliefs to personal involvement in human affairs. Those of you who saw or read John Osborne's play, *Look Back in Anger,* will recall that the alienation of the characters was a function of noninvolvement, and that the anger was focused upon the previous generation that had deprived young people of the desire to seek out causes and become personally committed to them. Don Quixote's greatness was not in what he fought but in the fact that he would not live without a cause. It is my hope that you will begin to see the need for this in your own life. It would be regrettable if you, like the generation that preceded you, refrained from giving your students a sense of human purpose.

The consequence of nonaffiliation and lack of sensitivity is powerfully portrayed in Katherine Anne Porter's *Ship of Fools,* a modern-day Tower of Babel. She portrays a shipload of distrust, fear, hatred, greed, and pomposity. Are we along for the ride in life, to take the trip to wherever it goes, or is there a time when we jump from the ship first, and look for a life preserver (which, by the way, we analagously carry with us at all times) afterwards? Again, to be or not to be—ourselves, or the ship.

We need not always accept the consequences of certain decisions for living that some novels indicate, but we do need to think about the choices that are represented. A best-seller of the last decade was Herman Wouk's *Marjorie Morningstar.* The central character of this romance is a very pretty young lady looking for a husband (or is it love?—this question is never quite resolved). She runs after her fantasy man, for whom she is ever so willing to surrender all her practical values. He turns out to be a paper lion, and Marjorie's original stability emerges victorious. Turning away from her attempt to shake loose the shackles of her middle-class upbringing, she enters a sensible maturity, which is like being able to see roses on your leg irons. My own cynicism here suggests my wholehearted disagreement with the author's conclusion entirely; I consider this particular work a great bomb. But on the other hand, the novel did require me to think about important questions of values, consequences, and choice.

What are the consequences, then, of holding before us such estimable values as courage, honor, victory, and the like? Of course, the answer will depend upon how we define each of the concepts. People of most countries and in most times, unable to deal with life in the abstract, have attached their values to social conventions. Since they have not defined courage for themselves they have permitted themselves to believe that courage is something that you are born with or get when you go to war.

There has never been a generation of men or women who categorically denied this association of courage and war, who have been willing to say courage is refusing to fight a war. However, there are some young men and women today willing to even pay the price of going to jail, who make such statements.

I want to spend this last section on the subject of the consequence of holding values, to look at the intricate relationships among values, war, teachers, and creative writers. I consider it important because I believe that, for hundreds of years, our teachers have produced men and women who were unable to say "no" to war. I read the other day about a teacher who was fired from her job because she encouraged a young man to refuse to be inducted into the army. My question is, then, Do we, as teachers, have the responsibility to do something about war or not?

Modern writers who have chosen the topic of war, and men and women who live it as their central theme have felt this kind of responsiblity. Their message was usually clear: that war is an insane, inhuman kind of experience, which men are too immature and ignorant to understand how to prevent. Antiwar novels have come out of most of America's wars. I do not remember ever reading, or hearing about a good prowar novel.

Among novels about the Civil War we had *Gone with the Wind,* and Crane's *Red Badge of Courage,* two portrayals of human waste and inhuman treatment of men and women. Remarque's *All Quiet on the Western Front* carried the same message about World War I.

World War II produced a sizeable portion of our contemporary writers, many of whom began their careers with a novel about the war. Mailer's *The Naked and the Dead* and Shaw's *The Young Lions* were outstanding among these. Their themes were similar; the waste, inhumanity, and most significantly, the absurdity of attaching qualities of nobility and heroism to the conduct of war. Later, Joseph Heller's *Catch 22* said it another way. Rather than talk about the horrors of war, he described the absurdity of it, where heroes are made only because they can't get out of it, and where nobility and courage are treated as the absurd struttings of big men with tiny brains.

As teachers we may want to consider our position towards war, especially if the lives of some of our students are potentially at stake. We may think that our students should consider similar questions of values involved in war. How do we help them ask questions, what should these questions be? We may find it politically expedient to refrain from giving answers, but we have the right to raise questions on this or any subject. Or if we don't, then we need to gain it.

Again the creative writer can come to our aid on the problems of war, to structure for us a set of questions which we need to think about, not the least of which is the real meaning of courage. If we can answer this set of questions about war, I believe we can transfer our insights to all our interpersonal relations.

3. Men and their institutions

Social life is now, more than ever before in history, institutional life. We have, as part of our industrial progress, achieved a stage of social differentiation which requires all human beings to fit themselves into available slots called roles. The independent business man (not that this is a type to be admired per se) is becoming obsolete. Most men and women in occupational life are bureaucrats, and most persons are somehow defined in relation to bureaucratic goals.

It is a terrifying condition, one that many writers have described. Since it is often difficult to raise one's head above the role demands which surround one, we often have to find our understanding in the experience of others. For ourselves, we are frequently raped without even feeling it. We must stand back to see that it has happened, and how it is happening. We frequently see what has happened to us by recognizing how similarly others are affected. Perhaps we are not really able to see parallels in our own institutional life to the themes portrayed in Orwell's *1984* or Huxley's *Brave New World*. But if we are sensitive to our own environment we cannot ignore similar tendencies, particularly in the way we are controlled, told what to believe, what to want, even what to need. If you are one of those who thinks this type of control is all just a means to an end, that is exactly what the stability of major institutions depends on you to think.

The novels that deal with the way institutions take over and dehumanize one's life are our most vital form of social criticism, particularly when these books are adapted for the screen. These works are effective precisely because they appeal to our feelings rather than to our heads. Intellectuals seldom make good social reformers. No one read or listened much to critics of the institution of slavery, but millions were touched deeply when they read Harriet Beecher Stowe's *Uncle Tom's Cabin*. No one listened much to those reformers complaining about adulterated foods, but Upton Sinclair's best-selling novel, *The Jungle,* provided the catalyst that resulted in the passing of the Pure Food and Drug Act. All in all, however, there are few major reform movements that arise as a response to a work of fiction, but many individuals begin to develop their commitments to social action in this way. If nothing more, some of them refrain from perpetuating a system they view as evil.

The institutions that appear to have the greatest impact upon personality development are the family, the job, and the school. Let's take a brief look at these separately.

Family Life: Most of us grow up in a conjugal family, consisting of parents, siblings, and often grandparents, aunts and uncles. Because we are so close to these individuals, because we are often dependent upon their love and care, we are seldom free to objectively consider the dynamics of family life.

We are unable to see, for example, how love can breed hate, how too much caring for a child can cripple him, how pleasing others can turn into a loss of self. I would refer you to Bruce Jay Friedman's *A Mother's Kisses,* Salinger's *Franny and Zooey,* or Roth's *Portnoy's Complaint* for a vivid, often painful description of some of these processes. Or go back to Joyce's *Portrait of the Artist as a Young Man* and Lawrence's *Sons and Lovers* for descriptions of the way in which family life can either provide for a man's destruction or for his consummate growth. The forces are the same, but their resolutions differ widely. The differences come from understanding the forces and dealing with them.

I believe that the understandings that we have of the forces of family life are eminently applicable to our treatment of students. If we recognize, for example, the dangers of dependency and the crippling effects of sibling competition, where persons mistake learning for getting the best grades, we can avoid producing these consequences.

Economic Life: What are the costs to us as human beings of earning a living? First of all we must understand that, in modern times, making a living is not only surival, or even comfort; it is status, power, security, and self-image.

But these are only concepts. Can you refer to some experiences which exemplify the way in which institutional economics has dealt with man? I think first of Shylock in *The Merchant of Venice.* I think of the way the Jew in Shakespeare's England was forced to define himself and his relationship to the Christian majority through his occupation as money lender and how such relationships are so often inhuman. I think of the indignity of labor when it becomes exploitation and recall Upton Sinclair's *The Jungle* and Steinbeck's *The Grapes of Wrath.*

Americans have always been fascinated by novels about the most glamorous of all occupations, working in Hollywood movies. I mention this category in order to suggest that the important value questions about man's relationship to his work is most dramatically raised in this context. When most people think about work, they think about money, glamor, and fringe benefits; and who offers more of these than Hollywood? There are some decent novels about Hollywood, however, which ask some very important questions about the price of fame and fortune, and the value of it. West's *The Day of the Locust,* Fitzgerald's *The Last Tycoon,* Mailer's *The Deer Park* raise these kinds of questions. I recall a chapter in Budd Schulberg's *The Disenchanted,* which dealt with Fitzgerald's Hollywood experience, that described a typical Hollywood orgy. (Remember, many young men think of occupational success as sexual power.) At one point in this mingling of the great and successful with the near-great and aspiring, a beautiful young starlet takes her clothes off and gracefully ascends the ladder to the swimming pool. Setting off her Venus-like profile against the full moon she stretches her glamorous body and springs forward, ending up in a disastrous belly flop. So much for Hollywood and glamor in work.

The question that teachers should be constantly asking themselves is what values towards work do they have to offer children. They should have some general approaches to answering this question. What are the real issues? What does money mean, what is the value of glamor, what about all this conformity; how much of myself must I surrender, how successful do I need to be, what is success really and what do I want to achieve? These are the themes that should be raised in the classroom, and these are the questions to which the teacher should have some answer for himself. Then, perhaps, he can help the student find one.

Educational Life: There have not been many successful books of fiction written about the classroom. Some books like Jonathan Kozol's *Death at an Early Age* and Herbert Kohl's *36 Children* have attracted readers from the general public as well as schoolteachers and students of education. The success of these books was partly due to their not being research reports. The message, drawn from experience, was communicated much in the form of modern fiction. The characters came to life, the action was vivid, feelings were stressed, and the problem was significant. Prior to this kind of writing about schools, significant books about contemporary education were rare. But there are some worth mentioning. First there was *Catcher in the Rye,* which we have already mentioned in several places. This was a view of private school education raising some important questions about the quality of interpersonal relations. A bit later appeared John Knowles's *A Separate Peace,* similar in content to Salinger's book, and concerning a young man seeking meaning and fresh air in a private school community. Then came a minor work with a major impact—Ivan Hunter's *Blackboard Jungle*— where the characters were incidental to the social forces stirring in the classroom. Readers found it distasteful but they would never quite forget it, especially since poor and black people are always insisting upon keeping the message of our guilt and responsibility before us.

John Hersey's *The Child Buyers* raised another issue; that is, to what extent do we who control society, by controlling education, have the right to treat children as soulless pieces of clay, to be shaped in whatever image we like? Here we have a terrifying portrayal of inhuman conduct that comes through as a very simple, quite gracious, everyday kind of business. What have we allowed the social elite, through our schools, to make of us? Do children have a right to remain different if they feel different? Have we considered this question for ourselves? How preposterous to run the lives of small children day after day, week in and week out, and never consider the ethical or moral question of whether we have the right to manipulate them!

Good writers, and important books like *The Child Buyers* raise important questions. Very seldom can we expect answers from others; we only seek their help in framing the questions. Each person finds answers in his own way and learns them because they are congruent with his style of inquiry and fit into his personal interests. Does this begin to make sense in terms of the critical question we are asking here; that is, what is a good, or significant, or relevant teacher?

4. A question of identity

A final kind of structuring that I will talk about here seeks some answers to the crucial question of identity. This is, of course, related to the general question of meaning and values, but is more specifically linked to the relationship between man and his culture. I am suggesting that it is useful to know, not only what you will become but what you are. In whose image have you been made? It is useful to know this in order to sharpen your perception of how the culture works through you as a teacher to shape the future.

Fortunately, the major works of the second half of the twentieth century are largely books about finding one's identity. There is much precedent for this subject. Many of the American expatriate novels of the twenties, as well as those written at home, were asking questions about what it means to be an American, what is the American experience. Hemingway chose a simple device to answer questions about what it meant to be an American: he went everywhere else and saw how he was different. Fitzgerald did practically the same thing, and then wrote the *Great Gatsby* to see how much of America he still had within him. In Ireland, Joyce, Yeats, O'Casey, and Synge explored their national identity. Earlier, Gorky, Turgenev, and Dostoyevski were inspecting their Slavic navels. These books have been important to me, despite my American identity, for they were able to communicate the richness and strength inherent in an ethnic or national identity. It is important to get in touch with the stream of life of which you are a part, even though you reserve the right to personally reject the burdensome qualities of your history.

Today the most popular books are written by Jewish and Negro authors. What can these offer us, especially if we are neither Jewish nor Negro?

The first point we should note is that these writers are all American Jews and American Negroes. Their experience is profoundly American, and through their adaptations we can observe the structure of American life.

Let me first say something about the writers themselves as a group and then a few words separately. The best of both the Jewish and Negro writers are those who can achieve some kind of detachment in order to inspect their experience and relate to it honestly. Although anger and bitterness may pervade much of the writing, literary integrity appears to prevail. The authors seldom lecture the reader, but provide action from which the reader draws the conclusions that the author hopes he will.

Good contemporary Jewish writers are many. I refer to them as Jewish not because they are, but because their work is dedicated to an exploration of their Jewish experience. The same holds true for the Negro writer. The best of the Jewish writers, in my opinion, are J.D. Salinger, Saul Bellow, Bernard Malamud, Norman Mailer, Arthur Miller, Philip Roth, and Bruce Jay Friedman. In combination, these writers can provide the reader with a rather extensive Jewish experience for himself. He can explore mother love, father control, ethnocentrism, family loyalty, the ethnic tradition, intellectual orientation, and social constipation (Mr. Portnoy's "complaint") and do so within the context of humor and very enjoyably reading. What he needs to look for, however, is a combination of cause and form. How does one's identity affect you and what are the contemporary forms it takes? In this way we can examine cultural influences while at the same time understand the American norm through the adaptations that are required. What does it take for a Jewish boy to marry a non-Jewish girl? What is the highly perceptive version of the kind of Anglo-Saxon female the American Jewish and black males think they need? We see this explored stolidly in Bellow's *Herzog* and humorously in Roth's *Portnoy's Complaint,* but both are deadly serious. What is the non-Jew's conception of the Jew, particularly when he observes him closely? How does this help the Jew or non-Jew define his own development? Malamud chooses this theme for his powerful novel, *The Assistant.* In Malamud's *A New Life,* in Roth's *Letting Go,* and in Friedman's *A Mother's Kisses* we observe small town life from the perspective of an urban Jew, perhaps the most urban of all urban types.

In a time when the sensitive American is becoming aware that he is an outsider in a nation of outsiders, the Jew speaks to him of exile and alienation. The American Jew, regardless of his successes within the normal institutions, is ever the outsider, even if, like Arthur Miller, he marries our biggest movie star. The Jew, unlike his counterpart the non-Jew, cannot find anywhere to fit in, and so he may search for encounter groups and Zen dens. He may, like Norman Mailer, explore the ghettos trying to be black or he may hide in suburbia, like Friedman's Stern, trying to be a white Anglo-Saxon. The kind of America which has maintained the Jew in his centuries-old wandering has managed to make of its own home-grown variety of Jew an outsider. For those who want to understand this process of alienation, to regain some of the American identity which has become so elusive, the Jewish writers provide many keys.

The black writer has accomplished much the same task. Through an exploration of his own racial experience, he has managed to capture and describe the American way of life and its effects on an outsider. There are currently many Negro writers being read by white middle class readers.

"What do the whites want?" these writers might ask. For a time, it appeared that they sought expiation for their guilt; they wanted to be flailed at every available whipping post. The whites came in droves to hear Baldwin's characters insult them in the Broadway play, *Blues for Mr. Charlie,* and they come in droves to let Leroi Jones rip at their flesh in his plays and poetry. Now, however, the monumental success of Claude Brown's *Manchild in the Promised Land* suggests that white America wants something more from the black man. He may, in his sterile and alienated state, want something called "soul." He no longer wants to be punished by the black man. I believe he wants to learn something from him.

Richard Wright wrote novels of social protest. His characters, like Bigger Thomas in *Native Son,* were created to dispel the stereotypes like Jim in *Huckleberry Finn,* and Uncle Tom. Ralph Ellison extended Wright's efforts and explored the experience of black men adapting to the urban North. The notion of invisibility, which he used to structure his book, *The Invisible Man,* communicated something important about the American way of looking at the world. If we can make good use out of a relationship with you, we will see you; if not, you are an invisible man. This invisibility can only result in alienation.

James Baldwin has capitalized extensively on the white man's need to face his guilt. He describes for his white readers all the economic, social, and sexual forms of white exploitation of the black man. His *Another Country* explores this theme from every conceivable perspective, and when the main character jumps off the bridge we all feel the sensation of having pushed him.

The nature of prejudice and what it can do to the man who holds it, much less the man to whom it is directed, is an important theme in Negro writing. The questions for us as teachers and learners are just these: What does prejudice do? Why do we do it? I do not want to analyze here the nature of prejudice, except to say that I believe it is a quality of a closed mind which, by definition, means that a person is closed to his own salvation. If we are alienated, frightened, frustrated, in a mood to change our social and psychological condition, we can attack niggers, longhairs, faggots, and commies. Or we can realise that the source of our alienation is conditioned in ourselves, not in others whom we resent. This understanding can be the beginning of the end of alienation.

Identity for the black man in America is a sense of dignity. It is the knowledge that he does not have to be the white man's servant or clown in order to get the white man's money. Identity is independence. Malcolm X's autobiography was, for many black men, a declaration of independence. The appeal of this autobiography to many thousands of white readers is that we also are looking for our independence, that we too have been enslaved and are seeking an identity that gives some meaningful continuity to our goals and tasks.

CONCLUSION

I have throughout attempted to refer you to works of fiction that I think you might have read. If I were able to talk with you I could have usefully changed my examples and made them meaningful to your questions. This is the value of learning from others rather than books. I have tried to emphasize themes which I think are important to today's college student, themes dealing with alienation, meaning, choice, purpose, and freedom. They are equally important to your instructors and some of you might take the chance of showing them how the same issues are relevant.

I have, as you might have guessed, spoken through my own major concerns, and if at times I seemed a bit overly enthusiastic about a particular point of view, it is because, in some respects, I am a true believer and given to fits of enthusiasm about my own conclusions. I hope that I do not leave you with a sense of futility, a sense that my meaning sounds noble but is too abstract to be meaningful. I think that this would represent a failure on my part, but perhaps a failure which is as necessary as trying.

Essentially what I was trying to do was have you understand the value of reading fiction as a way of developing self-understanding and commitment for your role as a teacher. Let me tell you how it transpired for me. I had been reading Hesse, as you can deduce from earlier remarks, about the same time I was considering my future at the University of California. I had operated for many years as one who was interested in surviving in the academic system, doing meaningless, or at best trivial, research, and taking only a marginal interest in students. At the same time I felt the demands of social conscience pricking at me to make the university responsible for ameliorating social injustice. Also, at this time, the university seemed in danger from political forces operating within the state. The governor, admittedly no friend to the university, appeared to be using the college as a political football. Many of my colleagues were leaving for other campuses, deciding that they did not wish to participate in the demise of the University of California. In short order I was considering offers from two other universities outside the state. I was encouraged, by those who wanted me to join their faculties, to get out before the deluge, before the ruin of the university. I would also have been paid better elsewhere.

But Hesse had obviously gotten to me. I found myself making statements about challenge, frustration, and despair as being necessary conditions for growth. What a fortunate time to be alive in this place where struggle is required and hopes were very dim! It all seemed to come together: how I had to come out from behind my protection (and it turned out that I was more protected against meaningful professional life than I was against the annoyance of students) and join the human race. I do not mean any of this as a personal catharsis, but I have to take the chance that you might not see it my way and believe that I am off on some big ego trip. I have come to accept as a value that there is no worth in not falling, but a great deal in getting up gracefully. This value, for me, came from Hesse and Camus and Gorky and Dostoyevski and Bellow and Baldwin and Ellison. It is also a sense of humanistic integration rather than academic alienation. Tolkien told it like it is: the forces of Mordor are darkening the skies all about us, and the future is very much in doubt. But there is hope, as long as Frodo lives!

6

curriculum and humanistic education: "monolism" vs. pluralism

Bruce Joyce

BRUCE JOYCE is an old friend who appears to suffer from the lack of humility that accrues from lack of failure. After reading his contribution, I more than ever felt that Bruce was the very best choice I could have made for a chapter on curriculum. Not only does he know the field better than most, he also knows the difference between (a) humanistic and engineering strategies; (b) humanistic goals and humanistic strategies; (c) humanistic goals and humanistic people. All he does not appear to understand (which is fine since if he did, he might not have written the chapter) is the difference between Christ and Christianity or Buddha and Buddhism; that is Christ as a person versus Christianity as a set of rules for fitting into a Christian society. This is knowledge and the need to either produce it or communicate it. I point this out because as I read Bruce's chapter, I kept thinking that learning or the kind of humanistic understanding that I have described in the introduction was something one couldn't produce if he tried to do so; and, even if it could be produced, I doubt if anyone could figure out a strategy for doing so in advance. This is to say that a truly humanistic chapter on curriculum couldn't be written. Or if it could, it would only be a picture of Gautama, the Buddha, holding his flower aloft, with his disciples nodding to acknowledge their understanding.

Since I did indeed want a chapter on curriculum and humanism I was quite pleased with Bruce's product. His version of humanism incorporates most qualities that have been attributed to the concept. Bruce cares very much about how people understand and he knows very well the difference between change scores on an achievement test and the light of true knowledge. He much prefers the latter and has worked for a long time trying to figure out ways of helping kids learn the kinds of things that can't be measured on an achievement test.

He is also very concerned about man's alienation and knows what it means to "work your own street" in search of a cure. Bruce's "street" is schools and schooling. He gives us a model of a curriculum that should reduce alienation, or at least conflict. My only concern about his conception of a means to humanistic ends is that it all sounds so damn well organized, and I suspect that anything that is so well organized has got to leave someone, or some part of one, out. I know it's an open model but that to me is almost like saying, it's a room with no walls. You can walk all the way around without bumping into anything, but how do you know you're in a room at all? Also Bruce's conception of the kind of schooling that is required to produce humanistic understanding, leading to a reduction of alienation, doesn't seem quite outrageous enough to cover all the bases. But then again, that might be my own hangup with structures and strategies. At least he has given us the best arrangement of the forms we are able to know, and one cannot really be expected to produce a new world out of old world materials. Unless it was some visionary who could see further than other men, or perhaps further than other men could possibly see.

Bruce is a person with courage, conviction, and commitment, and a bunch of children that he actually takes with him wherever he goes. He thinks that the false separation of worlds that bureaucrats create to keep themsleves apart from the children who are their clients is a fragmenting human experience. He would no more separate himself from the children he teaches than he would separate himself from those he raises. I suppose some of our more sophisticated skeptics would suggest that this stems from his inability to grow up. Bruce is much like a youngster, a good credential for persons working in education. But let me end this sketch where I began it. He writes, as he is, with enormous self-confidence in himself and in what he knows, and that, I think, is the one quality that will keep him from attaining humanistic nirvana, that special territory in the inner sky where the only curriculum specialist is the man who holds up the flower, and where others nod.

To plan for humanism at all may seem to be a paradox; at first blush deliberate unplanning or "decivilizing" may seem a more likely avenue to create an environment in which gentle self-actualization can take place.

Not to plan for humanistic growth, however, is to give the field to the philistines on one hand and the accidents of "natural" societal forces on the other. I do not know which is worse. The philistines would regiment children to economic purpose—and they *will* plan, and powerfully, a social system which reduces man to an economic entity and cultivate in children a utilitarian philosophy which will emasculate their humanitarian potential. The "natural" forces of society would mindlessly overpopulate the world and gather men into inward-looking social groups, national and tribal, unable to cope with the scale of problems generated by worldwide social forces. The resulting crises would force men into a collective materialism which might preserve life but would eschew humanistic development.

So plan we must, and in education it is the curriculum planner whose task it is to generate a field of humanistic planning. Although most curriculum theorists of this century would classify themselves as humanists and many are well aware of the forces mitigating against humanistic curriculum planning, such a field has not emerged to become a powerful force in education. Hence this paper will present an analysis of the reasons why the curriculum field has not succeeded in humanizing itself and will present a platform which, I believe, offers realistic humanistic direction to the field. A simple-minded definition of the humanists' objectives will be assumed throughout as the focus of the work of the humanist in curriculum. This definition sees humanism in terms of two interacting, mutually-dependent dimensions. Stated as goals of curriculum planning these are:

a. To create environments which enable individuals to actualize themselves on their own terms—emotionally, intellectually, and socially.

b. To create environments which help people reach each other and live with an expanding common consciousness—one which not only embraces the traditional liberal values of mutual respect and protection of the rights of others, but also reaches out to explore the development of expanded human experiences through new dimensions of relationships with others.

Both of these objectives assume that the child will have to learn to help shape a new type of human society that embraces possibilities of personal and social development rarely achieved in our present human community.

The possibility that curriculum planning can actually relate to such goals derives from the critical relationship between education and society. A human culture can be described as an elaborate set of problem solutions.[1]

---

[1] This is a common anthropological definition. See Ina Corinne Brown, *Understanding Other Cultures* (Englewood Cliffs, N. J.: Prentice-Hall, 1962).

Some of these solutions are addressed to physical problems (such as hunger and cold) and it is toward these that our economic and technological systems were originally developed. Other problems consist of meeting emotional needs, and some aspects of families and some modes of interpersonal interaction help to solve these for us. For each of us the culture largely defines the way we see problems and solutions, and also enables us to share reality with other humans. That is, those of us who share the same culture tend to see things in similar ways and to respond similarly to other human beings, although there is of course a wide individual variation within any cultural pattern.[2]

A culture is never complete. It is in continuous need for regeneration and reorganization. Within every culture there are certain problems that have never been defined adequately, and certain others for which there are no solutions, even though there are definitions. Within complex cultures such as ours, there is at all times a multitude of problems begging for help. Formal education systems have a potentially dynamic social role as a direct result of the incomplete and imperfect nature of the existing culture—the existing solutions to problems.

This opportunity exists, obviously, because education is a major agent in the transmission of culture. It fulfills the exceedingly important function (shared with other socializing agencies) of giving us humaneness, and transmitting to us a technology on which we can stand as we face the problems of human existence. Our present bureaucratic educational institution bids well to become increasingly effective at transmitting the general-purpose skills of the culture (especially reading and mathematics) and this is a role I would not want to undersell under any circumstances. (I am not *against* using the existing culture, although I do not believe it is perfect.) *However, the great dynamic challenge of the future is to develop entirely new modes of education, designed to help people create new solutions to problems, and to define problems that were not perceived before at all. Equally important, in a time when culture is growing ever stronger and more powerful and society is more urbanized and alienated, is to produce modes of education which can help people make contact with each other in new and stronger ways, and can help individuals to create lives which are unique, uniquely fulfilling, and socially productive—even transcendentally cooperative.*

Since the most visible and theoretically powerful leaders of the education community (John Dewey is the classic example) are well aware of the possibility of such goals and have been committed to some form of them, we have to ask ourselves why the field has not learned to create schools

---

[2] Leslie White's *A Science of Culture: A Study of Man and Civilization* (New York: Farrar, Straus & Giroux, 1949) presents the extreme technocratic view, but in so doing clearly defines the dimensions of dependence each of us has with respect to his culture.

devoted to humanistic goals on any wide scale. (There *are* some, but a pathetic minority.) Let us look at the field and its trends and see what we can discern.

THE CURRICULUM FIELD

The curriculum worker is part of a large cadre of persons who deal with educational planning, the training and supervision of educational personnel, and the development of educational materials. The collectivity of these persons, their expertness, and their activity constitute the curriculum "field." On the whole, curriculum workers engage in four kinds of activity: they plan educational programs, develop systems of instructional materials, train teachers, and supervise them. As any other worker, the curriculum specialist is greatly affected by the condition of his field.

The curriculum field is still relatively undefined. Curriculum planners have no agreed-on set of concepts or modes which are known and used by all hands. There is no lack of "prescriptive" curriculum theories—that is to say, ideas about what school programs *ought* to be. Nor is there any lack of curriculum.[3] On the contrary, there are a great many curriculum plans and a huge quantity of instructional materials built around curriculum plans. School districts, publishers, research and development centers, and others create curriculum plans and/or materials, train teachers, and build evaluation systems. This mass of activity is conducted by people who use a great variety of procedures. *Most* curriculum creators use intuitive procedures while some use highly self-conscious "systems" procedures. They also vary in the implementation devices and strategies they use. Some rely on curriculum guides as their chief vehicle, others use instructional materials, and still others use teacher training. Curriculum builders also differ in their view about freedom and control in curriculum matters. Some would create master man-machine systems in which rational decision-making procedures are administered by technocrats, teacher-technicians, or professional managers.[4] Others would give classroom teachers the central decision-making roles.[5] Still others would provide students with the central curriculum-

[3] For an authoritative definition of "curriculum," see Ralph W. Tyler, *Basic Principles of Curriculum and Instruction* (Chicago: University of Chicago Press, 1951).

[4] For example, see Robert J. Seidel and Felix F. Kopstein, *A Systems Approach to Development and Maintenance of Optimal Learning Conditions* (Washington, D.C.: Human Resources Research Office, George Washington University, 1967); and Robert E. Herriott and Benjamin J. Hodgkins, *Sociocultural Context and the American School: An Open-Systems Analysis of Educational Opportunity* (Washington, D.C.: U.S. Office of Education, 1969).

[5] Ole Sand, "Project on the Instructional Program of the Public Schools," in *Planning and Organizing for Teaching* by the National Education Association (Washington, D.C.: National Education Association, 1963).

making role.[6] A few curriculum specialists envision variations on all these, depending on what goals are to be sought.

The curriculum field has no overarching "metasystem," known to all or most of its practitioners, which enables comparison and choices among all the alternatives. On the whole, however, curriculum planners "do their own thing." For instance, systems planners build and test instructional systems while child-centered educators develop reflective teaching procedures and group dynamics experts refine sensitivity training procedures. Generally the reprensetatives of different persuasions do not talk to each other on a regular basis about the nature of the field.

Curriculum specialists of all types do have one thing in common: they have been coopted into the service of a bureaucratic, monolithic, largely dehumanized educational system and unless they change their orientations radically they will be unable to work for humanistic ends.

The curriculum worker has been bureaucratized by the same processes which have dehumanized functionaries in other social institutions throughout complex societies of the world. He has, in other words, increasingly become a servant of a system, largely impersonal in nature, which serves primarily to teach children the technological culture, and to fit them into the economic and status systems of the society. Although this institutional system is politically organized as many relatively small school districts, schooling throughout the United States and much of the rest of the world is actually so similar that we have essentially one large national system, that increasingly looks like one large international system as the eclectic world culture becomes more dominant, and the technologies of education become more widespread and homogeneous. It is not entirely outlandish to compare the giant education bureaucracy with the postal system, except that instead of taking mail from one place to another, it receives people when they are young, and delivers them when they are young adults, into the adult economics family and the social and political systems. As in the case of the postal system, things are delivered much as they are mailed. In education it is the characteristics of the children and their parents that account for the character of the delivered product.

The technologies (technology is used in the broadest sense to include scientific theories, the lore of practitioners, educational methods, and educational engineering) of curriculum development, instructional materials development, supervision, and teacher training—the four domains of the curriculum worker—have all reflected the progressive bureaucratization of education. Curriculum development,[7] despite a paradoxical concentration at

6 The general view of A. S. Neill; see his *Summerhill* (New York: Hart Publishing, 1960).

7 Sands, "Project on the Instructional Program of the Public Schools."

the theoretical level on personal and democratic processes, has been concerned with the planning and management of instructional systems and has increasingly turned toward the development and evaluation of system implementable on a national or international scale. Instructional materials development has been concerned with the improvement of devices designed to implement particular kinds of curriculums and to do so efficiently and economically. Efficiency usually is best served by wide implementation of standardized materials and these have, indeed, dominated the educational scene (the textbooks, primarily).[8]

The functions of the curriculum supervisor have become regulatory in every bureaucratic sense. In most school districts, supervisors and teachers are separated from each other by a wide gulf of function. In many cases they keep a distance that tends to perpetuate the bureaucratic nature of their relationship, and minimize spontaneous, creative encounters between them. (This is another paradox, since most supervisory theory also stresses democratic procedures and enhancing the uniqueness of individual teachers.)[9] Teacher training, operated chiefly by curriculum specialists, has leaned most heavily on student teaching, which is essentially an apprenticeship mode, designed to socialize the young teacher into the organizational patterns of the existing educational system and the roles of functionaries in that system.[10]

Present forces appear to be accelerating and sophisticating these trends. Content is gradually becoming more academically sophisticated, and instructional systems are now being developed that should be far more effective in efficiency, both from the point of view of the system, which wishes them to have a higher output, and in terms of the learner, whose

---

[8] Analyses of the standardization of textbooks are fairly common. For an analysis in one curriculum area, see Benjamin Cox and Byron Massialas, eds., *Social Studies in the United States* (New York: Harcourt Brace Jovanovich, 1967).

[9] C. W. Boardman and others, *Democratic Supervision in Secondary Schools,* rev. ed. (Boston: Houghton Mifflin, 1961).

[10] "6. A program of professional laboratory experiences should include some full-time student teaching to provide acquaintance with the range of the teacher's work and its interlocking relationships.

While the benefits of short laboratory experiences calling for observation and participation by the student are many, there are certain kinds of experiences all prospective teachers should have which cannot be had without some opportunity to spend full time in a school situation. Unless a student has such a chance, he probably leaves his college preparation for teaching without ever knowing what it is like to be responsible for a group of pupils for all their activities over a period of time. Many beginning teachers meet very serious problems because they have not had an opportunity during their student teaching to learn what it is like to carry complete responsibility for a group of learners in all their activities. This opportunity can be provided only when the student devotes his full time to student teaching." Florence B. Stratemeyer and Margaret Lindsey, *Working with Student Teachers* (New York: Teachers College Press, 1958), p. 50.

characteristics they will accommodate more efficiently. Cost accounting procedures are being introduced into education, not only with respect to economic factors, but with respect to the assessment of alternative educational procedures.[11] Increasingly, commercial firms are being drawn on to develop instructional materials development, evaluation systems, and cost accounting procedures. PERT procedures and PP&B procedures are being borrowed from the military-industrial complex and brought into the educational arena at an accelerating rate.[12]

In short, we are moving rapidly toward an industrial model of education, which is probably more efficient but even more bureaucratic in character than the inefficient model it is replacing. Even the recent humanistically oriented critics of schooling, such as Leonard,[13] Kohl,[14] Coles,[15] Kozol,[16] and others, while they have not been without effect, have been responded to in many quarters with the assertion that the ills they point to can be cured by making the system more efficient rather than by changing it in any fundamental way.

The curriculum specialist operated under many seemingly humanistic assumptions which coopted him to the service of the school bureaucracy. For example, the curriculum field assumed the classroom teacher in this school should have the initiative in matters of curriculum and instruction. Curriculum guides should suggest, but not control.[17] The community should be involved in all matters affecting its children. Cooperative planning should insure the inclusion of the student. The local educational authority, the neighborhood school, the child's teacher, and the child himself are the centers of power. The job of the curriculum specialist is to facilitate decision-making by these individuals. The field is to set before them the alternatives and the implications of the alternatives. The teacher is to be responsible and accountable, but he is to be considered the professional in charge. To violate his freedom would be a violation of professional ethics. This as-

11 Jack Wiseman, "Cost-Benefit Analysis in Education," in *Educational Investment in an Urban Society: Costs, Benefits, and Public Policy,* ed. Melvin R. Levin and Alan Shank (New York: Teachers College Press, 1970).

12 Werner Z. Hirsch, "Education in the Program Budget," ibid.; Melvin R. Levin, "Yardsticks for Government," ibid.; Desmond L. Cook, *Program Evaluation and Review Technique Applications in Education* (Washington, D.C.: U.S. Department of Health, Education, and Welfare, 1966).

13 George B. Leonard, *Education and Ecstasy* (New York: Dell Publishing, 1968).

14 Herbert Kohl, *Thirty-Six Children* (New York: New American Library, 1967).

15 Robert Coles, *Children of Crisis: A Study of Courage and Fear* (Boston: Little, Brown, 1967).

16 Jonathan Kozol, *Death at an Early Age* (Boston: Houghton Mifflin, 1967).

17 Sands, "Project on the Instructional Program of the Public Schools."

sumption neatly boxed the curriculum field within the limitations of the average teacher. If he did not know mathematics, or did not want to teach it, the field was stuck firmly on the horns of a dilemma, for had it not defined him as the center of power? If the teacher would not or could not teach inductively, the field was in the position of having argued that his was a world of free choice. He should create his own style, and if that style did not include induction, or an idea-orientation, or any other desirable element, no doubt his style provided its own compensation for his students. The student-teacher relationship had become sacred.

The curriculum field has made unwarranted assumptions about the school and its teachers. It was assumed that the social system of the school is democratic, and that the teacher wanted the responsibility for final curricular decisions. Thus, the curriculum field was then forced to live at the technical level of the local school (which prevented it from recommending anything requiring a high level of technical capacity, or a fundamental knowledge). In addition, the schools simply have not very often operated in a style remotely approaching democracy, and most teachers did not want the curricular responsibility that was thrust upon them.[18] (Not infrequently, curriculum theorists have railed against the textbook, told the teacher he was free, only to find him busily selecting *another* text.)[19]

Gradually, the curriculum assumed the more or less perpetual existence of the present curriculum areas because through those areas it could relate to the teacher. From time to time new ones were invented in order to pull the teachers toward different types of behavior. For example, the social studies and the language arts programs were invented to promote greater integration of subject matter and a more lively, problem-solving approach to instruction. Probably the most effective curriculum workers specialized in curriculum areas, because as long as one worked inside a curriculum area, he could affect the school if he were able to affect the instructional materials

[18] The studies of teaching behavior illustrate the general point. As James Hoetker and William P. Ahlbrand, Jr. pointed out in their review of the studies of reaching teachers who behave democratically with children are quite rare. See James Hoetker and William P. Ahlbrand, Jr., "The Persistence of the Recitation," *American Educational Research Journal* 6, no. 2 (March 1969): 145–68.

[19] "We have assumed, for example, that the most promising route of development for social studies is that identified in the literature cited earlier in this chapter—a route best described as the inquiry process. We accept Dewey's general definition...of this process as 'the active, persistent, and careful consideration of any belief or supposed form of knowledge in the light of the grounds that support it and the further conclusions to which it tends.' Furthermore, we have assumed that social studies content, practices, and purposes are reflected in large measure in textbooks, the basic material source of most courses." C. Benjamin Cox and Byron Massialas, "The Inquiry Potential of the Social Studies," in *Social Studies in the United States: A Critical Appraisal,* ed. B. G. Massialas and C. B. Cox (New York: Harcourt Brace Jovanovich, 1967), p. 7.

that went into it. Thus, as the mathematical content of textbooks was changed, those textbooks slowly taught the teachers, and slowly pulled them toward new methods. If textbooks changed too quickly, teachers had trouble with the material and rejected the innovation; but so long as curriculum specialists followed a policy of gradualism, they could actually make some minor changes. Thus it is that the most prominent members of the curriculum field (and by far the richest) engage in the production of instructional materials.[20] Unfortunately, as the curriculum field became tied to the curriculum areas more was lost than gained in terms of educational effectiveness, for as those areas have lost validity we have not been able to replace them. Thus, although most schools pay little attention to the creative and performing arts, education for greater interpersonal sensitivity, philosophy, and international concerns, among others, and although major efforts have been devoted to remedying this, it has been very difficult to change since so much effort has been committed to the established areas.

By far the most paralyzing effect of the bureaucratic assumptive world in which the curriculum specialist lived was that it tended to filter out all ideas which might have improved education but fit awkwardly into the school pattern. Because the curriculum developer assumed the school and assumed the teacher, he tended to confine himself to recommendations that were in the teacher's terms, or in the school's terms. He did not learn how to create different kinds of educational institutions embracing activities much different from the norm.

There is a sad pardox in this story. For most of this century the most active curriculum planners worked in an assumptive world which gave great prominence to a humanistic democracy. After Dewey,[21] they assumed that the school and the classroom operated as a democracy in which teacher and children worked together to apply the scientific methods to the betterment of society.[22] This practicing democracy would attend carefully to the needs of its members and to preparation for the active citizenship needed to develop a more humane and responsible society. That such a humanistic platform should be coopted by bureaucratic functionaries is both paradox and tragedy. Were it not that the existing school became coopted by the status system, and, hence, the economic system, the effects might not have been so bad. As it was, the school became the servant of the status system

---

[20] The example of the reading field is representative. See Allen H. Barton and David E. Welder, "Research and Practice in the Teaching of Reading: A Progress Report, in *Innovations in Education,* ed. Matthew B. Miles (New York: Teachers College Press, 1964) for a penetrating analysis of the social psychology of the leadership within that curriculum area.

[21] John Dewey, *Democracy and Education* (New York: Macmillan, 1916).

[22] Ibid.

and the curriculum worker, the servant of the schools, went along with the package.

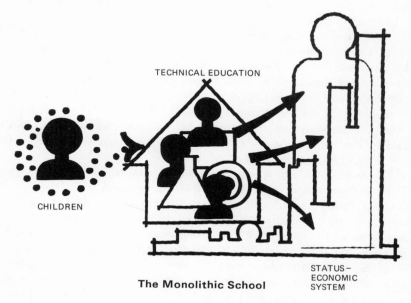

TECHNICAL EDUCATION

CHILDREN

The Monolithic School

STATUS –
ECONOMIC
SYSTEM

The situation has been most dramatically expressed by Edgar Z. Friedenburg in *Coming of Age in America*.[23]

Friedenburg argues that an open society—in which status hierarchy can be penetrated by an upwardly mobile individual—and a society which also is technological—in which status derives partly from technical achievement and capacity—places enormous pressure on its youthful members. If they are to rise in status (or to maintain the status of their parents, if they are middle class) then they must become technically proficient. As they drive themselves toward technical proficiency, they find that they are using themselves as instrumentalities. They are seeking their education, not for greater personal growth, but for its instrumental value; they are spending their youth, not to develop their individualization and humanistic potential, but to homogenize themselves technically in order to maximize their upward mobility. Furthermore, they are locked early into a competitive system, which pits them against their peers and makes their studies an instrument not of cooperation but of relative success-potential. By permitting itself to be locked

---

[23] Edgar Z. Friedenberg, *Coming of Age in America* (New York: Vantage Books, 1963).

into the vocational system, the school has come to be almost completely dominated by the status system. Its academic studies have been turned almost entirely into instrumental rather than intrinsic currency, and academic preparation has become the avenue to economic opportunity. Its practical studies have become a second track for the nonmobile. The effect of the status-orientation of the school has been to alienate many large groups from it. The consequences of poor preparation at one level carry such a heavy economic penalty—because of the doors that are shut at the higher levels—that the academically unswift are alienated (if not destroyed) by the system. Since academic ability and social class are positively related, another effect has been to destroy the confidence of lower class members in the very scholastic system that seemingly has proffered escape from the bottom of the opportunity-barrel, and then denied escape because of the way it was locked into the opportunity-system.

The curriculum field specifically has been coopted by the status system in a number of ways. First, it has learned to speak the language of "sequence," "prerequisite," and "mastery." Curriculum guides can scarcely be written in such liberal terms that they do not seem to imply that the studies listed for the younger children are essential preparation for the work to be given the older children. (The status ladder becomes an academic ladder!) Separate curriculum areas for vocation, commercial preparation of girls, college preparation, have appeared and are rationalized by the field. Evaluation has become a high art, and the curriculum field abounds in ways that evaluation can be used within curriculum framework to reinforce and extend status differences.[24] The language of curriculum is that of academic status-seeking (consider: "modes of inquiry," "structure of the discipline," "behavioral evidence").[25]

For the curriculum field, it is probably even more devastating that the status implications of progress in schooling have created such enormous pressure that it is very difficult to bring about any kind of curriculum change unless the public is satisfied that the change will not affect the status probabilities for its own students. If we try to change a mathematics curriculum in one suburb, for example, the parents will be afraid that the change will not be reflected in Educational Testing Services activities and that their children may be disadvantaged compared with those from another suburb whose curriculum might be admittedly less relevant to the students and the times, but might be more relevant to the examinations on which the gate-

[24] (a) Joel L. Burden and Kaliopee Lanzillotti, *A Reader's Guide to the Comprehensive Models for Preparing Elementary Teachers* (Washington, D.C.: ERIC Clearinghouse on Teacher Education, December 1969).

(b) Bruce R. Joyce, "Variations on a Systems Theme," *Interchange* (Fall 1970).

[25] John I. Goodlad, *School Curriculum Reform in the United States* (New York: Fund for the Advancement of Education, 1964).

ways to status so heavily depend. The curriculum theorist frequently responds to this problem by stating that specific prepartion for examinations does not affect the results very much, so parents and teachers need not worry about the effects of change. But no parent is likely to listen for long, and for small wonder: if one believed that education did not affect performance on the examinations, it would be only a short step to accepting the proposition that education does not matter very much in *any* way!

HUMANIZATION OF CURRICULAR TECHNOLOGY

The task of the humanist in curriculum is to free himself from the confines of the bureaucratic school and the sorting functions it performs for the status system, and develop instead the capacity to design and actualize a pluralistic education—the educational aspects of a pluralistic society.

The task is to move from educational routes which are largely characterized by bureaucratic procedures that sort students into the channels of the technical-industrial system into an educational panorama providing many avenues toward many kinds of personal and social development and which, through its pluralism, leads the other aspects of the society toward a world of alternatives and commitment to social improvement.

Thus:

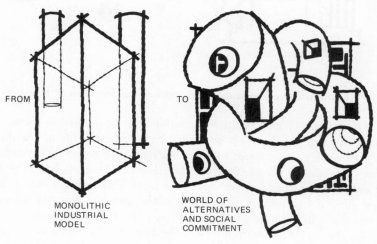

FROM — MONOLITHIC INDUSTRIAL MODEL

TO — WORLD OF ALTERNATIVES AND SOCIAL COMMITMENT

Because we have worked so long within the confines of the school as an institution and the teacher role as usually defined, this task will not be easy, for most existing curriculum theory and subtheories are straitjacketed by the existing structure of the school and that ubiquitous teacher role. What we need to erect are sets of engineering propositions which can be used to bring about a wide variety of educational environments, including the institutional forms which can nurture them.

THE SPECTRUM OF EDUCATIONAL MISSIONS[26]

The pluralistic world of education will be composed of many kinds of educational programs designed to further a large number of educational missions. The missions of the present school are tied to ascendency and survival in the technical-economic system. In place of this, a vast variety of missions must emerge.

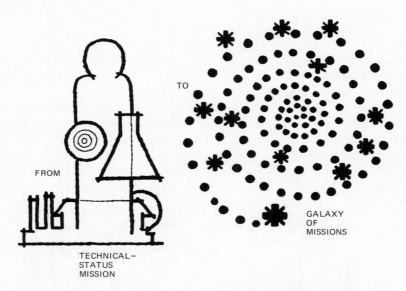

Monolithic to Humanistic Education: the Problem of Missions

The mission of an educational program can be defined in terms of the domains through which it (the program) enters into the life of the student. Since education is an attempt to enter one's life and change it or assist one in changing oneself, the product of education can be described as a developed capacity to respond to reality in new ways. The primary task in selecting an educational mission is to identify the domains through which the program will enter the life of the learner in order to change his responses to living in the world. The pluralistic education should represent many domains of possible development.

The possible domains of missions can be divided into three, with the caution that the categories overlap somewhat:

[26] This description of educational missions has been amplified in Bruce R. Joyce, *Alternative Models for Elementary Education* (Waltham, Mass.: Blaisdell, 1969).

1. We can attempt to improve the capacity of the learner through direct intervention in the personal domain (as through a direct attempt to improve his intelligence or to give him greater control over directing his own destiny);

2. We can attempt to enter the social domain, to assist him at a point where he is in interaction with his fellow man (as when we attempt to teach him social or economic skills); or

3. We can attempt to reach him through an academic domain, by teaching him academic skills and ways of dealing intellectually with complexity (as when we attempt to teach him the social sciences).

We can use these three categories—the personal, the social, and the academic—to sort out some of the possible direction of education. Then, for each type of mission we can learn what kinds of environments are likely to promote development in that domain. To assist us, we can turn to those educators who have specialized in creating environments appropriate to specific domains. For example, Rogers,[27] Maslow,[28] and others have developed approaches for achieving missions in the personal domain. The National Training Laboratory[29] among others, has developed principles to apply to the interpersonal domain. Psychologists like Ausubel,[30] Piaget,[31] and others have developed theoretical structures from which engineering propositions in the academic domain can be developed and developers like Schwab,[32] Taba,[33] and Suchman,[34] have developed engineering propositions with which academic missions can be approached.

[27] Carl Rogers, *Client Centered Therapy* (Boston: Houghton Mifflin, 1951).

[28] Abraham Maslow, *Toward a Psychology of Being* (Princeton, N.J.: Van Nostrand, 1962).

[29] Leland R. Bradford; Jack Gibb; and Kenneth Benne, eds., *T-Group Theory and Laboratory Method* (New York: John Wiley, 1964).

[30] David Ausubel, *The Psychology of Meaningful Verbal Learning* (New York: Grune and Stratton, 1963).

[31] For curriculum strategies built on Piaget's work see:
(a) Edmund Sullivan, "Piaget and the School Curriculum: A Critical Appraisal," Bulletin no. 2 of the Ontario Institute for Studies in Education, 1967.
(b) Irving Siegel, "The Piagetian System and the World of Education," in David Elkind and John Flavell, eds. *Studies in Cognitive Development: Essays in Honor of Jean Piaget* (New York: Oxford University Press, 1969).
(c) Hanne Sonquist, Constance Kamii, and Louise Derman, "A Piaget-Derived Preschool Curriculum," to be published in *Educational Implications of Piaget's Theory: A Book of Readings,* ed. I. J. Athey and D. O. Rubadeau (Waltham, Mass.: Blaisdell, in press).

[32] Joseph Schwab, ed., *The Biology Teachers Handbook* (New York: John Wiley, 1965).

[33] Hilda Taba, *Teaching Strategies and Cognitive Functioning in Elementary School Children,* Cooperative Research Project no. 2404 (San Francisco: San Francisco State College, 1961).

[34] J. Richard Suchman, *The Elementary School Training Program in Scientific Inquiry,* Report of U.S. Office of Education Project Title VIII, Project no. 216 (Urbana: University of Illinois, 1962).

The result of this work is an array of potential curriculum theories which can be applied to the creation of alternative educational environments. The figure below displays the theoretical model of such an enterprise:

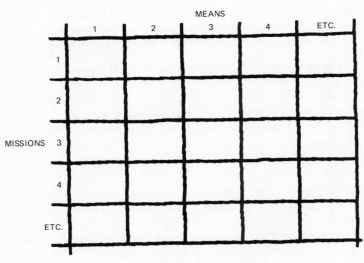

Missions-Means Matrix

Just as missions can be categorized into the personal, the social, and the academic, so it is with approaches to the creation of educational environments. Approaches vary according to which view of reality is emphasized. The *personalists* view reality from an individual perspective, and concentrate on environments which *help* the individual create his reality and his worldview. The *interaction-oriented* emphasize the social negotiation of reality and focus on environments which facilitate social processes. A third category is that of the *information-oriented,* who emphasize the symbolization of knowledge and concentrate on environments which improve our symbolic capacity to process information. A fourth approach focuses on how culture shapes behavior, and concentrates on the manipulation of the social environment to shape external behavior.

Hence, four types of approaches to the creation of educational environments can be related to three categories of educational mission.

The family of "personalists" includes those theoreticians and practitioners who focus primarily on the individual's construction of his own reality. Thus they focus on the development of the individual, and speculate on the environments which might affect his personality or his general ways of relating to the world. Therapists especially tend to share a concern with the distinctive ways each person constructs his world; they see human nature in terms of individuals.

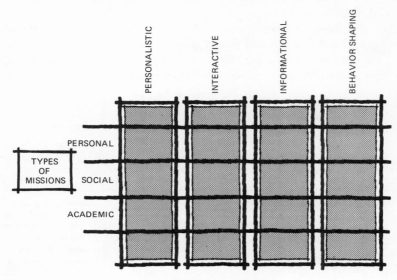

Types of Environments

The second family, those educational theorists and practitioners who focus on the processes by which groups and societies negotiate rules and construct social reality, see education as a process of improving the society. Many in this group have suggested an ideal model for society and procedures for creating an education which can help bring that model to a wider audience.

Others who emphasize social behavior concentrate on interpersonal relations and the dynamics of improving them. The approaches to education in either case have a distinctly social character.

The *information-processing* category consists of educational theoreticians and practitioners who are concerned with affecting the information processing system of the student. It includes those who have developed educational procedures designed to increase general thinking capacity (that is, the capacity to think abstractly or to think inductively). It also includes those who focus on ways of teaching students to process information about specific aspects of life. For example, many educational theorists believe that a major mission of education is to develop approaches to the teaching of the academic disciplines, so that the student learns to process information the way the academic scholar processes it and thereby achieve the intellectual power of scholarship.

The fourth group focuses on the processes by which human behavior is externally shaped and reinforced. Their major efforts have been devoted to understanding the shaping of human behavior and how education can be be built on an understanding of processes. The major theorist in this area is B. F. Skinner.[35]

It is to these four families that curriculum workers can turn for ideas about educational missions and means. The following is a list of some educational theorists and approaches from each of the four categories, grouped according to the domain of mission that each one favors.

TABLE 1.   A list of educational approaches, grouped by orientation and domain of mission

Approach	Major Theorist	Orientation (Person, Social Interaction, Information-Processing, or Behavior-Modification)	Missions for Which Applicable
Non-Directive	Carl Rogers[36]	Person	Development into "fully-functioning" individual (however, broad applicability is suggested, for personal development includes all aspects of growth).
Awareness Training	Shutz,[37] Perls[38]	Person	Increasing personal capacity. Much emphasis on interpersonal development.
Group Investigation	Dewey,[39] Thelen[40]	Social-Interests	Social relations are permanent, but personal development and academic rigor are included.
Reflective Thinking and Social Inquiry	Hullfish and Smith,[41] Massialas and Cox[42]	Social Interaction	Improvement of democratic process is central, with more effective thinking the primary route.

[35] Individually Prescribed Instruction, Learning Research and Development Center, University of Pittsburgh, Pittsburgh, Pa.

[36] Rogers, *Client Centered Therapy.*

[37] See William Schutz, *Joy: Expanding Human Awareness* (New York: Grove Press, 1967).

[38] Fritz Perls, *Gestalt Therapy: Excitement and Growth in Human Personality* (New York: Dell Publishing, 1965).

[39] Dewey, *Democracy and Education.*

[40] Herbert Thelen, *Education and the Human Quest* (New York: Harper & Row, 1960).

[41] H. Gordon Hullfish and Phillip Smith, *Reflective Thinking: The Method of Education* (New York: Dodd, Mead,, 1961).

[42] Cox and Massialas, "The Inquiry Potential of the Social Studies."

TABLE 1. (Cont.)

Approach	Major Theorist	Orientation (Person, Social Interaction, Information-Processing, or Behavior-Modification)	Missions for Which Applicable
Inductive Reasoning	Taba,[43] Suchman[44] and others	Information-Processing	Primarily designed to teach academic reasoning, but used for social and personal goals as well.
Logical Reasoning	Extrapolations from Piaget (See Sigel, Sullivan)[45]	Information-Processing	Programs are designed to increase thinking, but also are applied to moral development and other areas (See Koblberg)
Psychoanylistic	See L. Tyler[46] and others	Person	Personal emotlonai development is primary and would take precedence.
Creative Reasoning	Torrance,[47] Gordon	Person	Personal development of creativity in problem-solving has priority, but creative problem solving in social and academic domains is also emphasized.
Academic Modes	Much of the Curriculum Reform Movement (See especially Schwab and Bruner for rationales)	Information-Processing	Designed to teach the research system of the disciplines, but also expected to have effect in other domains (e.g., sociological methods may be

[43] Taba, *Teaching Strategies and Cognitive Functioning.*

[44] Suchman, *The Elementary School Training Program.*

[45] Siegel, "The Piagetian System..." and Sullivan, "Piaget and the School Curriculum."

[46] Louise Tyler, "A Case History: Formulation of Objectives from a Psychoanalytic Framework," *Instructional Objectives,* AERA Monograph no. 3 (Washington, D.C.: National Education Association, 1969).

[47] E. Paul Torrance, *Guiding Creative Behavior* (Englewood Cliffs, N.J.: Prentice-Hall, 1962).

TABLE 1. (Cont.)

Approach	Major Theorist	Orientation (Person, Social Interaction, Information-Processing, or Behavior-Modifcation)	Missions for Which Applicable
			taught in order to increase social understanding and problem-solving.
Programmed Instruction	Skinner[48]	Behavior Modification & Theory	General applicability; domains of objectives.
Conceptual Systems Matching Model	D. E. Hunt[49]	Person	An approach designed to increase personal complexity and flexibility.

The purpose of the curriculum field is to develop general knowledge about how to bring educational missions and means together in the real world. It is the creation of pluralistic educational environments that is our business. We need the ability to specify alternative missions, to create the

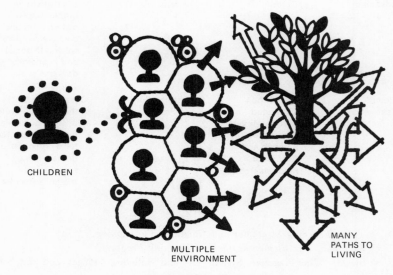

CHILDREN

MULTIPLE ENVIRONMENT

MANY PATHS TO LIVING

The Pluralistic School

[48] B. F. Skinner, *Verbal Behavior* (New York: Appleton-Century-Crofts, 1957).

[49] David E. Hunt, "A Conceptual Level Matching Model for Coordinating Learner Characteristics with Educational Approaches," *Interchange* 1, no. 2 (June 1970).

environments that will accomplish those missions, and to carry out the engineering necessary to create the material, the social systems, and the instructional systems that will actuate them.

The result will be an array of environments, each serving students in a particular kind of way.

In practice, students will create their own school by selecting from a wide offering of planned educational programs. To see how this might work, let us look at several modes of education—curricular modes, we shall call them—and see how they might be brought together in a student's life. (They represent only a few of the possibilities.)

THREE CURRICULUM MODES

One kind of curriculum mode that we will learn to engineer can be called the individualized self-teaching school or the cybernetic system mode. It is characterized by preplanned, largely automated materials, utilizing self-instruction by individuals or groups for whom instructional activities have been prescribed, again by an automatic assessment system that also feeds back progress reports to the learner. The cybernetic mode will present to the student a large array of self-administering courses or programs in many areas. He will put together much of his education by selecting from this bank of alternatives.

A second curricular mode centers around individual counseling to help the learner structure his own educational goals and activities. The learner might be led to encounter some kinds of preselected problem situations, but learning is seen as personal. Continuity comes through the action of the student as he generates purposes and activities. We can call this the tutorial mode.

A third curricular mode involves group inquiry. Groups analyze problems, try on ideas from the various disciplines, and explore social values. The scholarly endeavor of the group and its interpersonal processes are included as subjects for study. The disciplines are learned by practicing them. Democratic process is valued. Feedback is collective and emergent. Content may be partly preselected and partly produced by active inquiry and dialogue on the nature of society.

Each of these curricular modes can be adapted to perform unique and important functions in education. Blended, they can offer a common general education, the development of personal talent, and the humanizing effects of cooperative inquiry into critical issues. Let us examine them individually and then see how they can be used together.

The cybernetic systems mode

We are more certain of some educational objectives than others. The cybernetic mode is appropriate in areas of curriculum where:

(1) we have relatively stable agreement about cognitive or skill objectives. That is, we are relatively sure that we want to accomplish the objectives and will want to accomplish them for some time to come. A good example is skill in the four fundamental arithmetic operations with integers and rational numbers. For the next few years (not forever!) it seems safe to say that we want most, possibly all, children to develop reasonable proficiency in this area. Skill in reading is another area of which we are sure that in the forseeable future all possible learners should be brought to a high level of competence. It is not necessary for elementary school facilities or individual teachers to decide annually that the arithmetic operations or reading skills will be taught. We can stabilize these and certain other areas for a long period so far as general objectives are concerned.

(2) we can construct adequate self-instructional devices for the vast majority of students. "Self-instructional" should be broadly defined here. One can learn many things by reading about them. Books are self-instructional devices. *Programmed instruction* should be included. Units using films, tapes, and other media have been developed. Computerized games can teach many things. Simulation techniques will expand self-instructional possibilities greatly.

(3) we can develop automated feedback systems for keeping the learners and responsible adults informed of progress. Programmed instruction has an edge here, because of the precision with which objectives are specified and ordered and the easy amenability of the process to "embedded" tests. However, precise automated evaluation is possible nearly any time that objectives are clear and self-instruction is possible.

(4) the area can be learned as well alone as in a group. Many aspects of social dancing might be acquired in response to films and computer-controlled instructions, but much of its appeal would be gone. On a more serious side, controversial issues, drama, and improving social and sociointellectual skills require group activity for a good bit (rarely all) of the instruction. Learning map skills, on the other hand, does not *require* group interaction or very much didactic presentation by a teacher.

(5) pacing of instruction is important. For example, in any curricular mode, many arithmetic and reading skills are achieved at enormously different rates. In fact, teachers working alone with traditional materials and normal pupil-teacher ratios have been unable to achieve adequate individualization of instruction in most skill areas.

With respect to the social atmosphere in this mode, the norms would stress independence and industriousness. Students would need to learn to judge their own progress and "reward themselves" for progress. An air of calm support and mutual help would be important, as well as openness about progress. Teachers would function as facilitators and troubleshooters.

To summarize: where we have curricular objectives that are very stable, but are achieved effectively by self-instruction that can be monitored by automated feedback systems, we can apply cybernetic principles to create instructional programs. *Such programs would not work for all students* (no curricular mode does), but they could work effectively for many. Effective diagnosis would result in placing some children with tutors, remedial specialists, and teachers in groups. Subprofessional technicians can be trained to work with the children and the feedback can be scrutinized constantly by a specialist who would sound the alarm for students for whom the program wasn't working.

Because of the negative reaction of so many educators to automation, we must stress again that the cybernetic curriculum need not be a deadly array of sequenced "programs." It can be a rich multi-media program, diversely using film games, books, programs, and other devices.* Also, it would not be appropriate for all parts of any curricular area. For example, while much science instruction might be automated, instruction requiring a cooperative attack on original problems could not be accomplished this way.

The cybernetic mode would undergo constant revision as objectives change and technology improves. At any given time it would represent a bank of programs which students could dip into the construct part of their education. (High schools, for example, might offer an array of short courses in each curriculum area. By selecting a combination of programs in a subject, a student could create his own layered program in required and elective areas.)

To create this bank of possibilities, systems planning procedures would be employed.

The tutorial mode: the idiosyncratic curriculum

The creation of tutorial modes challenges the curriculum worker in different ways. The old story about Mark Hopkins and the log has long been the symbol for a delightful and wise teacher, the idea of having one's personal teacher. We are always trying to find ways to give students personal attention, whether by individualizing reading programs, providing guidance counselors, or offering the opportunity to learn the French horn. The ratio of pupils to teachers has been against us, however, and so has the idea that the "curriculum" must be "covered."

---

* The distinction between computer-assisted instruction and computer-monitored instruction is instructive in this regard. Computer-assisted instruction uses computer-controlled devices as the interface between the program and the student and is appropriate only within the cybernetic mode. Computer-monitored instruction orchestrates a wide range of devices, including books, films, etc. The combination— CAI plus CMI—enables the student to employ many learning devices within a program and can be employed in many curricular modes.

The cybernetic curriculum mode puts books and machines to work, freeing manpower for the development of curriculums devoted not to the individualization of common learning but to the development of personal talents and interests. The idiosyncratic curriculum is appropriate for those ends that:

1. are defined by the learner in his personal quest for understanding and self-development.
2. need personal counseling to assure definition and availability of any special resources and advice which the learner needs.
3. while they might be achieved in group activity, are accomplished socially only through interest groups (in the generic sense of the term). In other words, where personal interests are sufficiently congruent enough, group inquiry serves idiosyncrasy.

An idiosyncratic curriculum might be achieved by assigning students to a kind of tutor whom we could name—an academic counselor—who meets with each student regularly and helps him define personal educational goals and the means for achieving them. In some cases he might serve as a more traditional tutor. In other cases he might help the student to locate a special teacher, resource person, or community resource, for help on a particular problem. If a student were studying justice, the counselor might help him find a court where he could watch cases. If the child were interested in the French horn, the counselor would help arrange for a music teacher.

The counselor would help the child develop a program of wide personal reading (we don't want him stopping with what we provide in the cybernetic curriculum). Also, the counselor would help him get together with others of similar interests (it's not much fun putting on plays or learning modern dance by yourself).

Our academic counselor could have overall charge of ensuring that the child's life in school is a good one and that he receives help with out-of-school problems. If he shows talent or creativity, the counselor would see that it receives nourishment. If things aren't going well for the child in the cybernetic or group inquiry portions of the educational program, the counselor would be able to intervene drastically if necessary, and help change the child's program.

We might envision some teachers who would function solely as academic counselors, each with an assigned quota of students. Available to them would be subject specialists of many kinds. Developing the functions of the academic counselor for the six- and seven-year-old should provide some interesting research, since relatively few people have tried this sort of relationship with the younger child. It should be evident that such a mode would emphasize rewarding initiative and exploration. Seeking, probing, questioning would be highly valued. The technical support systems would need to be responsive to the demands of a great many students seeking a great many ends.

The curricular worker will have to face an enormous variety of tasks in order to depict and engineer tutorial modes. The possible tutorial roles, possible support systems, and alternative ways of bringing students together with tutors and resources provide a dizzying matrix of important engineering questions to be resolved.

The personal discovery curriculum belongs to the student. It can exist because of energy saved by the cybernetic curriculum. Both of these modes emphasize the learner as an individual. That is not all he is, however, so we need another curricular mode.

The group inquiry curricular mode

The inquiring group was at the core of the progressive movement's approach to education. The group of students, with their teachers, would learn democratic skills and scientific method simultaneously while they explored their world and developed commitment to the ideals of democracy. Until the academic curriculum projects began in the 1950s the chief thrust for social reform was provided by the legatees of the progressives. An overwhelming proportion of curriculum supervisors in the schools of today was influenced by this tradition.

Its Achilles heel has always been its dependence on teachers with extraordinary skills. Given the supply of talent available to education, the demands made were simply too great for the average teacher. He could not know about enough domains of knowledge and handle groups well enough to cope with the range of educational objectives.

However, group inquiry as a mode is extremely useful when:

1. group skills and interdependence are to be acquired. The democratic way must be learned *in situ*.
2. the learner should test himself against the ideas of others. Controversial issues and contemporary social movements, for example, need the interplay of diverse reactions to events. Many kinds of thinking can be learned if we have to balance our ideas against those of others.
3. group dynamics is an important learning agent. The power of the reference group, for example, can accomplish many things. The intellectual and social climate of the school is a consequence of the group process. Students can teach each other a good deal about social life. Drama, debate, sciencing are social and dependent on social feedback as well. International games require groups.
4. individual differences are advantageous. A homogeneous group studying its society would probably develop much less vigor and heat than a heterogeneous one.

As in the case of the other model, the curriculum worker has to face a large number of tasks in order to engineer the setting for academic inquiry. Teaching strategies have to be developed, studied, modified. The kinds of teachers who can employ them need to be identified. Academic inquiry in the various disciplines needs to be compared and contrasted. Ways of combining or separating them have to be clarified. Alternative technical support systems can be studied. The creation of each mode requires the use of systematic planning techniques and a range of instructional technologies.

A SPINNING OF DREAMS

As if the task of creating and studying curriculum modes were not enough, the curriculum worker needs to develop plans for constructing well-balanced educational programs which can be orchestrated to serve (or be served by) a wide variety of students.

To illustrate this task hypothetically, let us construct a design for a school (remembering that "school" means "pattern of education" not a specific building) whose basic organization consists of four teams of teachers and clusters of support systems built around each of the three curricular modes. One team will use the cybernetic mode, one the tutorial mode, and two will employ group inquiry.

The basic education layer

In the first case, let us build a self-instructional mode, using cybernetic principles and consisting of self-instructional units of many kinds which give the learner the option of developing himself in a number of areas. First of all, for reading skills, then for arithmetic, then for world history, let us build a highly sequenced course within this mode. Let us also make available courses in several foreign languages, in art history, music history, and literature. The staff of this team will need to learn how to build alternative routes for students who are unable to teach themselves by this mode. They will need to be experts in diagnosis and in the training of aides who will do much of the work in these realms. The support systems clearly will have to be massive self-instructional systems employing many media, including television, tape, programmed instruction, conventional books, workbooks, language laboratories, activities packets that instruct people on projects to be carried out, and many other things.

The personal layer

Second, let us build a tutorial mode of the kind that we described earlier. The team administering this mode will be skilled in training people to counsel with children and to facilitate their personal inquiry. Each youngster will need to contact his tutor several times a week and the tutors will need to call in consultants as the students develop interests in problem areas beyond their particular competencies. The support systems for this mode will need to include an enormous library, to utilize many media, (television, tape, contact films, motion picture films, filmstrips, slides), to develop books of many sorts, and to make arrangements so that the students can reach out beyond the walls of the school for instruction and for information.

The sciencing layer

Let us also include a scientific inquiry system. In this mode, skilled group leaders will lead groups of children to inquire into significant problems and, in the course of that inquiry, will teach them the modes of inquiry and the structures of the academic disciplines. Each child should be engaged in several groups during each year. The support systems for this layer need to include the products of the academic reform movement, the systems for teaching the discipline, to the children. Since many of these teachers will be expert in their discipline, it is probably more important to provide laboratory facilities, excellent libraries, and aides who can construct needed materials and help the youngsters get the necessary data and ideas. In this mode, each group will identify problems and attack them at its relative leisure. Scientific inquiry should not be hurried, and it is through dialogue and debate that the structures of the disciplines become clear and the modes of inquiry become explicated.

The dialogue layer

The fourth layer of this school will be devoted to a dialogue on the nature of the society and on its future. In this mode again, skilled group leaders will help children identify and study serious social problems. Also television programs will bring to the youngsters information and analysis about contemporary events on a weekly basis. At present, activities in such a mode would deal with the problems of the cities, poverty, building an international community, and the like. The teachers need to be skilled in group inquiry and to be backed up by support systems and materials which include not only magnificent library facilities of the kind described for the preceding layer, but also by people who can help construct materials when these are needed. Some aspects of this layer can be accomplished through the mass media, as indicated before. Television programs can bring to the students of an entire city information and opinion about certain events, and this should be done regularly. Other activities should be done at the group level where clusters of youngsters attack and try to solve problems that seem worthwhile to them.

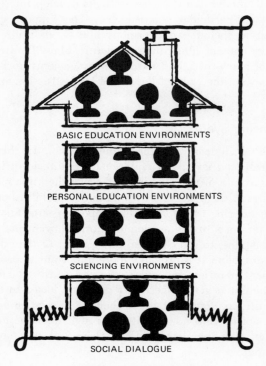

The Four Layer School

The balance in a multilayer education

In such a school teachers would work in teams. As a result the student is not exposed simply to the personality and opinions of one person at a time, but is a constant participant in a dialogue about what to do next and how to do it. If one teacher cannot help him learn the skill he needs then he can turn to others. If one teacher has strong opinions about some segment of academic inquiry, or about society, then that person's opinions can be balanced by those of the other members of the team. Furthermore, such a school balances the possibilities in the life of the learner. He is not dominated by skills, nor by the dialogue on society. He has the opportunity to participate in all of these. Also, because each teacher does not have to be responsible for all kinds of learnings, it is possible for the teachers to become experts and to teach each other the skills needed to operate in their particular mode.

In today's schools, too many teachers perform too many functions and students are clustered together in such a way that enormous effort has to be expended to treat them as individuals. In the multilayered school, some activities would be organized for individualization, others for group inquiry, and there need be no conflict between the two. Furthermore, the mass media, instead of being argued about as an alternative to the classroom teacher, can be utilized to perform its most effective functions.

The political organization of such a school should provide places for students to share in steering committees that operate the support systems, create materials, and shape the ways that students select curriculum alternatives. For example, the library should be operated by a faculty, student, and teacher aide committee that keeps in continuous touch with the needs of the students, the needs of the faculty, and the demands that are made on the staff. All the other support systems, too, should have steering committees of this kind so that the governance of the daily life of the school is a cooperation among all the members of the community.

Furthermore, the "school" should link students throughout the nation and even the world to engage in the social dialogue necessary to bring about pluralism in all aspects of life. Film, television, and print media now enable us to study with others far removed from us in space—an essential if we are to face social problems beyond the scope of our village or urban neighborhood.

As an example, let us look at a brief description of a curriculum plan designed to capitalize on television's capacity to link students all over the country in a study of a serious problem that faces them all—the problem of alienation.

A COMPREHENSIVE CURRICULUM APPROACH TO THE PROBLEM OF ALIENATION

This curriculum is part of the fourth layer of the school: the social dialogue.

THE MISSION: A WAR AGAINST ALIENATION. Our mission is to bring together the young people of America in a war against alienation that divides men in a mass society.

Since the term "alienation" has been rather loosely used in the popular press—although generally it refers to the sense of aloneness and disaffiliation among men in a mass technological society—we should take some pains with its definition; but to avoid a long digression from the substance of this paper, we will eschew a dissertation on its nature and assume that the reader of this paper is familiar with Durkheim, Weber, Keniston and the other analysts of the phenomenon.

Kenneth Keniston has become a spokesman for the factors which compound youth's dilemma against this general background of cultural alienation. He has pointed out that American society makes extraordinary demands on its members. In the first place they are asked to adapt to chronic social change. America is never still. Ideas come in and out of fashion at a dizzying rate. The insatiable media search continuously for new sensations and ideas and fads and transmit these as fast as they are discovered. Second, American society is extremely fragmented. At present, particularly, it seems like a collection of minority groups. Caste and class combine with ethnic stratification. The matrix we have been describing above in which there is a great sense of social separation in general, provides a condition in which individuals have to attempt to achieve a sense of personal wholeness in an extremely fragmented situation. In the third case, there is an extraordinary discontinuity between childhood and adulthood in a situation of extreme competitiveness (which itself increases alienation) and great uncertainty. The adolescent is required to make decisions affecting his entire life during a period in which he is very young and while faced with an almost impossibly complex economic and social matrix through which he must find his way.

The purpose of the comprehensive curriculum which we propose will be to reduce the sense of alienation and to decrease the fact of alienation by enabling young people to make life more personal and more filled with the dialogue in which they and their elders examine this aspect of society and attempt to do something about it.

The general behavioral objectives for the curriculum

It is not possible in a document of reasonable length to provide the detailed behavioral objectives necessary to develop a complete curricular approach. However, it is necessary to provide enough behavioral objectives to give the reader a clear idea of the direction which we are recommending.

1. The student can apply Keniston's conceptual framework for analyzing alienation between contemporary society. The achievement of this objective would be demonstrated by the student's ability to use Keniston's concepts to describe behavior in the contemporary society, including exemplars from his own behavior and those of his associates, and the ability to point out or demonstrate exemplars of alienated and nonalienated behavior.
2. The student can apply conceptual systems for analyzing bureaucratic behavior in contemporary society.
3. The student can engage in a dialogue with peers and elders over the problem of alienation and affiliation in the society.
4. The student can formulate a plan for reducing alienation in a situation in which the student has involvement. This includes working together with others in the school situation to create a less alienated and more authentic and affiliated mode of behavior within that institution.

These are really very general objectives which are only designed to give the flavor of the specificity with which our mission should be approached.

The teaching strategy

Our strategy is designed to capitalize on the unique advantages of television to enable people all over the country to engage in a simultaneous study of matters of concern to all. It will use television to apply democratic process principles to the problem area. The strategy is engineered from the principles of the Group Investigation model articulated by Thelen. The strategy hinges on the possibility of using open-circuit television plus television tapes to induce the students from all over the area to which the curriculum is directed (we will speak of the nation for illustrative purposes) to engage in the simultaneous study of alienation. This nationwide student body would develop ways of attacking and defeating alienation and replacing bureaucratic contact with authentic personal contact and meaningful interpersonal relationships. The key idea is the radical one of trying to induce a national cooperative inquiry into the problem area—to apply democratic process to what would result in cooperative groups all over the nation being related to each other by means of television, working in the same area. Let's see how this cooperative study on a nationwide scale might work.

Phase one   The strategy begins with televised confrontations with the problem situation. These confrontations can be in the form of dramatizations of puzzling incidents related to alienation. An example would be the Kitty Genovese incident in which apartment dwellers in New York heard and, at times, watched a young woman being stabbed to death in the courtyard of an apartment house but declined to get involved even to the extent of calling the police. But alienation comes in many forms less dramatic, and a good many of the confrontations should deal with the less dramatic but equally important incidents of human behavior which exemplify the alienated condition. Alienation is so widespread in the contemporary human scene that the task of generating the dramatization should be discouragingly easy. Driver behavior, for example, or commuter behavior in subways, behavior in large organizations, competitive situations, all abound to provide dramatic material.

Our suggestion is that the curriculum sequence begin with the presentation of a number of dramatizations in which various types of alienated behavior are illustrated. These should include routine behavior toward others, the failure to respond or get involved in social situations, withdrawal, criminal behavior of various kinds, interpersonal situations in which individuals do not respond to one another with warmth and authenticity, and others.

Phase two   In the second stage, students should begin to make clear their reactions to the situations. For this purpose classes of youngsters in high schools and junior high schools throughout the country could react to the incidents and groups of them could be brought together to make television tapes or to have discussions which would be broadcast live in which they would share their various reactions. A dramatization should stimulate a wide variety of reactions and the variety itself should be puzzling to the student. Some students will not see the alienating effects of competition, or cliques, etc., whereas others will feel it keenly.

Ideally, classrooms all over the country would discuss their reactions to the confrontation dramatizations and then representatives from various regions of the country would appear on television to describe their reactions. This would set the stage for the next phase of the work—planning inquiry into the problem area.

Phase three   At this point, using a nationwide hookup, social scientists could meet with the students in the studio and help them to formulate inquiry into their reactions to the situations they had observed. Some of the scholars could introduce them to frameworks for analyzing various phenomena in the alienation complex. Television tapes could be prepared also and distributed to local classrooms to provide suggestions for lines of study into the phenomena.

This phase could be shaped so as to induce groups of local students in classrooms all over the country to study not only the confrontation dramatizations and the questions they raise, but also to expand their range of study into their community life. They could then begin to study the same phenomena in daily life that they are studying by means of their analysis of the confrontation dramatization.

As the study proceeded, classrooms could communicate problems and progress by television. Again the nationwide hookup could be used to provide consultation with social scientists over the study problems as they developed. For example, if a group of students in New York, Los Angeles, and New Orleans were studying bureaucratic behavior in large organizations, the social scientist might appear on the television hookup and present to them ways to go about their study. Simultaneously television tapes could be made and distributed to the local schools providing further and perhaps more detailed advice.

As the studies proceeded, students could begin to share their findings with students in other parts of the United States. Other students could comment on the findings and the social scientists could have their commentary as well. The results of the students' study could be compared with the results of the scholarly study. Keniston, for example, could compare the findings of his analysis with those that are being turned up by students in various parts of the United States.

As soon as the studies were considerably developed and had been discussed and analyzed thoroughly, it would be time for the next phase.

Phase four In phase four, the television medium would be used to challenge the students to two kinds of efforts. One would be to formulate plans to reduce alienation in some aspects of their lives. A second would be to formulate plans which could be applied on a nationwide scale to reduce alienation.

Over the nationwide network students and experts could present their plans as they were formulated, criticize the plans, and discuss their implementation. Groups in various parts of the United States that were formulating similar plans could be addressed over the nationwide network or through specially prepared television tapes to provide consultation from experts. (During all the phases up to this point, quite a number of programs would continue to introduce theoretical and student-generated ways of looking at the alienation problem so that in the course of the phases a rather complete coverage of the area would be ensured.) Considerable time would be taken with this phase so that alternative approaches to the reduction of alienation could be well aired and analyzed.

Phase five In this phase local groups would begin to put into effect their plans for alleviating some aspect of alienation within the orbit of their competence. As the plans were put into action, they would be reported over the nationwide network and particular local groups would prepare television tapes which would be sent to other local groups reporting their progress and problems. As the progress and problems were reported, experts would address the local groups over the nationwide network and, also, would use the medium of video tape.

Simultaneous with the local activity, a nationwide organization of children would be started using the nationwide network and representatives of the local groups throughout the country would be put together to select some aspect of alienation for a nationwide frontal attack.

Phase six In this phase the local efforts would continue and the nationwide effort would be inaugurated. The nationwide network would be used to coordinate the efforts, to keep the students from various areas of the country in contact with one another, and to develop and refine further plans. Using the nationwide network, aspects of the plan could be put into effect simultaneously all over the country. For example, let us suppose that one aspect of the plan was to increase warmth in hitherto impersonal relations such as the way that one relates to restaurants, waiters, and waitresses. Over the nationwide network, ways of doing this could be discussed and the students could set a target date for implementing the new form of behavior. Then, simultaneously, all over the United States, restaurant employees would find that young people were acting differently toward them. The students would know the plan was being implemented throughout the United States, they would have the reinforcement of the nationwide community and the obligation of holding up their end of the game.

Phase seven Phase seven would consist of reports from local activities and the preparation for further national action. In addition, students would be taught how to evaluate their efforts; that is, how to determine whether or not they would be becoming less alienated in interpersonal relations and in inducing less alienation in other people.

Curriculum mode The combination of nationwide television with the cooperative inquiry strategy would result in an educational mode never before seen; that is, a cooperative inquiry which would have local and national aspects and which would involve all the young people of the country in the simultaneous study of problems that affect them very deeply. If this mode were successful, the students utilizing the nationwide network might select other areas for examination and study. Problems of urbanization, international understanding and relations, developing careers, learning to relate with others, sex and marriage, could be selected. The television-mediated cooperative inquiry mode, enabling a dialogue among representatives of all the children of the nation and permitting them to interact with experts and their elders, might generate a national dialogue on problems of personal and social significance, in which the strength and optimism of the young could be combined with the technological knowhow of the old to produce what really could be a significant effect on the American society.

Curriculum engineering plans of this sort differ from the usual in that they begin with education (missions and means) and create the institutional form from the specification of the environment. If we confine ourselves to those environments which "fit" the format of the present school, then no pluralism will result—we simply will embellish the technical monolithism of the past. On the contrary, our efforts should be to increase on a continual basis the options that are available to the population and the flexibility with which they can be made available. As more options are developed, making more and more kinds of education commonplace, and giving students the power to educate themselves in increasingly humane ways, then the curriculum worker will be making his contribution to the search for an increasingly humanistic education. He will be helping people to clarify alternative educational missions or purposes and to select from among them; he will develop alternative curricular strategies for achieving those missions; and he will develop the means of institutionalizing a very wide range of missions and means in an increasing variety of institutional forms.

Hence, the curriculum worker will have an array of technologies which he can bring to bear on educational problems so that the society and students will have a layer range of options. Presently, schools present very limited alternatives to children and these alternatives are focused to help them to technical proficiency. The wider range envisioned here will enable students to create much of their own education and a large proportion of its remainder to be devoted to a dialogue on the humanization of their society.

7
educational
guidance

Carl Weinberg

My humanistic perspective in this chapter is that of the social reconstructionist. Humanism must be contained in the environment rather than in the intentions of persons or in the goals of programs. I talk about a therapeutic environment where persons can grow and develop their vast potentials. I talk particularly about a version of guidance that is almost identical to a perspective on education. Unfortunately, we are in a stage of educational development when this notion is not as obvious as many of us beleieve it should be. Persons do talk about curricular functions, administrative functions, and guidance functions. All of these could be identical, particularly if we are talking about the construction of a therapeutic environment.

It must be kept in mind (although at times I tend to forget it myself) that it is idle speculation to talk about the construction of a therapeutic environment without simultaneously talking about the destruction of an alienating environment. We educationists do not have the luxury (and it is not our fault because we entered late in the game) to build from scratch. And it is not so much because all the curriculum structures have been formalized or because bureaucratic offices have been established. It is because we are dealing with people who have been socialized to believe in the institutions that are detrimental to the mental health of children. I am even talking about the parents of these children who, if my calculations are correct, would be the hardest to convince that their children are being undermined. In the main, the majority of persons who educate or are educated are unable to see their predicament because they are not educated to see at all. They are taught only how things have been done, and they have never been able to choose an alternative.

I am most pessimistic about the possibility of advancing my version of the guidance function into public schooling as it now exists. Nonetheless I felt compelled to set it forth so that, in case some chink in the monolithic armor of public education shows up, new propositions might be considered.

GUIDANCE AND SOCIAL RECONSTRUCTION

Most persons who have attended schools providing guidance counselors think that educational guidance is what those people do. I used to think so. For many years I believed that school counseling was a matter of getting students to straighten out so they wouldn't give their teachers too much trouble. Then I read some books that told me all the things that counselors are supposed to do, and I will summarize these shortly. Later I began to think there were better things for counselors to do than what they are typically expected to do. These ideas will be the focus of this chapter.

Educational guidance can be defined as a process where students are helped to overcome barriers to their educational progress. Most of you who have made it through the school system relatively smoothly may not be aware of these barriers. Choosing a curriculum, meeting the requirements, being grouped, being told about colleges, are all strategies intended to aid this smooth passage. Many students, however, regardless of ability, have difficulties either learning or adjusting to the classroom situation. They come up against a different set of barriers, and guidance people try to help them overcome these. These persons may be teachers, administrators, or counselors. Most educational personnel, including other students, play some part in the guidance process, although the counselor is the official person responsible for the guidance activity.

Let us begin by looking at what these persons do, keeping in mind that guidance, in the sense which I will use it here, is conceived more broadly than what school counselors do. In the process of describing the activities of school counselors, I want to consider some problems inherent in conducting such affairs. These problems are potential dysfunctions of such activities. It will be remembered, from chapter 3, "School and Society," that dysfunctions are the negative consequences associated with achieving certain functions. It is here where we begin to consider the human, or "inhuman," effects of some aspects of a formal organization.

THE FUNCTIONS OF GUIDANCE[1]

Data collection

Students are complex phenomena and one function of educational guidance is to make some sense out of them. Therefore, we apply labels to their separate characteristics so we can understand them better. Since we have little information about these characteristics to begin with, we collect

---

[1] Many of the ideas contained in this section are derived from my chapter, "The Functions and Dysfunctions of Guidance," in *Social Foundations of Educational Guidance* (New York: Free Press, 1969).

data. On the basis of these data, we make decisions on what needs to be done to best guide the child.

We usually collect four kinds of data, which implies that, for the purpose of guidance, students have four dimensions. Somewhere within these dimensions we can find cues to the source of student difficulties, or suggestions for the most constructive individually-oriented guidance.

Physiological Data: This type of information about the student is collected through physical examinations and from interviews with parents or observations by the teacher. Data on hearing, eyesight, stamina, weight patterns, disease history, and coordination might suggest some physical basis for educational difficulties. We are all familiar with the difficulties some students have in seeing the board or hearing instruction and recognize the fact that many students are reluctant to reveal their deficiency.

Psychological Data: These involve observations about student behavior made by teachers and counselors. These observations are often in the form of interpretations such as "well adjusted" or "immature." Usually psychological data are reported as scores on standardized psychometric instruments, such as personality tests. The kind of data frequently used to assess student difficulty are patterns of *nervousness,* reflected by habits such as nailbiting or frequent needs to go to the bathroom; patterns of *aggression,* signified by pushing or hitting; and patterns of *withdrawal,* indicated by daydreaming, sleeping, and refusal to participate in group activities. Sometimes the more Freudian-oriented teachers and counselors observe personality syndromes revealed in creative projects of a student. The student using only dark colors in his artwork may be diagnosed as morbid or harboring some deep self-destructive tendencies. This kind of assumption, however might be readily checked by examining the colors available in his paintbox!

Sociocultural Data: These are items relevant to the student's social background, his place and participation in several forms of social life. Some sociological factors would be race, nationality, religion, family size and make-up, and socioeconomic level signified by the occupation or education of his parents. Schools usually emphasize family patterns and conditions and ignore some possibly significant factors about the student's peer associations. A broken home is usually a telling data, as is an alcoholic parent. Since we almost always expect problems to show up when students come from a socially disorganized home, we perhaps read symptoms into the child's otherwise normal behavior.

Educational Data: These are facts dealing with the child's education history. We look particularly to patterns of achievement and adjustment in the classroom. Scores on standardized achievement and IQ tests used for grouping students are felt to be specially meaningful, perhaps because, regardless of what they measure, numbers are quite simple to work with. Participation in school activities, such as clubs, is often felt to be a good indication of the child's integration in the school.

Inherent in the process of data collection is the assumption that the data mean what we think they mean. We assume that a score on an IQ test tells us a student's capacity. We assume that a broken home means a disorganized and difficult home life. We assume that if a child is black, or chicano, or Puerto Rican he is inadequately socialized. We assume that if a child is aggressive, he has a personality problem. We prefer to think that children who restrain themselves from displaying emotion are well adjusted.

You can see the dangers that I have begun to hint at. Assumptions may be useful as guidelines but it may be detrimental to the child to ascribe legitimacy to these assumptions prior to extensive inquiry. Actually the whole process of classification, which is a natural outgrowth of the data collection, can be defeating to the goals of educational guidance. Preconceptions of students often become "self-fulfilling prophecies," where the child begins to behave according to the expectations we have of him. If he has a low score on an ability test, we expect him to achieve less, and he often does. Preconceptions of this sort have frequently been applied to nonwhite students where our expectations for individuals are influenced by our notions of the educational achievements of black people in general.

Evaluation

Evaluation, as a guidance activity, is the process of making sense out of the data and determining whether or not the student's problem is being resolved. Usually the solution to a problem is judged, or evaluated, according to the prominent values of the school. If the problem concerns a disruptive student, the school may judge the counseling a success when he stops disrupting the classroom. When institutionalized compliance is valued above individual expression, the evaluation criteria are predetermined and the student's problem may remain unsolved.

Evaluation involves diagnosis. We judge the meaning of the data in order to diagnose the source of the problem and decide on its treatment. In the case of the school, what the data mean and how the problem is evaluated are determined by the values the school wishes to preserve. Learning—the prime goal of the schools—and improved learning—the prime goal of guidance—is assumed to be indicated by the child's passage through the grade system and the achievement level he attains. His capacity for generalized learning is not the issue. If he figures out how to get good grades without learning anything (an adaptation to which you can all relate), then he has met the criteria of evaluation.

Evaluation, like counseling itself, has become an institutional function intended to preserve the institutional status quo. The success of any guidance counselor is determined by the extent to which he supports the primary functions of the school. Should he begin acting in ways that might be conducive to the child's mental health but endanger the equilibrium of the school, his job will be seriously threatened.

Understanding the dysfunctions of guidance evaluation can proceed from this kind of analysis. In helping to preserve the school in its present form, guidance serves to recast, or rehabilitate, many students to fit better into the system which has failed them in the first place.

The advisor-predictor role

Once the counselor has developed some preliminary hunches about the source of difficulty he begins to counsel the student. He makes an educated guess that a certain kind of interaction will be productive. He usually has in mind various suggestions to help the student work his way out of difficulty. Sometimes he will offer these suggestions openly; at other times he will structure the interaction so that the counselee will come up with these suggestions for himself. Dysfunctional counseling occurs when the basis of the counselor's hunch is influenced by factors outside the counselee himself.

The kind of advice offered, or ideas that the counselee is encouraged to generate for himself, are usually linked to the structural organization of the school and its available opportunities and facilities. The kind of organizational pattern of which I am speaking is, for example, the way in which we divide students into future doctors or future auto mechanics. Once we make these decisions, we are somewhat bound by them. It is highly disruptive to both the individual and the system to reroute him because we gave him bad advice in the first place. What the student can do to solve his educational problems becomes more and more limited as he moves along the educational conveyor belt. The dysfunctions of this assembly line conception of educational progress should be obvious. By the end of their long road through the school system, many students find themselves discontented with their direction. They will be unable to change because they have based their decisions on the same factors their counselors used. The whole notion of time, for example: the school runs a course of twelve years prior to higher education, and students need to get out of school whatever they can during this time period. In high school, the student must make a curricular decision, because that is how high schools are organized. He may be very unready to make such a decision but the system requires it. Counselors have to help them make this decision by this time, even if the students are totally unready for it. Another basis for counselor decisions, and consequently for the student's own decisions, is what the student is likely to be most successful at, regardless whether it will make him happy. It is here that counselors and students alike are caught up in the web of status striving. Teaching elementary school, for instance, is seldom a profession considered by men because of its limited status. Male students would be more apt to choose law, medicine, or engineering whether or not they are interested in the field, and they then undergo a boring higher education trying to convince themselves that this is exactly what they want.

Much of the counseling advice is how to survive in the environment and centers on helping the student become a "good citizen." After all, this is what society and the school both need and approve of. Students are encouraged to make decisions to fit into the school program and then develop strategies for pursuing program goals. In this way, the advisor-predictor role operates to control the amount of deviance that our social system experiences. The dysfunctions of fitting-in are numerous. Many people can't fit in and, rather than be defined as failures, they attack the system they have failed. Many people, however, do manage to fit in, although they might sacrifice their individuality and creativity to do so.

The disciplinarian role

Professionally, the idea of discipline is no longer associated with punishment. Realistically, however, an objective description of what counselors actually do may involve punishment as a way of maintaining control.

When I use the word "discipline" professionally, I refer to what it means according to the guidance books, the established norms of professional associations such as the Pupil Personnel and Guidance Association, and the attitudes of college faculty who teach the guidance courses. Counseling practice involves a whole range of disciplinarian attitudes, from total involvement in structuring the punishment to total uninvolvement.

Discipline can broadly be conceived in two ways: (1) as controlling deviant behavior (this need not involve punishment), and (2) helping the student gain self-discipline in order to achieve his goals. How the counselor interprets discipline will determine the quality of his interaction with the student.

If a student is referred to the counselor for disrupting a classroom (a large bulk of the average counselor's caseload) the situation might be resolved by short-term directive counseling, usually consisting of the counselor telling the student how to change his behavior. Or the counselor can explore the student's attitudes underlying his disruptive behavior. This might require a longer-range nondirective counseling of allowing the student to talk about the problem in his own way at his own pace. In nondirective interaction, the counselor does not intrude his own judgments or values about the student's behavior.

If counselors feel responsible for maintaining control in the school, or even consider this more important than discovering the source of a student's disaffection, the dysfunctions of counseling can be severely detrimental for students. Again, we return to the institutional goals of forcing students to fit into traditional patterns, regardless whether these patterns are conducive to individual growth and development.

Within the framework of a control ethic it becomes necessary to stereotype deviants. Often deviants become defined by the number of hours they spend in the detention room or the number of their referrals to the counselor. This produces what we might call the "horn effect" (opposite of "halo effect") where those who have been identified as deviants carry the invidious definitions made of them into all their present and future classrooms. Although counselors have the opportunity to stop this vicious cycle, they more often help to perpetuate it. If a counselor believes that maintaining control is one of his more important functions in a school, he undermines his other professional functions as student advisor. The students will now consider the counselor part of the bureaucracy of the school and will deal with him in the same guarded manner as they deal with other administrators. The openness and honesty required in a good counselor-student relationship will be impossible to achieve.

Parent-surrogate friend

One of the assumptions underlying the guidance function is that students sometimes require an individualized interaction. Counselors are supposed to offer students that warm personal touch so blatantly absent in the average classroom. Counselors, as you all have experienced, appear in your educational life about the time you move out of the self-contained classroom. Their personalized attentions are an attempt to counterbalance the more formalized aspects of secondary education. In higher education, counseling offices are almost exclusively devoted to offset the depersonalization that characterizes our typical large universities.

Meeting emotional needs, then, is an important guidance function. It can serve the system by accommodating frustrations that might otherwise become translated into aggression against the school. Meeting emotional needs at the elementary school level is usually left to the classroom teacher (most elementary schools do not have a counselor). As a parent surrogate, the elementary school teacher usually applies the same sanctions that parents use to guide and control their children. That means, simply, that if the child misbehaves, the teacher withdraws his affection. This, the promised rewards of love and caring are held out to the child like a carrot for a donkey. Many aspects of classroom life are parallels to life at home. Students compete with each other, like siblings, for the affection of the teacher. For the individual, learning may become defined almost exclusively as competitive achievement. Children will learn anything if it will meet with the teacher's approval. In this way they early begin down the garden path of seeking grades—one measure of the teacher's approval—and eventually confuse this entirely with an education. Counselors are usually taught to encourage students to make their own decisions based upon an evaluation of their own capacities and needs. Many students, grateful for a personalized touch, may attempt to place the counselor in the role of the all-knowing parent and, as children do with parents, shift to him the responsibility for decision-making. The guidance ethos requires independence of the counsel, and assumes that independent decision-making is a healthy outcome of a good interaction. However, there is considerable temptation on the part of the counselor to assume the parent-surrogate role and thereby maintain the student in a dependent attitude. This effectively prevents the students from learning how to exercise freedom.

Integration

I do not mean racial integration here, although this may be a part of this particular function. Racial integration connotes a bringing together of different races in order (at least in our society) to improve the opportunities of the nonwhite group. Integration, in the more general sense I use here, refers to the process of organizing conditions in the school so that all members have a place within it and, thereby, know their relation to each other and to the structure of the school.

Integration is an important function of counseling—perhaps the most important that I will use—and therefore I will dwell upon it, giving what I consider to be the school structure on integration and how counselors facilitate it. I shall also comment upon an ideal conception of integration as it might relate to the life of the student.

Counselors attempt to fit persons into the routine activities of the school. In the average high school, counselors organize classes, usually based on homogeneity of ability or interest. Schools have programs. Within these programs are required courses. Some required courses, like Math or English, will be common to all programs. Counselors need to integrate students by suiting them with one of the available programs, a set of courses leading to graduation. In order to ensure a "scientific" basis for integrating students, counselors rely upon data, such as test results and achievement patterns. Counselors often participate in organizing the program of extracurricular activities and fitting students into it. Counselors ask of each student, "Where does he belong within the structure of the school?" Seldom do they ask, "How can we reorder the structure of the school to accommodate his unique qualities?" Asking this, the counselor would have to rise above his institutional role, and see the school as a flexible institution, as being able to be manipulated rather than the child.

I now have to ask you, the reader, to consider the way in which you have been integrated into your educational system. Haven't you been asked to find where you fit, to choose among the existing programs and courses? Haven't you frequently been limited to certain courses and certain kinds of instructors? And haven't there been many activities in which you have had to participate without choosing? It is not that the school assumes it knows best the way you learn best; it is only that educators have not yet discovered how to maintain a formal organization that permits students much flexibility in the way they use it.

The real meaning of integration, as it applies to students rather than systems, involves a congruency of belief and experience. A student is truly integrated into a system if he has the power to influence the system's decisions that affect his life. A student is integrated into a system if he understands why he is doing what he is doing. Only then does he become a participant. A student is integrated into a system if he believes in it, and believes that its goals are worthy and the means of attaining them are appropriate and right. A student is integrated into his institution if he feels that he is not alone in his conception of how the school should be. Ultimately, he is integrated into the school if his experiences are congruent with his conception of himself, that he is doing what he should be doing, wants to be doing, and is most capable of doing.

Counselors will fit you in nicely enough, but how many of them are able to reorganize institutional structures to integrate you in the various ways mentioned above? It is this function of counselor as reconstructionist that will be followed up extensively in the latter part of this chapter. At this point, however, we should look at the way a school counselor defines student problems and how he solves them.

THE SOURCE OF STUDENT PROBLEMS

We have talked about the functional activities of guidance and counseling. Now let us take a look at some of the theories and ideas that counselors use in defining their relationship to students, particularly those having a problem.

When we meet somebody in some kind of difficulty we usually attribute some reason to this difficulty. If a person is depressed, it is usually for some reason. Some persons, of course, walk around in a state of constant depression, which is not lifted regardless of the changes he or others make in his life.

Chronic depression also has an explanation behind it, although it is usually much more complex than for the routine depressions we encounter. For most people, feeling badly, or functioning badly, can be linked to a specific condition, which, if alleviated, will effect a change in the mental state. Problems of money, love, low school grades are examples: if the person gets money, finds or refinds his love, or improves his grades, he will usually feel better and function better.

When students approach the counselor with a problem, he needs to assume a source for the problem and then help by focusing on that source. If the problem is poor functioning in school—as it usually is—the source is usually hidden. Seldom do students know what the cause of their difficulty might be. But the counselor usually begins with some assumptions about what the reason is likely to be, since student problems, like most human problems, follow regular patterns. As a result of observing these patterns we come up with theories, which, for the purpose of counseling are seldom more than hunches or assumptions about the source of the problem. But most professional counselors operate in terms of these assumptions.

Persons who are untrained in the behavioral sciences and, for purposes of our example, are unfamiliar with Freudian psychology usually attribute some *common sense* explanation to another's problems. Most people use this common-sense strategy in helping to solve their own problems: I can be happy if only I can get "enough" money, find the "right" girl, get a "good" job. Counselors frequently have to work according to this kind of common-sense approach, since time is usually short and schedules cramped. Counselors will accumulate a set of common-sense assumptions about how students may overcome barriers to their educational progress. Many of these assumptions are expressed as ethical prescriptions, such as "Be good and you'll feel good." Most public school counselors are former teachers and are used to thinking in terms of these moralistic prescriptions. This kind of approach often prevents them from seeing the possibility that well-behaved students can also have problems. For this reason, most students who are assumed to have problems are those who are problems to the school.

Because professional counselors are usually trained in some aspect of the behavioral sciences, they look for the source of student problems in terms of the principles of these disciplines. Typically, counselors utilize psychological facts and ideas to explain deviant behavior. The most commonly used notion in the classification of student problems is that of defense mechanisms,[1] and all disruptive and maladaptive behavior can be linked to them. There are two classes of defense mechanisms: defenses against anxiety, and defenses against frustration. Anxiety defenses include—

> *repression:* In this instance the person reacts to his anxiety by pushing the anxiety-producing stimuli out of his conscious mind, into the subconscious mind. Usually the person will deny the existence of certain inclinations he knows to be bad. In the classroom, many students deny or repress normal inclinations to express their emotions. It is typical of such students to feel uncomfortable or even angry when others give into such feelings. Students who repress their feelings, while not disruptive of classroom routines, usually have a more serious problem than those who do not, even though the disruptive ones may come more quickly to the attention of the counselor.
>
> *projection:* This strategy to offset anxiety occurs when persons attribute

[1] For a detailed discussion of the mechanisms of defense see Anna Freud, *The Ego and the Mechanisms of Defense* (New York: International Universities Press, 1946).

to others feelings they cannot accept in themselves. If a student has feelings of dislike for himself he may attribute these to others: "Everybody hates me. The teacher doesn't like me." This student finds himself in a constant battle with others and justifies his aggression towards them in these terms.

regression: This strategy occurs when persons, faced with anxiety stress and unable to deal with it in mature ways, revert to responses which were appropriate at a former stage of development. An older child throwing a temper tantrum would be an example. Students may cry or pout or close themselves in an impenetrable shell. They may refuse to learn, as they earlier refused to eat.

reaction formation: This is a process whereby the person, unable to live with one feeling or set of feelings about an object, does an about-face with his feelings. Finding love unacceptable, or threatening, he turns the feeling to hate. If he finds sex terribly exciting he may twist it about and find it loathsome. Many school deviants have used reaction formation to diminish the danger of their failure. The strategy goes something like this: A student becomes anxious about doing well in school. To reduce the anxiety, he denies that he wants to do well. To reinforce this, he tells himself that school isn't important. He may even convince himself that he hates school. If he then fails at something he hates, or deems unimportant, the failure is unimportant. Unfortunately, since this is only a defense, it has a shallow foundation. Persons need to keep convincing themselves, feeding the fire of their antischool attitudes. Many destructive acts are committed in these terms.

Defenses against anxiety occur beneath the level of awareness. If persons were aware of what they were doing they wouldn't do them so easily. Another set of defenses are those which are at the level of consciousness; that is, we know what we are doing. These usually occur at a point of frustration when we would prefer to be doing something other than what we are doing, or in another way. For example, daydreaming in the classroom usually indicates that the child is not interested in being there, at least not at that moment. At the same time, the child knows exactly where he is, even if his dreams have taken him to an enchanted land. The mechanisms of defense against frustration which are the most common are—

rationalization: This is the process of giving good reasons for real ones. It is, in effect, a way of closing down the thinking processes. We feel like doing something but we also feel that we have to have a good reason for doing so, so we invent one. If we didn't let ourselves get away with this we might inquire how best to bring our emotional lives in harmony with our institutional lives.

compensation: This is a process whereby an individual makes up for some real or imagined defect by exaggerating some other aspect of his personality. Sometimes this compensation is carried to excess, and persons get caught up in their own illusions. The most common example is that of Napoleon who needed to become a great leader to compensate for his short stature. In everyday life, we have examples of the coward who acts like a bully, the insecure man who boasts about his accomplishments. One form of compensation that frequently applies to scholarly or creative activities is *sublimation,* whereby a person expresses personally unaccept-able or unattainable impulses in constructive forms. If Toulouse Lautrec, for example, had achieved his sexual desires he might not have used these energies in his painting. Many students, unable to find outlets for their emotional needs, sublimate them by putting all their psychic energy into their studies. A second form of compensation is fantasy. Unable to achieve certain gratifications in reality, we substitute our fantasies for the real thing. Often persons create an elaborate fantasy life, and thereby close themselves off from learning how to live happily with the possible.

displacement: This process occurs when we are unable to find an acceptable outlet for our frustrations and we then turn it towards some-one we don't mind venting it upon. The average organization man, for instance, cannot vent his hostility towards his superiors; neither can he express it to his "inferiors" since he needs their respect. He can, how-ever, vent his hostility towards his wife, and this may be the explanation for many divorces. The student who finds expressing anger to his parents unacceptable or inappropriate, may take it out on his teacher; or the teacher may vent his hostility towards his students. We come to believe that there are only certain acceptable outlets for our emotions of love, hate, sadness, and fear, and for many of us, life becomes a search for legitimate displacements.

Psychology provides counselors with a range of concepts and ideas that they apply in estimating the source and structure of a problem. The in-fluence of Freudian psychology has caused them to look towards the home environment for clues to various problems. Freudian interpretation of parent-child relations appears to hold the greatest promise of revealing the source of an unhealthy condition. Of less consequence to most professional counselors are the concepts and ideas of sociology which provide other ways to view the source of student problems.

Sociological explanations for student problems

Here is where I begin to get into my personal thing. What I find most exciting about the whole field of educational guidance is speculating upon the social forces that produce students problems, and speculating further about how social action can do something about these forces. But before I get into my argument about how guidance can and should become a social reconstructionist activity, I want to point out some ways in which these social forces get in the way of almost everybody's education.

First of all, we were talking about assumptions that counselors have about the source of student problems, and I mentioned a psychological basis for these assumptions, centering around family experiences and a number of defense mechanisms. Another way of viewing student problems would be to assume that students experience difficulty because they have not been socially prepared to meet the expectations of the school. This is the *adjustment*-vs-*adaptation* dichotomy. In understanding the difference between these two concepts, you can begin to understand how psychological and sociological perspectives differ.

Adjustment is a process of bringing the personality into line with itself and with the environment. Adjustment problems exist when the psyche, or mental state, of an individual cannot handle his daily experiences. Maladjustment occurs when the person employs strategies which do not reduce, but rather increase the tensions of coping with everyday life. An example of a maladjustment is when a person is constantly forgetting about tests and assignments, because confronting the situation produces tension or anxiety.

Adaptation focuses upon the role rather than the personality. An adaptation problem is produced when there is some stress or conflict inherent in the role. Maladaptation occurs when persons play a role inappropriately. An example of this would be a student treating his teacher in the same way he treats his parent. Many problems of maladaptation occur when students use their peer group as the reference point for how to behave in school. Cursing or being aggressive may be appropriate behavior among one's age mates, but teachers find it distracting in the classroom and those students become defined as problems. With this version of cause, the source of the student's problem seems to be that roles demanded by institutions are incompatible with those demanded by the social units. Although the student himself may be quite psychologically fit, his problem lies in his socialization to perform in appropriate ways.

Let us now choose a sample problem and apply our separate interpretations. Take the following case:

The case of herman

Herman is fourteen years old, in the eighth grade of a junior high school. Herman's father is a lawyer; he has two older brothers, one in college, one in law school.

Herman's grades are Cs and Ds. He refuses to study and treats tests as a joke. He is the class "clown," leaping at every opportunity to make fun of some classroom situation. The other students laugh heartily at Herman's comments to the point where everything he says arouses laughter. Teachers have commented, for several years, in much the same way about Herman's academic performance; his achievement would be better if he would stop clowning. Herman has never failed a subject; only in Physical Education has he almost failed. For the past few years, however, his grades have never been above a C.

Here we have a fragmentary description of a student who would be defined as a problem in most schools. For our purposes, it is not important to know more about Herman. We are only interested here in exploring the preliminary interpretations of this student's problem. Let us take our interpretations separately, making it conditional that whatever interpretation we choose determines the course of helping. I shall comment about the kind of helping strategies that are implied by each interpretation as we go along.

Psychological Interpretation: Herman makes fun of school as a way of devaluing what he cannot do well at. This is a reaction formation, fostered by the anxiety he feels coming from a high achievement family. Herman is reacting to a combination of pressure in the home and lack of success in the classroom. This failure to achieve, and probably his disapproval at home, leaves him with a deep sense of insecurity. His clowning is an attempt to endear him to others. At this point, belonging has become more important than achievement.

This interpretation suggests that the following action be considered for Herman:

1. He must be given some kind of security related to achievement, rather than popularity. He needs some educational activity where he can achieve so that the reaction formation will be unnecessary
2. We need to find some way to reduce the pressure that Herman experiences from his parents in order to decrease his anxiety
3. He needs to be integrated into some activity group to give him a sense of belonging.

Sociological Interpretation: Herman is neither a class leader, an achiever, an athlete, nor a failure. He has chosen the role of clown because it provides what he considers to be his unique advantage over others. For Herman, the peer group appears to be the most significant reference group in his world, more important than either his family or school in competing for his loyalty. To resolve the inherent conflict when one's behavior does not meet the approval of one's institutional affiliations, one establishes priorities. In some ways, Herman is a victim of a social arrangement that places low priority on the act of releasing tensions in the classroom. In some situations, this capacity would be highly valued; unfortunately for Herman, school is not one of them. Herman is caught in a situation which values least what he does best.

This interpretation of the problem suggests that Herman needs a situation where his capacity for humor can be rewarded and cultivated. He could be placed with a teacher whose classroom flexibility is such that Herman's patter would not be defined as disruptive. This would be a situation where extensive verbalization of every sort is encouraged. This means that small group discussions would be emphasized. We must communicate to Herman that his clowning is inappropriate rather than neurotic in that context. Through ongoing discussions, the counselor would attempt to explore other ways for Herman to adapt to classroom routines, and ensuring the viability of his style, help him seek alternative outlets.

Social and psychological motivations

All behavior is motivated by some goal or purpose. The contrast between sociological and psychological definitions of behavior can be further illustrated by comparing two conceptions of motivation. Many students "misbehave," that is, they perform certain acts which school personnel consider disruptive. Students ordinarily know that this behavior is disruptive. Why do they do it? What are they trying to achieve? Perhaps, if we take the psychological view, we can say that they are seeking an outlet for their frustration to stabilize their personality. Frustration is hard to live with; typically, it leads to aggression. Or, taking the sociological perspective, we can talk about an alternative status system. If status cannot be achieved by the typical institutional means, then students often build their own society based upon acts of deviance. Another sociological interpretation would be that the student is only motivated to be consistent with his pattern of socialization which, in many homes (particularly lower-class homes), may be incompatible with the behavioral expectations of the school.

If Johnny has difficulty in learning to read it can either be that he has a block against it (he sees himself as incapable and goes about defying others to change him) or that he has not been socialized to value reading. If we take the psychological explanation we have to get Johnny to change his self-concept, or improve his self-image, perhaps through success activities. If we take the weak socialization-to-reading-values version, we have to work on his attitudes, perhaps by encouraging him to emulate a successful role model from his neighborhood.

At this point I want to state that my purpose in presenting an alternative to traditional psychological interpretations of behavior is not to argue the value of one over the other, but only to awaken persons to the possibilities inherent in the sociological view. Students live in a world of social forces and identities, all of which contribute to their adaptations to everyday living. Now, more than ever, when new concepts of race, social class, adolescence, and political commitment, to mention but a few, are changing traditional social arrangements, we need to appraise sociological effects.

The counselor as reconstructionist

Counselors have been typically referred to in professional circles and literature as pupil personnel workers. They are responsible for the mental health and welfare of students and any way to advance this goal should be considered their legitimate domain of work. Our present times seem to call for alternatives to traditional ways of counseling. Students live under more stress from various sources than ever before. From parents, school authorities, and other students they experience the traditional pressures for academic performance. They must make occupational decisions at a time when the values of professionalism are being seriously questioned. Many students do not now look forward to status careers for the sake of security as they once did. The value of security itself is being questioned. At the same time, the occupational world is being transformed by technology and specialization and a college degree may not be enough occupational preparation. If one is to delay gratifying the urges of living until receiving a college degree, one might still be short of what is needed. The medical student is the prime example of delayed gratification: after four years of college and four years of medical school, he is now required to specialize—another few years of putting off living! Furthermore, students are participating in political and social life more than before. They begin serious relationships with the opposite sex earlier and are required to make decisions about political and social responsibility earlier. They are more on their own and must make more decisions. They want more freedom, which always implies more responsibility and more choices. They have experience with drugs, sex, and confrontations with legal authorities. Young men are always being subjected to the draft. Adolescents are often in conflict with the whole adult society. Schools are being viewed as much as control institutions as learning ones. In the constantly shifting sands of everyday living young people need to find some solid ground. They are less prone to turn to their parents than they once did, and they are less able to depend upon the establishment for truths about how to live their lives. They are prone to reject the whole spectrum of contemporary social life. What can we offer them? Individual counseling? There are not enough counselors to go around, and the present youth culture has a monumental distrust of adults in general.

The time has come for a preventative view of mental health. It is logistically impossible to do a good job of helping all the students who need the support of pupil personnel workers. If many students are experiencing similar difficulties it should be more efficient to deal with the problems rather than the individuals. By dealing with causes, we should be to eliminate many problems at the same time, and consequently relieve the anxiety connected with them.

A therapeutic environment

Counselors have, for many years, been defining their work as a form of therapy; that is, they help people who have become sick. Building a therapeutic environment is a preventive mental health version of a counselor's responsibility; that is, we try to maintain an environment that will help students work out their own conflicts while, at the same time, prevent the school conditions that make students unhealthy.

One of the assumptions underlying my whole approach to student personnel problems is that we produce many of the problems we try to solve. The school is simply not a healthy place for children or other living things. Let us examine some of the mechanisms by which the school undermines the mental health of its students.

(1) *Differentiation:* The school separates persons according to qualities they possess or we assume they possess. Such factors as IQ, interest, and achievement patterns are the bases for differentiation. At a more subtle level, schools differentiate students according to race and economic status. Since educators do not know how to integrate human differences within a school context, they emphasize these differences in a segregated context. We force persons to relate to others who are similar and make it difficult for them to interact comfortably with those who are different. The way we have segregated our students provides them with the framework of the self-fulfilling prophecy which I discussed earlier (see page 206). That is, we encourage students to form a conception of what they can and cannot achieve and to stay within the confines of that definition. If they should attempt to test that self-conception, they experience anxiety, doubt, and confusion. Think of your own situation as college students. Try to consider rejecting a professional goal, turning, instead, to some manual trade where you will live as a member of the working class. Or even, if you just begin by considering dropping out of college, can you see yourself facing the future without a college degree? Many students would have serious difficulty making such a decision. The world is not your oyster. A person without a degree has fewer choices and anxiety increases as you try to multiply those limited alternatives from which to choose.

(2) *Subservience:* Students are early socialized to consider themselves subservient to the rules of the institution and the authority of the teacher. They are conditioned to believe adults know what is best for them. Should they rebel against this definition of their position, we have a host of sanctions awaiting them, from actual punishment, such as suspension, to disapproval, perhaps leading to social isolation.

Teachers have time-honored ways of getting other students to gang up against the deviant. By these means students come to learn that the social world is made up of superiors and subordinates. Questioning this arrangement produces anxiety, and we are not taught to deal with our demands for freedom in an anxiety-free way. This is why we so badly mess it up when we finally have it. The whole student rebellion, in fact, consists of less than five percent of the college student population. The reason most others do not participate, regardless of the issues, is that they are afraid to question, much less challenge, the carefully-taught belief that students do not have the right to participate in decisions that affect their lives.

(3) *Competition:* Another pattern which is conducive to producing mentally unhealthy students is the structure of competition. Students are

forever being thrust against each other in the never-ending battle for approval, love, grades, honors, and access to college. Competition is usually detrimental to anyone's mental health—that of the winners as well as the losers. The losers suffer by developing a sense of inadequacy. The winners suffer by developing a self-image that can only be maintained by constant winning. Many college students fall apart because their high school success patterns are not repeated in college. Human beings appear to need affiliation with others; they need to care about and be cared about by others. The competitive mode of educational life is divisive and alienating. The most serious consequence of this pattern, in my view, is that persons are forced to learn whatever others tell them is good for them to know, since they are learning to be evaluated by these others. Within this framework there is no possibility to develop an interest in learning for its own sake, nor is it likely that students will explore their own capacity for learning. The relationship of mental health to learning is, to me, a matter of developing yourself and your learning capacities in ways most congruent with yourself. Competitive learning is a matter of everybody learning the same things in the same way so they can be judged. When anxiety becomes part of the learning process— as it must if one is always being evaluated—then it is certain to interfere with the learning process. For these reasons, school is an anxiety-producing place for many students. The only ones to get out of the anxiety pattern are those who flunk out. Those who stay in must learn to live with their anxieties.

(4) *Conformity:* Students learn quickly that the best way to avoid negative sanctions is to do what everybody else is doing. This, of course, is encouraged by educators because it is the simplest way of ensuring conformity. Conformity is a process of shaping your motivations and inclinations to correspond with the range of acceptable behaviors. Persons usually push to the center because they are confused and doubtful as to the limits of the range; that is, if the amount of individualism that you permit yourself is always in doubt, you are most likely to guard against expressing any of it. Denying ourselves the opportunity to be fully human is truly an unhealthy condition.

The best example of this in the classroom is the way we take special pains not to express any of our feelings. We guard against expressing joy, or sadness, or pain. We don't laugh too loud, never squeal with delight, and never never cry. The fact of conformity itself is not necessarily the serious problem; it is what we conform to. In this case, we conform to expectations of behavior that are restrictive of most of our human emotions. By guarding our expressions of feeling, we find ourselves, before long, not feeling anything. The easiest way to prevent our violating our proscriptions for expressing feelings is simply not to feel. The human mind is amazingly adaptable. It is very sad that we ask it to perform so many tasks that deprive us of our humanity.

(5) *Unidimensionalism:* Schools assume that, since children cannot think abstractly, it would only confuse them to be oriented as cultural relativists. This means that we give children a set of *do*s and *don't*s that define the world. These rules quickly become translated as *should*s and *shouldn't*s. We don't want to mess up their little minds by exposing them to a whole set of shifting standards that will apply in some cases and not in others. The school sees as its function the ethical socialization of children. Teachers believe that it is their rightful responsibility to care for the morals of the larger society by implanting these in the heads of the young. Children must learn all the restrictions on their personal freedom that are necessary to contain them in a capsule of virtue.

Since it is very difficult to explain to children the various conditions under which sexual behavior is or is not acceptable, we teach them that sex is wrong, and many of them grow up believing it. Even when they experience it, they do so with the feeling that they are doing something wrong. We convince them that it is wrong by institutionally ignoring any reference to sex in school and by severely punishing students who want to use the school grounds to experiment.

Students seldom learn, during their educational experience, that certain values are functional in certain societies and not in others. It is almost always a matter of communicating a conviction that things are either right or wrong in themselves. As students accept and internalize these values, they then experience anxiety whenever they have a thought or feeling about violating their beliefs. We have taught them, for instance, that industriousness is an important value and they feel guilty and anxious for the rest of their lives when they wish to be idle. Having been taught to respect constraint, they experience anxiety when they feel like letting go. Valuing success, they have difficulty accepting themselves when they fail. All we need to do to prepare students to live comfortably with their feelings, and with social and ethical differences, is to instill in them a sense of the diversity of human possibilities. But schools do not want to do this.

Essentially there are three reasons why educational institutions undermine the mental health of students: control, efficiency, and motivation. Let's examine each reason separately.

Control: Control can be thought of, euphemistically, as the management of large numbers of persons, in this case primarily students, although other personnel may be similarly managed. Very simply, educators view their institution as a mechanism that needs to run smoothly. When its resources or philosophy are challenged, the institution becomes threatened. Any violation of the normal school routines represents a threat. The deviance of one child, while handled as an individual case, is interpreted as a single case of the larger threat of disruption. If we permit one deviance to remain uncontrolled, the threat can become widespread. This kind of institutional thinking suggests that educators assume that students and others, if left to their own devices, might want things to operate in a different way. "Then, why shouldn't they?" becomes the logical question. The only possible answer to this is that educators cannot flexibly handle a range of different motives and inclinations.

Alternative structures to those which are maintained in the schools—specifically those that might encourage a wide range of adaptations to the school—violate the educator's sense of stability (as if stability was somehow a holy notion!). Stability, according to this way of thinking, then becomes an end rather than a means, and the success or failure of a school year is determined by the extent to which we have avoided any problems. The reason—and not a good one—for this adaptation is that most schools do not operate with a sense of human goals and therefore have not developed ways of evaluating their attainments in terms of growth or learning. Lacking these goals, educators make the absurd assumption that we are getting somewhere if the machine does not break down.

Another assumption underlying the control structure of education is that children are somehow better off if we limit their freedom. Since we know what is best for them, we know that too much freedom may get in the way of their educational experience. All we really do know, however, is that if we control them adequately they will follow our rules to the extent that they will make it through our system.

Efficiency: The major instrumental function of education is to move large numbers of students through the schools and into the adult roles they are to play in society. This is a monumental task, but schools have been accomplishing it for many years. It requires the kind of efficiency that would probably break down if student needs got in the way.

Look at it this way. How does one herd large groups of students down a long corridor to the outside world? And what would happen if some decided along the way that they wanted to stop the process and save themselves from the slaughter at the other end (this is just an analogy)? Suppose those in protest wanted not just one, but many paths to the outside? Then we would have to build them, you would answer. But we don't know what they would look like, or whether we could afford to build them. It is more efficient to go along with the same way we have always done it, with one direction, one set of standards, and one outcome—graduation. Rather than be completely vague about the alternative routes, let me suggest here that it is possible to conceive of an educational experience unrelated to graduation, to units, to access to college or a professional school. But is this efficient, if our function is getting kids *through* an education rather than *into* one?

My answer is, "Yes, most efficient," but I would need to change the goals and conception of our function. Efficiency is a matter of achieving goals in the best possible way. If our goals lie beyond any concern for the personal well-being of students, then what we have is adequately efficient.

If our goals concern turning out healthy and happy citizens rather than just working people, then our process is horribly inefficient.

Unfortunately, efficiency has become completely wrapped up in the dollar. Human beings—students, in this case—are educated on a cost-per-student basis. The kind of education we want, or educators want, is determined by the amount of money we are willing to spend on it. The kind of education we may need in order to handle the affective, or emotional needs of students may require that we cut the size of our public school classes from 40 to 15. But if we say we can't afford this, we are saying we cannot afford to give kids a decent educational experience. But then again, what is a decent educational experience? (From the content so far in this chapter and in the book you should have a good idea.)

What I am really saying is that educators and the public cannot financially afford to make education a healthy experience.

Everybody is looking for, and sometimes willing to accept, new strategies for correcting some deficiencies in the schools, as long as we can do it without raising property taxes.

Differentiation of students into categories, with concomitant psychic costs, is a matter of efficiency. It is always more efficient and cheaper to educate a large group at the same time than a number of persons individually. It is also easier to counsel a student who has already chosen his academic or vocational curriculum, than one who hasn't. It is, if we get right down to it, much more efficient to run the lives of others rather than take the chance that, if left to their own devices, they will come out the kinds of products we promise the public trust they will be.

Motivation: Educational structures and strategies of the type I have analysed here provide students with motivation to achieve, and motivation to conform. The competitive mode of earning grades in the classroom is of the former type. The motivation to develop a set of academic and personal-social skills that will help you fit in is of the latter.

Teachers establish standards and then force students to compete with each other for the various rewards of achieving these standards. In schools today there is no single force as effective as competition to motivate students to keep their noses to the grindstone. This is why we continue to employ strategies that work, although we recognize they may have enormous dysfunctional consequences. Unfortunately, we hesitate to question whether the goals for which they work, much less the process, is really worth it.

Students need to be motivated to assume adult roles, to become a part of the larger society. We teach them to do this by choosing a career, attaining the education required for that career, and being morally committed to responsibly fulfill that career. If students do not respond to the educational processes as they are expected to, they risk losing the esteemed place in adult society that we have promised them. They are motivated to conform because they want the same things their role models have. They know about status, about a good income, about security. We can feed them almost any kind of education and they will swallow it because they want to belong.

A therapeutic environment

I have said that I believe the function of a pupil personnel worker is to provide a therapeutic environment. Instead of concentrating our energies to help kids overcome the hangups we have caused, we need to provide them with an environment that does not produce hangups. The kind of environment I want to describe is one that will reduce students' anxieties and conflicts and provide a context in which those already troubled can get well. I firmly believe the problems that students typically have today are best resolved by their personal involvement in a meaningful environment, rather than by therapy.

The pupil personnel worker comes to this task in the context of an already well-structured institution. His job must be to reconstruct it, to change the existing patterns of interaction, and to conceive of and execute new ones. With such a reconstructionist view of himself, the counselor must work to convince other members of the educational bureaucracy that change is not a personal threat to them.

To avoid the stigma often associated with persons working for change, sometimes radical change—that they do not have a concept of the new but only a hatred of the old—we need to conceive of this therapeutic environment in the most concrete terms. Let me suggest some possible components of this therapeutic environment that pupil personnel workers should create.

(1) *A Nondifferentiated Environment:* Students will not be placed into categories based upon artificial designations of their qualities, such as achievement level, IQ, or occupational interest. Curriculum choices as such will not be the typical structure, although students may take special interest courses. In this way a student who may wish to become an engineer is free to take courses in auto mechanics without jeopardizing his course requirements for college entrance. In the elementary school, small ability groupings will be replaced by interest groupings and children who want to read about farms, for example, will aggregate themselves into one reading group and those who want to read about cars into another.

The philosophical basis of this component is a concept of classroom interaction based upon emerging differences of style and background rather than produced differences of age or ability.

(2) *Interpersonal Interaction:* A therapeutic environment is one that guarantees maximum interaction among students and between students and teacher. At the same time the interaction must not be linked to grading or other traditional evaluation schemes. Students should be encouraged to question the routines of the classroom, to discuss with each other in an open forum the way they are affected, to discuss with the teacher the rationale

behind his requirements, to ask for clarification of expectations. As part of this ongoing dialogue, children should be encouraged to define themselves as individuals and avoid the personal and social binding that occurs as a result of attempting to fit into the student roles. The outrageous assumption that should guide this kind of interaction is that it is all right for children to be children, they do not have to become little adults on the first rung of the socialization ladder. Actually, a therapeutic environment would define childhood as a very special period of life and children should explore with each other what it means to be a child. As children who find it unnecessary to deny themselves in order to meet a set of impersonal expectations, students can easily discover their commonality with others, which is always a therapeutic condition.

(3) *An Expressive Environment:* The classroom should be a place where one's human needs and inclinations are not stifled. Children should experience a whole range of expressive feelings and be given opportunities to express them. They should be allowed to cry, or curse, or bang their fists on the desk.

We can ask them: What are the sounds of delight, pain, sorrow, frustration? Although we now give them exercises to strengthen and loosen their bodies, we ignore their feelings. A good five-minute arm wrestle, with all the accompanying grunts and groans and laughter—as long as we don't let them get hung up on winning or losing—frees the mind for learning better than a hundred pushups would. The assumption here is that one learns more completely if feelings are integrated with purely cognitive understanding. Because we ignore these feelings, learning becomes a process of acquiring impersonal facts. It turns out that students who do well in school today are those who can ignore their personal involvement with knowledge and concentrate on memorizing facts to earn the grade. This is not a growth model of education; it is a survival model, which usually interferes with growth.

(4) *A Cooperative Environment:* We have seen how education has evolved into a competitive structure where learning is a matter of beating out the other guy for the system's rewards—approval, honors, grades. A cooperative structure would permit students to learn in their own way, individually or in a group, with an agreed-upon guarantee to respect one another's efforts. There would be no standards to differentially evaluate students as members of a group. Standards may be applied, however, and evaluation may occur by students assessing their rate of progress, but no rewards will be linked to these standards. Within this structure, the role of the teacher would be to assist students in a resource capacity, and help define their objectives and problems. A guidance teacher, then, would take his cues for behavior, for both the goals (of the class) and means of attaining them, from the students. On the basis of his assessment of this, he then recommends structures

for classroom activities. Students, who are being prepared to function in a democratic society as adults, are seldom given a democratic experience. A cooperative classroom structure would, ideally, be an experiment in participatory democracy. It is amazing how students can become involved in their education if they have something to say about what kind of education it will be. At the same time, the alienation and anxiety encouraged in an authoritarian environment can be eliminated. Students are more and more struggling to be free of the institutional concept that they must play a subservient and inferior role throughout their education. A democratic structure would be one where students do not have to either rebel or grow up to change their position. It is a pity that so many students spend so much effort trying to just make it through their education that they do not find the time or the opportunity to enjoy it.

CONCLUSION

These have been some suggestions for creating the kind of environment that would avoid producing and maintaining typical student problems. The pupil personnel worker who wishes to function as a change agent should best be guided by the problems themselves. He needs to ask, "What kind of anxiety do students experience and why?" and "What can we do to eliminate it?" If we take the view that students have to learn to get along in a sick circumstance then we are contributing to the maintenance of that circumstance—we are "cooling out" a possible force for change. To me, what to do for the future is obvious: we have to remake the present. Pupil personnel workers, counselors, guidance workers—whatever we want to call them—must see their task within a professional framework. Their major responsibility is the mental health of students, not the organizational functioning of the school. Today, these two tasks are mutually exclusive; they need not be in the future.

8

business administration and education

Kouji Nakata

KOUJI NAKATA comes to his version of humanism through his personal encounter with the study of organizations and organizational life. He was, coincidentally, caught up in the humanistic movement, from the professional side, when his field of business administration became involved with the inside world of the bureaucrat. When he saw that personnel relations involved more than the impersonal aspects of bureaucratic role, Kouji became interested. From his background in business administration, Kouji began to look at education as the logical recipient of some of the ideas being generate in his discipline.

Kouji was swept up by the sensitivity, T-group movement as these ideas became part of his academic area. But, like the rest of us who contributed to this book, he did not let his studies get away without bearing a direct relationship to the way he wants to live his life. The point is that our academic and personal life must be conjoined in a purposive manner to achieve our personal integrity and congruity. This is Kouji's struggle, much like it is our struggle and the struggle of students we attract to our classes.

Kouji has moved away from where he was about a year before he wrote his chapter. I remember when he used to believe that helping people relate to each other in an honest and meaningful way was where it was at. Since then he has tried to work at an action level, hoping to integrate, through organizations and educational systems, his ideas with action programs. The point is here, that he does not believe that relating meaningfully is enough, and if this kind of relating does not go beyond the point of simply feeling good about people, he doesn't want to get involved in the first place.

His chapter strikes at a number of issues which are central to the humanistic movement. Some of his ideas are similar to others in other chapters. His unique contribution consists in the way he is able to link his personal humanistic commitments for change and dignified living to the use of knowledge in formal organizations. Kouji tries to make sense of the more formalistic aspects of the humanistic movement in his treatment of organizations and strategies, such as senstivity training and organizational development. His treatment of bureaucracy as a personalizing rather than depersonalizing environment suggests some hope in an otherwise bleak outlook for persons working in large organizations. The conclusion that we all need to draw and to understand is that, if industrial organizations can be made to approximate humanness then there is still some hope for schools. Kouji's unique contribution is to make that possibility explicit.

THE CHALLENGE OF EDUCATION FOR
LIVING IN A CHANGING WORLD

It is my belief that, in the social sciences, what people choose to write about and how they write about it should be deeply connected to their own unique experiences as human beings. Integrating this personal perspective with the text adds a sense of richness and understanding far greater than just the statement of impersonal positions on a specific topic. To write in this way means to include the process and struggle one goes through that leads to a particular insight or conclusion. It is another kind of knowledge or knowing that helps the process of learning to become an active participant in the discovery and use of knowledge, instead of being only a passive recipient of knowledge.

For this reason I find it necessary to begin with a short statement on my own relationship to the field of education and the part it plays in the larger concerns of my life. Education is far more to me than a mere field of study. I entered and continue to participate in the field of education with a deep sense of personal caring and commitment. This is because I approach it as the process through which individuals can grow and develop the vast potentialities that lie within them. My concern is for the future of man in the kind of world emerging today.

To see the communication of knowledge as the passing on of data, theories, models, and conclusions by themselves, feeds the common and dehumanizing misconception that education is primarily the accumulation and memorization of a body of facts. Certainly, this represents one of the results of education, but a vastly more important goal is learning about the *human process of education*—of learning how to learn, how to release and utilize the creativity that lies within us and, most important, how to integrate knowledge and education in our daily lives to become more fully the person we want to be in an increasingly complex technological society.

Our educational institutions have certainly not been the only, or the best, settings for encouraging this process of education, personal growth, and discovery, but they are becoming more critical because of the increasing dominance of technology in our culture. In order to function and have some impact on our society, it is becoming more and more necessary to develop ways to maintain human values and protective creative capacities in an environment which, by its technological nature, is not deeply committed to these principles.

KNOWLEDGE AND TECHNOLOGY

The creation and application of new knowledge is the backbone of technological advances. Industry seems unified around the slogan "Knowledge is power." But in this sense, knowledge is only knowledge—raw data—and should not be confused with its consequences. What we need, in addition to knowledge, is *understanding,* which is the personal interpretation of knowledge. It is understanding that transforms knowledge and gives it meaning and a sense of perspective or relative significance in the light of personal values and goals. Seen in this way, technology might escape its tendency to become bureaucratized and thus avoid succumbing to the self-serving quality that is inherent in bureaucratic structures. Theodore Roszak has written of this danger of self-defining technocracy if its use is not guided by enlightened leadership.

> But for our purposes here it will be enough to define the technocracy as that society in which those who govern justify themselves by appeal to technical experts who, in turn, justify themselves by appeal to scientific forms of knowledge. And beyond the authority of science, there is no appeal.... In all these arguments, the technocracy assumes a position similar to that of the purely neutral umpire in an athletic contest. The umpire is normally the least obtrusive person on the scene. Why? Because we give our attention and passionate allegiance to the teams, who compete within the rules; we tend to ignore the man who stands above the contest and who simply interprets and enforces the rules. Yet, in a sense, the umpire is the most significant figure in the game, since he alone sets the limits and goals of the competition and judges the contenders.[1]

It is in our schools that I feel we must begin ensuring that our society will not become unidimensional in its technical and scientific goals and values. The warnings of this occurring, like so many things that are realities today, began as fantasies in such books as Orwell's *1984,* and Huxley's *Brave New World.* Today they are the warnings of serious and concerned professionals in all fields. Rene Dubos, professor of microbiology and pathology, Rockefeller University:

> Our society is highly expert in controlling the external world and even the human mind, but our relationship with other human beings and the rest of creation are constantly diminishing in significance. This society has more comfort, safety, and power than any before it, but the quality of life is cheapened by the physical and emotional junk heap we have created. We know that life is being damaged by the present social conditions, but we participate nevertheless in a system that spoils both the earth and human relationships.[2]

[1] Theodore Roszak, *The Making of a Counter Culture* (Garden City, N.Y.: Doubleday, 1969), pp. 7–8.

[2] Rene Dubos, *So Human an Animal* (New York: Scribner's, 1968), p. 6. (Copyright © 1968 Rene Dubos; quotations reprinted by permission of Charles Scribner's Sons.)

David Riesman, a noted sociologist:

...But the scientific and rationalist temper of our meritocracy (a society built for maximum productive efficiency) may undermine the morale of even those within its protection; it has no religious base. Is America's romance with practicality and efficiency enough to sustain it? Men serving a system with no goals other than its own further advance to have no transcendent aims. They are vulnerable to an inner and outer attack that criticizes them for sustaining a self-perpetuating structure, rather than helping to cure the diseases of society.[3]

Norbert Wiener, founder of the science of cybernetics:

... (For men) to throw the problem of his responsibility on the machine, whether it can learn or not, is to cast his responsibility to the winds, and to find it coming back seated on the whirlwind.

I have spoken of machines, but not only of machines having brains of brass and thews of iron. When human atoms are knit into an organization in which they are used, not in their full right as responsible human beings, but as cogs and levers and rods, it matters little that their raw material is flesh and blood. *What is used as an element in a machine, is in fact an element in the machine.*[4]

We have advanced far enough in our scientific and technological capacities to make great strides towards the elimination of poverty, towards the prevention of pollution. And we should be able to plan social living in such a way as to reduce the number of atrocities of daily living to which we are all subjected. But we choose not to do so. This is because we value other things more. Men travel to the moon while other men still die of malnutrition and other diseases of poverty in our cities and rural areas. Our government would rather sacrifice wildlife and ecological balance than buy back offshore drilling leases. There are countless other examples of this value system that places scientific and material gains above gains in individual freedom, equality of opportunity, and the preservation of the quality of our physical and social environment.

It is through our educational institutions that I hope we can stop the misuse of technology. We need new kinds of men to be in control and power, men of vision, able to view technological advances within the perspective of higher human values.

One of the advantages of having taken my graduate work in the behavioral science area in a school of business administration and in a

[3] David Riesman, "Notes on Meritocracy," *Daedalus* (Summer 1967):897–908.

[4] Norbert Wiener, *The Human Use of Human Beings* (New York: Avon Books, 1967), p. 254. Copyright 1950, 1954 by Norbert Wiener; reprinted by permission of the original publisher Houghton Mifflin Company.

department of social and community psychiatry is that I have had the opportunity to deal firsthand with the growing adjustment problems that our rapidly changing environment is causing. In the most basic way, both of these departments are involved in a process of reeducating adults to cope more effectively with a highly complex and technologically oriented society. It is from this experience that I have turned to education in hope of providing in our schools an education which is relevant and helpful to those who are to live in a rapidly changing and highly technological world.

In summary, my basic concern is to find ways in which the individual can achieve some sort of personal fulfillment within an environment increasingly characterized by technology and change. Further, it is my belief that the educational system must become a prime agent in bringing about this end. To do so will require that current educational goals and even educational thinking be redefined.

"TIMES THEY ARE A CHANGIN'"

> We have modified our environment so radically that we must now modify ourselves in order to exist in this new environment. We can no longer live in the old one. Progress imposes not only new possibilities for the future, but new restrictions. It seems almost as if progress itself and our fight against the increase of entropy intrinsically must end in the downhill path from which we are trying to escape. Yet this pessimistic sentiment is only conditional upon our blindness and inactivity, for I am convinced that once we become aware of the new needs that a new environment has imposed upon us, as well as the new means of meeting these needs that are at our disposal, it may be a long time yet before our civilization and human race perish. . . .[5]

It's a different world that is emerging. I don't care who you listen to,—the president of General Motors or Bob Dylan—the message is clear: the times are a-changin'. Look around you, go to the kitchen, read the paper, watch the TV—try to keep in touch with all the new things that are happening, try to understand them all. It's impossible. Even worse, it's becoming more difficult, for change itself is becoming more complex and rapid.

A whole new field is coming into existence, the study of the future—people trying in every way possible to predict what is to come. Most of the predictions are frightening. Here's how Herman Kahn and Anthony Wiener, two people who have thoughtfully and systematically surveyed the past and present to project the future, see the situation:

> The purpose of this paper, however, is to focus attention on some of the new problems created by technological and economic progress. Through

[5] Ibid., p. 66.

such progress such issues arise as:

the accumulation, augmentation, and proliferation of weapons of destruction;

the loss of privacy and solitude;

the increase of governmental and/or private power over the individual;

the loss of human scale and perspectives and the dehumanization of social life or even of the psychobiological self;

the growth of dangerously vulnerable, deceptive or degrading centralization of administrative or technological systems;

the creation of other new capabilities so inherently dangerous as seriously to risk disastrous abuse; and,

the acceleration of changes that are too rapid or cataclysmic to permit successful adjustment.[6]

We don't have to read projections about what it will be like fifty years from now to be concerned; just open our eyes. Let me give one example from experimental psychology, a study of what happens when you crowd animals together. It is frightening, to say the least.

The sex mores of the rats in the sink were disrupted, and pansexuality and sadism were endemic. Rearing the young became almost totally disorganized. Social behavior of the males deteriorated, so that tail biting broke out. Social hierarchies were unstable, and the territorial taboos were disregarded unless backed by force. The extremely high mortality rates of females unbalanced the sex ratio and thus exacerbated the situation of surviving females, who were even more harassed by males during the time they came in heat.[7]

It is even more frightening to see the same kind of behavior starting to occur in our major cities, only this time it is human behavior.

If we take a close look at some of these predictions for the year 2000, we see that they are not star-gazing kinds of predictions, but are, instead, conservative projections based on current trends. Even in my short life span, I've seen space flights go from the funny papers right into reality. The now imagined and the yet unimagined are just around the corner. To look at the conservative predictions are enough to get a feel of what's coming tomorrow.

Here are a few of the changes Kahn and Wiener see for the future:

[6] Herman Kahn and Anthony Wiener, "Faustian Powers and Human Choice: Some Twenty-First Century Technological and Economic Issues," in *Environment and Change: The Next 50 Years,* ed. W. R. Ewald (Bloomington: Indiana University Press, 1968), p. 103.

[7] E. T. Hall, *The Hidden Dimension* (Garden City, N.Y.: Doubleday, 1966), p. 32.

"Dangerous Personal Choices"[8]
  a. Sex of children.
  b. Genetic engineering enabling you or someone else to choose what kind of child is to be born.
  c. Super-cosmetology (nose jobs, face lifting, and enlarging breasts are just the start).
  d. Lengthy hibernation and the preservation of corpses for later revival.
  e. Psychedelic drugs ("better living through chemistry").
  f. Electronic stimulation of pleasure centers as well as electronic programming of a persons personality.

"Degradation of the Environment"
  a. Radioactive debris from both peaceful and war related nuclear explosions.
  b. Increased CO_2 in the atmosphere.
  c. Waste heat.
  d. Other wastes, debris and just plain garbage.
  e. Excessive urbanization.
  f. Insecticides, fertilizers, food additives, etc.

"Intrinsically Dangerous Technology"
  a. Modern means of mass destruction.
  b. Nuclear reactors-fission or fusion.
  c. Biological and chemical "progress" especially biological and chemical weapons.
  d. Molecular biology and genetics.
  e. Mind control.

The area that is especially meaningful to me is the threat to privacy. Privacy may be a luxury which may increasingly diminish. Some of those things which might become outmoded include:

  a. *The right to idiosyncratic* thoughts, utterances, values, way of life, style and manners and method of self-expression.
  b. *Isolation or protection* from selected aspects of the physical enivornment; from selected aspects of the social environment as pressures and/or intrusions by individuals, organized private groups and business, and political and governmental organizations.
  c. *The right to withhold information;* to make many family and personal decisions, *by oneself.*
  b. *Enough elbow room;* in order to be unobserved occasionally, for aesthetic purposes; in order to get things done, and *as a value in its own right.*[9]

Most frightening is the following statement by Kahn and Wiener:

Perhaps most crucial, choices are posed that are too large, complex, important, uncertain, or comprehensive to be safely left to fallible

8 Kahn and Wiener, "Faustian Powers and Human Choice," p. 113.
9 Ibid.

humans, whether they are acting privately or publicly, individually or in organizations. . . . Choices, however, that become inescapable once these new capabilities have been gained.[10]

These aren't the only influential people suggesting that it would be more effective for us fallible human beings to leave the decision-making that controls how we live up to the computer. I, for one, do not want a computer determining what kind of world I am to live in. The next logical step would be for it to tell me what to do. I would then simply be another variable in the service of progress.

People too are changing. It would be unrealistic to assume that the enormous social, political, economic, and technological changes have not had a significant impact on all of us. Television, the pill, drugs, nuclear weapons, are only a few of the significant changes that have affected personal values, goals, expectations, and ways of relating to the world. These are changes of particular relevance to education. For the teacher it means understanding people who grew up in a markedly different world than their own. McLuhan has done some of the pioneering work in examining these differences.

> The young student today grows up in an electrically configured world. It is a world not of wheels but of circuits, not of fragments but of integral patterns. The student today *lives* mythically and in depth. At school, however, he encounters a situation organized by means of classified information. The subjects are unrelated: they are usually conceived in terms of a blueprint. The student can find no possible means of involvement for himself, nor can he discover how the educational scene relates to the "mystic" world of electronically processed data and experiences that he takes for granted.[11]

As Eric Trist points out, the contemporary environment is becoming increasingly characterized as a "turbulent field" as it moves into a new phase of development called the post-industrial society.[12] This turbulence is the result of both the increased complexity and size of the total relevant environmental field, as well as the increased interdependence of the parts and the unpredictable connections which arise between them as a result of the accelerating but uneven rate of change.

He is talking about what most of us have already experienced. It

[10] Ibid., p. 103.

[11] H. Marshall McLuhan, *Understanding Media: The Extension of Man* (New York: McGraw-Hill Paperback, 1965), p. vii; © 1964 by McGraw-Hill Book Company.

[12] Eric Trist, *The Relation of Welfare and Development in the Transition to Post-Industrialism* (Los Angeles: Socio-Technical Systems Division, University of California, 1967). See also chaps. 13, 15, 16 in *Towards a Social Ecology* by F. E. Emery and E. L. Trist (New York and London: Plenum Press, 1971).

doesn't take long in grappling with such problems as the war in Vietnam, poverty, and racial inequalities to feel the full impact of the enormous size and degree of complexity of our society. Trist goes on to say:

> This turbulence grossly increases the area of relevant uncertainty for individuals and organizations alike, and raises far reaching problems concerning the limits of human adaption. Forms of adaptation, both personal and organizational, developed to meet simpler types of environments no longer suffice to meet the higher levels of complexity now coming into existence.[13]

Trist makes the point that changes in social patterns are not only desirable, but absolutely necessary if we are to achieve a level of adaptability to a world of rapid technological change and characterized by repeated and protracted environmental crises. The new patterns he projects into a post-industrial world are not simply an idealistic vision but, in Kenneth Clark's phrase, "survival imperatives." The emergent patterns that Trist sees, particularly in cultural values and organizational philosophies, are remarkably congruent with the goals and demands of humanistic educators who have reached their conclusions from quite different points of view. A brief summary of Trist's proposals for adaptive changes follows.[14]

Changes in emphasis of social patterns in the transition to post-industrialism

Type	From	Toward
Cultural Values	Achievement Self-Control Independence Endurance of Distress	Self-actualization Self-expression Inter-dependence Capacity for Joy
Organizational Philosophies	Mechanistic forms Competitive relations Separate objectives Own resources regarded as owned absolutely	Organic forms Collaborative relations Linked objectives Own resources regarded also as society's
Ecological Strategies	Responsive to crisis Specific measures Requiring consent Short planning horizon Damping conflict Detailed central control Small local government units Standardized administration Separate services	Anticipative of crisis Comprehensive measures Requiring participation Long planning horizon Confronting conflict Generalized central control Enlarged local gov't units Innovative administration Coordinated services

In examining the question of what education can do to help individuals and the society as a whole to creatively and constructively adapt to

13 Ibid., p. 5.
14 Ibid., p. 34.

this rapidly changing technological environment, my own conclusions support those of Trist. In the following sections I would like to focus on two particular elements which I feel to be essential to bringing about the kinds of necessary change and central to any truly humanistic approach to education, the development of a more broadly informed and integrated intelligence and the ability and courage to make moral decisions.

THE DEVELOPMENT OF INTELLIGENCE

> A truly educated person is trained to mesh his intelligence with his feelings in a disciplined whole. He cannot deny or subordinate either his brain or his heart because each is essential to the effective functioning of the other. Our colleges must provide the opportunity for students to test their courage to stand alone, to accept the risk of alienation and aloneness that comes with the anguish and torture of the search for moral commitment and disciplined, intelligent action.... Wisdom and moral sensitivity tempering human intelligence are not now ethical abstractions, they are survival imperatives.[15]

What Kenneth Clark is saying is nothing new: it simply is not heard by those who make decisions about education or "miseducation," to use Paul Goodman's description. Not only is Clark not heard, his commitment to a reevaluation of educational goals is embarassing. His writing style is the antithesis to the traditional style of a professor writing about education; in this case, someone forgot to take out the emotion: words like courage, accept the risks, aloneness, anguish, torture, moral sensitivity, and commitment. Clark should be taken as an example: it's about time we all began talking about what happens to the whole person and quit naively assuming we need only concern ourselves with the cognitive-rational development of students.

Clark indicates that education today fails students in two major ways. First, education has mistakenly chosen to focus on the development of intellect (thought functioning independently of emotions), and not on the development of intelligence, which is the capacity to feel as well as to reason as an integrated individual. The second point he makes is that this capacity to deal with life as a whole person through moral and intelligent action is becoming a survival imperative in the face of a rapidly changing technological and social environment.

One of the most vehement antiintellectuals on the current scene is Eric Hoffer. The first time I read his *The Temper of Our Times*,[16] I really couldn't understand his dislike and mistrust of intellectuals. I excused it as

[15] Kenneth B. Clark, "Intelligence, the University, and Society," *The American Scholar* 36, no. 1 (Winter 1966–67): 32.

[16] Eric Hoffer, *The Temper of Our Times* (New York: Harper & Row, 1967).

his own form of snobbery. This may be partially true, yet I have come to understand that his is a very tenable warning against the overemphasis of academic detachment, scientific objectivity and general amoral positions on human struggle. It's the same perversion of only relying on "intellect" and not on "intelligence," the "hardness of heart of the educated" that worried Gandhi. And it seems to me that this very problem is at the crux of the problem with what is so loosely called education today.

I am not saying that all intellectuals are hardhearted rationalists, but that I do see these tendencies being reinforced as correct behavior in our schools. My own experience as a student of the behavioral sciences has forced me to confront the scientific values of objectivity and detachment. The result of this experience for me is again beautifully summarized by Kenneth Clark.

> How is it possible to study a slum objectively? What manner of human being can remain detached as he watches the dehumanization of other human beings? Why would one want to study a sick child except to make that child well?[17]

The detachment of many researchers reflects a value system that makes it possible for scientists to cut themselves off from the emotional and spiritual parts of themselves and from the world outside their laboratories. René Dubos is one of a growing number of scientists who are crying out in anger against a dehumanizing science. He along with others are not advocating doing away with science and technology and returning to more primitive states, but instead are working towards a more balanced integration between technology and humanitarianism.

> I should be expressing in the strongest possible terms my anguish at seeing so many human and natural values spoiled or destroyed in affluent societies, as well as my indignation at the failure of the scientific community to organize a systematic effort against the desecration of life and nature. Environmental ugliness and the rape of nature can be forgiven when they result from poverty, but not when they occur in the midst of plenty and indeed are produced by wealth. The neglect of human problems by the scientific establishment might be justified if it were due to lack of resources or of methods of approach, but cannot be forgiven in a society which can always find enough money to deal with the issues that concern selfish interests.[18]

> Scientists shy away from the problems posed by human life because these are not readily amenable to study by the orthodox methods of the natural

---

[17] Clark, "Intelligence, the University, and Society," p. 28.
[18] Dubos, *So Human an Animal,* p. 3.

sciences. For this reason, such problems are not likely to yield clear results and rapid professional advancement.[19]

I am sickened by a value system that justifies, to the destruction of other values, an amoral "science for science's sake," that only accepts scientific methodology as credible, that lauds objectivity and detachment to the exclusion of other human characteristics. For me, to do this is to lose touch with my humanity.

Many people have chosen to concern themselves only with the rational side of man because it is less threatening, more certain, and more controllable than the emotional. My point is that man is not solely a rational-cognitive being. To encourage people to believe this is not only grossly misleading, but detrimental to their capacity to develop as whole and creative individuals.

Education, as it is structured in most of our schools today, has failed to accurately integrate emotional development with intellectual development. We have unrealistically, and harmfully, separated out a person's rational capacities from the rest of his self. Even worse, we teach our children to keep their emotions out of their thinking, implying that personal emotions and feelings are less important and reliable than good, clear, rational logic.

Good decisions are based on good information. The assumption that rational-cognitive information is the only good information is built on an inaccurate perception of human behavior. This is an incredible state of things, for we know well, both through years of research and common experience that there are other kinds of relevant information that affect our thoughts and behavior—intuition, unconscious processes, feelings, emotions, extrasensory perceptions, as well as spiritual and mystical experiences. All of these elements when fused together make possible decisions and actions which open up the possibility of acting as full human beings. Modern education, nevertheless, has unrealistically fragmented man's learning and living processes and, worse, has chosen to emphasize only one part of an immensely complex human process.

The societal danger of this monomania of the rational can be well documented.

> There is a horrible example in history of what the Educated Society might easily become unless the university commits itself to the education of the whole man. It is the destruction of one of the world's greatest and most creative civilizations, the China of the T'ang and Sang period, by the imposition of a purely verbal, purely intellectual, purely analytical education on man and society, the Confucian Canon.
>
> Within a century, this commitment to the purely intellectual in man destroyed what had been the world's leader in art as well as in science,

19 Ibid., p. 216.

in technology as well as in philosophy. We are today in a similar danger—for we, too, tend, under the impact of the triumphs of organization and the analytical mind, to downgrade everything that is direct, immediate, and not verbal.[20]

When we limit knowledge by a reliance on external rational-cognitive proofs, we consider knowledge as an object or possession, something that we add to ourselves, and not as *part* of ourselves. I abhor this compartmentalization of the human effort. There will always be knowledge which we treat as external to ourselves (spelling and arithmetic, for instance), yet there is also learning which is not separate and common, but uniquely ours: learning that has been integrated into the unique values, emotions, goals and feelings that make up our personalities.

Knowledge, in this distinction, refers to ideas which require either empirical or logical validation. Learning refers to the sense persons make of these ideas within their own experience. Knowledge is something like the food; learning is like the act of eating and ingesting it. The source of ideas, however, may be either external or internal. If these ideas (or knowledges) emerge from the outside world they must then depend upon that outside world for their validity. That is, they must be supported, either rationally or empirically using references from the outside world. Sometimes however, ideas emerge from the inner recesses of our being. They emerge out of some process of thought and feeling, conscious and unconscious which we cannot trace. These ideas are also knowledge, and their validation only requires them to be meaningful within the persons unique experience. A person's intuitions and dreams are two sources of this kind of knowledge, and they are as valid and useful to the person as cognitive-rational knowledge. The education of the whole person requires learning to use both external and internal sources of knowledge. Our educational system is built on the valuing of the accumulation of extrinsic knowledge. Too often we judge ourselves and others in artifical and dehumanizing ways. For example, the lack of degrees or lack of high grades in no way affects the intrinsic value of a human being, but the identity crisis which results from not having them would certainly lead us to think otherwise.

Further, the assumption that the great scientific innovations and discoveries are based solely on technical and intellectual processes, is unsound. Again, we have been led to believe that it was Einstein's genius, implying some kind of extraordinary power quite apart from him as a person, like an especially large computer, which explains his discoveries. It was a lot more than information retention and manipulation; any com-

[20] Peter F. Drucker, "The Rise in Higher Education," in *The Revolutionary Theme in Contemporary Education,* ed. T. Ford (Lexington: University of Kentucky Press, 1965), p. 93.

puter is capable of doing that. Polanyi, physicist and philosopher, describes the point quite clearly in the following summary.

> So we see that both Kepler and Einstein approached nature with intellectual passions and with beliefs inherent in these passions, which led then to their triumphs and misguided them to their errors. These passions and beliefs were theirs, personally, even though they held them in the conviction that they were valid, universally, I believe that they were competent to follow these impulses, even though they risked being misled by them. And again, what I accept of their work as true today, I accept personally, guided by passions and beliefs similar to theirs, holding in my turn that my impulses are valid, universally, even though I must admit the possibility that they may be mistaken.[21]

The point Polanyi is making is that even scientific knowledge is personal; it is not something detached, but is intimately connected to the person who discovers it, as well as to the person who later uses it. He also points out and illustrates that these scientists who were extraordinarily creative and productive were so because they were able to make decisions in the absence of satisfactory knowledge, relying on hunches, intuition, faith, personal courage, self-confidence, and boldness of gambling.

Another important aspect of this creative process is commitment. Carl Rogers, in expanding Polanyi's point that personal knowledge is also committed knowledge, also uses Einstein as an example of what commitment is.

> In my judgment, commitment is something that one *discovers* within oneself. It is a trust of one's total reaction rather than of one's mind only. It has much to do with creativity. Einstein's explanation of how he moved toward his formulation of relativity without any clear knowledge of his goal is an excellent example of what I mean by the sense of commitment based on a total organismic reaction. . . . This commitment is more than a decision. It is the functioning of an individual who is searching for the directions which are emerging within himself.[22]

This kind of committed, organismic response represents the extension of human power to its furthest reach. It is the noncognitive elements which complete this process. Clearly, any realistic definition of intelligence must take into account the personal, nonrational elements of thought. And perhaps chief among these is commitment, for commitment is necessary if intellect is not to become uncreative, sterile, and potentially dysfunctional. It is the role of humanistic education to keep this need for the development of all the aspects of human intelligence clearly in focus.

[21] M. Polanyi, *Personal Knowledge* (Chicago: University of Chicago Press, 1958), p. 145.

[22] Carl Rogers, *Freedom to Learn* (Columbus, Ohio: Charles E. Merrill, 1969), p. 273.

TO ENCOURAGE MORAL DECISIONS BASED
ON PERSONAL AWARENESS

For me, the whole point of developing the capacity to integrate your feelings with your rational thinking is to be able to make moral decisions. It is this concept of moral man that Szasz describes as the central focus of his definition of humanistic psychology.

> To the extent that people have freedom of decision, and to that extent only, they live as moral beings. This, I use the term "moral" in the sense of choice or decision-making behavior, not in the sense of following a code of ethics.[23]

Szasz goes on to point out the similarity of this concept with Piaget's concept of the morality of the autonomous personality. This is in contrast to the morality of the heteronomous personality which depended on external sources for norms of conduct and control.

In addition, I choose to focus directly on the actual decision process because it has been my experience that talking about doing something and actually doing it are two different phenomena. A man tells me he feels the problem of the blacks and thinks that we should break down the racial barriers. This is what he says, but it is many times quite different from his actions when he becomes personally involved. It is only at the actual time of making a decision that our true feelings and attitudes emerge. Only at the point of decision do we get a true reading on our emotional reactions. It's one thing to predict how you will intellectually and emotionally respond. In reality your reaction may be an entirely different thing.

We learn in an integrated way through the actual experience of making decisions. It's a different, and I think a more important learning, than studying about the workings of various idealized models of reality. As the world around us changes at an increasingly faster rate, it becomes more critical to learn *how to make decisions,* than how to make the best decision. Educationally, this means an experimental and reality-based learning process which provides the opportunity to make choices instead of spending years studying how it is supposed to be done.

Another reason for my focus on personal decision-making is a growing realization that the problem of being able to have and feel the freedom of making decisions is at the crux of the adjustment problems modern man faces in a highly technological society. The work of Rollo May is the most

---

[23] T. Szasz, "Moral Man: A Model of Man for Humanistic Psychology," in *The Challenges of Humanistic Psychology,* ed. J. F. T. Bugental (New York: McGraw-Hill, 1967), p. 45.

relevant in describing the casualties of those who are unable to cope with a rapidly growing technological environment.

> Indeed, the central core of modern man's neurosis is the undermining of his sense of responsibility, the sapping of his will and his ability to decide. It is more than an ethical problem: the modern individual so often is convinced that even if he did exert his will—or whatever illusions passes for it—his actions would do no good. It is this inner experience of impotence that constitutes our critical problem.[24]

To me, the ability to make moral decisions is based on the personal awareness of who you are and what you want out of life and how these are affected by the environment in which you live. I am also personally concerned about the question of how we, as educators, choose to relate to what is happening in the world around us.

The problem with opening ourselves up to all that is happening around us, especially the negative aspects, is that it is easy to be overwhelmed. I have had to quit reading the front page sometimes because of the frustration and pain it had caused me. It takes a great deal out of me just to face the issues openly—to feel the full impact of their implications. To become overwhelmed and threatened by much of what is happening around us is common. Some of the resulting common defenses to such issues as the Vietnam war, police brutality, racial inequality, student unrest, etc., are simple black-and-white explanations, scapegoating, denials, rationalizations, idealism, and withdrawal from involvement.

Reality is seldom simple. Instead, it is like an endless web of complexly interwoven links, constantly changing at an increasing rate. As an example, look at the classroom: try to change the kind of education the children are getting. First, there is the problem of turning the kids on, which usually does not come naturally because all of us are well-trained and conditioned in another way of teaching and learning. Read *36 Children* by Herbert Kohl[25] to get some idea of the struggle one exceptional person had in turning on a few of his students. It wasn't easy for him or the children to adjust to this new way of relating.

How about the principal who steps in and has control over what you do in the classroom? There is also the local school board, and the wishes of the parents and the general public. In California, there is a Superintendent of Schools, the States Board of Education, and the governor. There is the reality of limited finances, required books, and tests, and externally established teacher-student ratios. There is also the realization of Kohl

---

24 Rollo May, "Love and Will," *Psychology Today* 3, no. 3 (1969): 47–48.
25 Herbert Kohl, *36 Children* (New York: Signet Books, 1968).

that just one year of teaching a child may not be enough to significantly affect his life.

So this is the picture of reality. It is a disgusting and potentially immobilizing reality. But there is another reality for me and that has to do with me as an individual. Aside from the rational weighing of the "realistic" possibilities of various actions, a more important and more subjective consideration is how *I* want to live my life. Subjective considerations, like subjective knowledge, carries its own special kind of validation. It is not so much what I eventually want to be or what I want to accomplish that requires subjective validation, but how I choose to confront and interact with the world: whether to be active or passive; whether to try to change it or give it up; whether to fight for what I want or go elsewhere; and, if necessary, test my courage to stand alone. I am not trying to be dramatic. This is way I experience my struggle to have an impact on the environment in which I live, and my validation of my subjective knowledge is attained when I achieve congruity between my beliefs and my action.

My value system says that it is better to see the world as it is than to ignore it. If you don't know what is going on, how can you do anything about it? I am not about to let other people make decisions which significantly influence my life. I am also saying that to be able to keep our eyes open means that we have to have the capacity to creatively and constructively cope with what we see. If it threatens you, it's only natural to implement some form of defense to protect yourself.

To bring all this back home, it seems that we—you and I—have to make choices about how we want to live and how we want our world to be. Because of the enormous complexity and increasing rate of change, these choices are becoming painfully difficult. The threat of feeling powerless, alienated, overwhelmed by the sheer size and inertia, as well as by the complexity and speed of change is real.

If one of the principle aims of humanistic education is to develop human beings capable of moral choice and action, then we as educators must be exemplars of that process. We must make those conscious choices of whether our lives are to be fragmented or unified, authentic or hypocritical, autonomously or heteronomously determined in the processes we hope to foster.

One thing which we must avoid is the kind of coping behavior which leads you to grab on to tangible products, things that you can understand and control: like teachers wanting "well-disciplined" and conforming children in their classroom—ones who don't cause trouble. It also leads us to gravitate toward unitory and quantifiable criteria, such as grades, for such intangibles as happiness and fulfillment.

Conformity is the enemy of education, and the attempts to achieve it are a defensive response to threatening complexity and uncertainty. Conforming is easily rationalized because it is more efficient to produce all shoes from one pattern than it is to produce ten million uniquely different shoes. It's called economy to scale—the more you produce of a product, the lower the cost of each item. You don't have to deal with new and different things because everything is the same. Conformity is an efficient and comfortable way of dealing with complexity and uncertainty, but costly in terms of individual freedom.

For a teacher to encourage individual freedom and to provide the frequent opportunities for choice makes the educational process a significantly more difficult enterprise. However, at the same time, it changes the process from pointless, boring, and value neutral (or negative) to something in which we can invest ourselves with a sense of dignity and worth.

The final goal, then, is to provide an educational setting in which the possibilities for choice are provided, in which the kinds of information needed for making these choices is available, and in which the support is provided which enables people to take the risk of choice, knowing that learning occurs as a result of failure as well as of success, and fearing neither. The current system of rewards and punishment based on right answers must be broken down, for it breeds the fear of failure which blocks individual risk-taking necessary for development and growth. It builds a dependence on authority figures to determine and dictate the speed and content of one's development and, in general, one's actions. It is training and conformity, not education. It assumes that individuals do not have within them the capacity to grow and develop or learn by themselves but, instead, require external motivation and direction. This, to me, is intellectual arrogance based on the fear of having to confront fully the true complexity, uncertainty, and emotionality of another human being.

It is clear that to protect against failure is, at the same time, to protect against success. The fear of failure immobilizes you, leading you to try only those things which are certain, not things which are new and uncertain and are on the frontiers of our development and learning. It must surely be evident that it is just that kind of willingness and ability to deal with the new and the uncertain that will be required of future generations.

How can we begin implementing these changes in education? I think it demands a large scale effort on the part of our entire school systems. Individual efforts, no matter how dedicated and successful, are not sufficient as long as the basic and predominant methods of the educational system remain unchanged. What is needed is for educational organizations to make drastic changes in their basic bureaucratic nature in order to accommodate and facilitate a more humanistic education. I can offer no panacea, but I can suggest one organizational form that looks the most promising and has already begun to prove its appropriateness in a variety of very large organizations.

ORGANIZATIONAL DEVELOPMENT:
AN ALTERNATIVE TO BUREAUCRACY

Educational institutions on the whole are bureaucracies. That is, they are predominantly characterized by the following:

1. A well-defined chain of command.
2. A system of procedures and rules for dealing with all contingencies related to work activities.
3. A division of labor based on specialization.
4. Promotion and selection based on technical competence.
5. Impersonality in human relations.[26]

At least two major problems result from the use of these fairly structured and rigid forms of organization. First, such organizations are contrary to the basic nature of teaching.

> ...teaching demands effective bonds between teacher and student which are foreign to the enactment of a bureaucratic office. Moreover, such relationships tend toward personal, i.e., particularistic, ties between teacher and student; yet the teacher must also judge the accomplishment of his student impersonally, i.e., universalistically. Thus, ...the intrinsic nature of teaching runs counter to the bureaucratic principle of school organization and that, paradoxically, to perform adequately in his office the teacher is forced to violate the rules of performance.[27]

Secondly, bureaucratic forms of organization are ill-adapted to the rapid change the environment now demands. As Bennis points out, it is a form more suited for the days of the Industrial Revolution than it is for today's complex and uncertain technological world.[28] The bureaucratic "machine model" is efficient in managing routine and predictable activities, but its basic rigid design fails in flexibly responding to rapid changes in its environment.

At an even more basic level, it seems incompatible that education, which focuses on the development of individuals who are open to change and who are able to creatively and constructively respond to a changing world, can occur in a bureaucratic structure which resists change and is basically reactive, rather than proactive to the problems of our society.

Organizational development emerged from the efforts of a number of

---

[26] Warren Bennis, *Organizational Development: Nature, Origins, and Prospects* (Reading, Mass.: Addison-Wesley, 1969), p. 19.

[27] E. E. Bidwell, "The School as a Formal Organization," in *Handbook of Organizations* (Chicago: Rand McNally, 1965), p. 979.

[28] Bennis, *Organizational Development.*

applied behavioral scientists to design a more viable organizational form for a rapidly changing industrial sector. It is a very recent approach to the human side of organizations. Basically, organizational development is a complex educational strategy intended to change the beliefs, attitudes, values, and structures of organizations so that they can better adapt to new technologies, markets, challenges, and the dizzying rate of change itself.[29] But, it is far more than this, for underlying its methods is the attempt to integrate individual needs for growth and development with organizational goals in order to make a more effective organization.

As Bennis points out, organizational development is built on three basic propositions:

> The first is an evolutionary hypothesis that every age develops an organizational form most appropriate to the genius of that age and that certain unparalleled changes are taking place which make it necessary to revitalize and rebuild our organizations.
>
> The second is that the only viable way to change organizations is to change this "culture," that is, to change the systems within which people work and live. A "culture" is a way of life, a system of beliefs and values, an accepted form of interaction and relating. Changing individuals, while terribly important, cannot yield the fundamental impact so necessary for the revitalization and renewal I have in mind—if our organizations are to survive and develop.
>
> Thirdly, a new *social* awareness is required by people in organizations along with its spiritual ancestor, *self*-awareness. Organizations are becoming collectively aware of their destiny and their path to guiding their destiny. This proposition asserts that social consciousness is more difficult to induce than personal awareness, but more essential in the kind of world we are living in.[30]

In comparison with the value system that underlies bureaucracies, organizational development offers alternative values which I think are basic to the process of humanistic education. Instead of the bureaucratic values which stress rational task-oriented behavior and deny humanistic and democratic values, organizational development stresses the importance of personal feelings, which are the basis of trustful and authentic relationships. Without such relationships, the organization as Argyris and Bennis[31] point out, becomes a breeding ground for mistrust, intergroup conflict, rigidity and other behavior destructive to both the effectiveness and growth of individuals and groups.

---

[29] Ibid., p. 2.

[30] Ibid., p. v.

[31] Warren Bennis, "Goals and Meta-Goals of Laboratory Training," *Human Relations Training News* 6, no. 3 (Fall 1966): 1–4.

Organizational development also offers a significant departure from current practices in its shift away from the traditional highly individualistic personal orientation which has characterized our educational and organizational systems toward a heightened awareness of collective goals and the subsequent refocusing of emphasis beyond the individual person or organization. It is basically an ecological approach. This represents a breakthrough in organizational thinking, one that offers some increased hope for the survival of our institutions in new and more appropriate forms.

In terms of its historical roots, organizational development grew out of a need for a more comprehensive and practical approach to organizational change than the use of sensitivity training groups. For this reason, much of the change methodologies involved in organizational development are focused at the interpersonal level and involve similar techniques and values as those in sensitivity training. Because of the focus placed on man's emotional life as opposed to the traditional educational strategy which focuses exclusively on man as a rational-cognitive being, it is highly controversial.

Overall organizational development, though it may contain sensitivity training as a part of its program, is much more balanced in considering both rational and emotional sides of man. It is more centered in reality —on real life and on-the-job problems—than sensitivity training. For example, two of the major components of organizational development are team-building and resolving intergroup conflict. In the first case, the goal is to help a group of people who normally work together become a more effective working team. In the second example, the goal is to resolve conflicts between groups that normally interact and depend on each other for certain services. Specifically, in an educational organization, such as a school, these could be a particular classroom, or subgroup in a classroom, which make up a learning team; or in the latter case it could be a group of teachers, administrators, and parents trying to resolve their conflicts and work out a more effective relationship.

The central assumption of organizational development—that educational strategies must deal with both the realities of man's rational side and his emotional side—is especially applicable to educational institutions. Even more important are the underlying values of organizational development. These are the basics that need to be internalized in order for any organizational development program to be successful. They are also values that, I think, should be a part of humanistic education. Some of them I have mentioned already. Others I have taken from Warren Bennis's list of metagoals, or values, of laboratory training and from Tannenbaum and Davis' paper, "Values, Man, and Organizations." (1969)[32]

[32] Bennis, Ibid.; R. Tannenbaum and S. Davis, "Values, Man, and Organizations," *Industrial Management Review* 10, no. 2 (Winter 1969): 67–86.

1. *To take a holistic view of man.* This means to move away from artificially and conveniently considering only specific fragments of the total person. There is more to the life of a student than his rational capacities, or the way he acts in school, or the scores he gets on tests. It means to do away with labels, such as "failure," "poor worker," "low motivation," "disadvantaged," which are handed down from teacher to teacher and become self-fulfilling prophecies.

2. *To move away from a view of man as essentially bad towards a view of him as originally and basically good. To move from the distrust of people to trusting them.* This implies getting away from the tightly controlled classrooms where education has become more discipline and coercion than discovering and creating. It is to rely on a child's natural motivation to learn, understand, and grow as a person, instead of on external motivations. It is to challenge the traditional forms of organizations that are designed to control, limit, push, check up on, inhibit, and punish persons assumed to be basically bad and untrustworthy.

3. *To move away from the avoidance and negative evaluation of individuals towards their confirmation as human beings.* When feedback is given to others (students), it is too often negative and destructive of the individual rather than focused on the perceived shortcomings of a given performance. For example, grades become a reflection of a person's general worth as a human being: "good boys" get good grades and do what the teacher tells them. At a more mechanical level, it is widely accepted in psychology that positive reinforcement leads to better results than does negative reinforcement. Confirmation is positive in nature, but is far more significant than a positive reward or reinforcement. It is to deeply care about and confirm the basic humanity of another person that supercedes normative judgements about personal differences.

4. *To move from resisting and even fearing individual differences towards accepting and creatively drawing out and utilizing them.* This is in the spirit of the original definition of education, which is to draw out the uniqueness of an individual and opposed to the usual definition, which is closer to training for conformity. The process of accepting and utilizing individual differences is much more difficult, but necessary, for it lies at the very heart of democracy.

5. *To achieve authenticity in interpersonal relations.* This implies a relationship that enables each party to feel free to be himself. This relationship, in turn, implies more open and honest communications. The value of authenticity encourages individuals to be themselves and to communicate inwardly and with others as freely as possible.

6. *To move from a primary emphasis on competition to a greater emphasis on collaboration.* Here the traditional authoritarian teacher-student relationship is minimized, and participation, involvement, and the self-direction of students are encouraged. In this spirit of collaboration, both teachers and students become learners. Learning to work with people, instead of against them, in the solution of a problem, is an important skill to apply to the massive and complex problems that are emerging in our society.

7. *To have a spirit of inquiry.* One element of this is to approach problems with a hypothetical spirit, a feeling of tentativeness and caution, and respect for probable error. Another is experimentation, the willingness to expose ideas and positions to retesting and modification. At the core is the willingness to risk oneself, to be open to error and change, both essential qualities of creativity and growth.

8. *To expand consciousness and choice.* The educational process should be designed to create conditions that encourage a person to think about his behavior, to expand his consciousness and awareness of human phenomena, and to think about how he chooses to act and live. The basic assumption is that knowledge makes men free and allows them to choose and follow their own destinies.

I have purposely left out the mechanical details of various organizational development techniques and leave that to those who are more experienced and qualified to do so. Moreover, it is my feeling that it is the internalization of the underlying values, and not necessarily the inclusion of particular structures and techniques, that is important. I make this point because there always seems to be those who adopted the techniques, but who do not fully adopt and live the underlying values. The techniques and methodologies should be continually changing and improving, and are thus always secondary or intermediate goals in the educational process.

The goals of organizational development, particularly as applied to schools, is the creation of a structure and environment which makes possible the emergence of more autonomously functioning individuals who, at the same time, are able to work toward collective ends. It is just such people that are desperately needed to deal with the grave crises that are our daily companions. It is the development of these skills that will enable us to use technology effectively to combat our problems. Technology *is* a weapon in our struggle to find ways of dealing with the enormous difficulties besetting us. But, unless we can educate people who can effectively wield that weapon, it may just as easily be turned against us as against our adversaries— pollution, maldistribution, social disorganization, and a generalized dehumanization of our environment.

TOWARD A MORE HUMANISTIC EDUCATION

By way of conclusion, I would like to take a final look at humanistic education, not as a necessary corrective to enable us to deal with a world in crisis, but as a human process. It is really a reminder of what to me is a crucial point: that the final achievement of the goals of humanistic education are reached only by the quality of life that infuses the educational process. And that, of course, is the quality of the people who participate in it.

Humanistic education, at its best, is an attempt to encourage the growth and learning of all those involved—students, faculty, and admin-

istrators. The focus is on the people and relationships involved in the educational process, such that a course or curriculum may only be considered humanistic to the degree that the persons involved—teachers and students—are fully human.

To design and structure a humanistic curriculum or a humanistic school is the wrong approach. Rather, we should focus on the development of educators who are more humanistic, allowing them, in turn, to design their own schools and curricula: This is because humanistic education is essentially a human process, guided more by transcending values than by the accomplishment of specific behavioral objectives. Seen in this light, humanistic education is clearly not just teaching more "humanistic subjects." Humanistic education can neither be simply another technique, or a curriculum revision. It is rather, requiring of a teacher that he be a fully functioning human being, one who has

> ...experienced optimal psychological growth—a person functioning freely in all the fullness of his organismic potentialities: a person who is dependable in being realistic, self-enhancing, socialized, and appropriate in his behavior; a creative person, whose specific forms of behavior are not easily predictable; a person who is ever changing, ever developing, always discovering himself and the newness in himself in each succeeding moment of time.[33]

For most teachers, this does not require that they teach something new in a new way as much as it requests that they be more fully themselves. That, to me, is humanistic education.

Finally, humanistic education implies the holding of deep-seated values. The simple statement of a belief in a set of values, however intellectually and emotionally defensible and defended, is not adequate. The level of communication is, in large part, dictated by the level of concern for, and commitment to, these values. Catechism does not create Christians, and the mindless repetition of slogans of the mechanical application of "humanistic" techniques do not make humanistic educators. Men learn from men. They are unmoved by professional or mechanical excellence, but respond to the embodiment of professed values as they take concrete form in another person's life. William Arrowsmith's comments on the decline of teaching in the humanities makes an excellent summary of what is needed in humanistic education.

> It is men we need, not programs. It is possible for a student to go from kindergarten to graduate school without ever encountering a *man*—a man who might for the first time give him the only profound motivation for learning, the hope of becoming a better man. Learning matters, of

[33] Rogers, *Freedom to Learn*, p. 295.

course; but it is the means, not the end, and the end must always be either radiantly visible, or profoundly implied, in the means. It is only in the teacher that the end is apparent; he can humanize, because he possesses the human skills which give him the power to humanize others. If that power is not felt, nothing of any educational value can occur. The humanities stand or fall according to the human worth of the man who professes them.[34]

In the final analysis, the success of a humanistic education rests primarily on the presence of humanistic teachers. It is not the techniques you know, nor the material you have available; it is how fully human you are in your interaction with students. We must unlock ourselves from the dependence on rigid curriculums, assignments, and other designed experiences. They all assume that we need external structures and motivations to facilitate learning and growth. We must give up that complete sense of responsibility for a child's learning, and give the child a chance to respond, to begin developing his potential, to get turned-on, to live.

[34] William Arrowsmith, "The Future of Teaching," *Journal of Higher Education* 38, no. 3 (March 1967): 133.

9

educational research

Philip Reidford

PHILIP REIDFORD is for me—and this was as surprising to me as it might be to you—the most difficult of all the authors to describe, since he is a very dear friend. Why that is I'm not really sure. It may be a case of missing the forest because of the trees. It is also possible that so much of what I see in Phil, I see in myself, and consequently dismiss it as right or natural. This is certainly egocentric, but still explanatory. Another reason why Phil is quite difficult for me to describe is because his personality is built up by contradictions rather than consistencies. It's one thing to make sense of patterns, but quite another to find a pattern in inconsistencies. Let me try to explain this.

My first important encounter with Phil was the time I was able, with his help, to talk him out of quitting his job and going to India to talk with the people in the streets of Calcutta. We agree to this day that it was right that he shouldn't have gone at the time since he had not yet learned the possibilities for humanistic living in the university. He may decide, and soon, that these possibilities are exhausted, but he agreed he needed to discover this for himself.

Phil has only recently, like a seesaw, settled at his balance point after years of going up and down between belief and disbelief, conscience and form, acceptance and outrage. More than most of us—because, in part, he had received a "gentleman's" education—he found it difficult to accommodate his personal needs and desires to the requirements of formal bureaucratic living. He had been taught style, and learned it well. It was hard to give up.

Phil ran away from the United States for a couple of years, running away from college and from the traditional expectations of his family. He went to Sicily in search of a saint and worked there with the people in an educational capacity. His thoughts turned back towards the United States and towards further education when he decided he could not help children very much with good will alone. He did not know then, as he does now, that he was closer to doing the kind of job he envisioned, with no degrees at all, than he was after he completed his Ph.D. in educational psychology.

Phil's humanistic perspective, at least in the chapter on research, is one that asks us, as researchers in education, to do something important. What is important is what helps people learn better and become better human beings. He suggests a number of strategies that researchers might use to guarantee that what they do is useful. They are often difficult strategies, but important research, like important human growth, only occurs after great effort.

Finally, I would like to point out that Phil did not find this task highly rewarding. He found it difficult, laborious, frustrating. It is difficult to talk about research in a humanistic way, since almost no researchers that I know have been able to integrate their definition of persons as human beings with the researcher's definition of them as subjects, like rats in a maze. But, like the ethical man he is, he attempted to give a faithful presentation of the research activity, reserving his humanistic interests for emphasizing the utility of the task. He might have gone further—as I probably would have, except I don't know the basic routines of research as well as he does—to say something about the possibility that research, trying to deal with persons objectively can never be valid in the humanistic sense. That is, when you equate what a person does with what he is, what he says with what he thinks, what he is with what he feels then you have replaced the living person by the researcher's symbolic representation of him.

Although Phil is not far from this position, he is not sure he wants to get closer. He has recently stated his belief that science is science and life is life, and it is quite possible to believe in both as long as you don't think one has anything to do with the other. This, too, has been part of his balancing act. In the classroom he has been known to lecture and run encounter groups in the same week, and in between, turn students on to making films and taping the sounds of life that we never hear unless we tune in. His academic survival is very touch and go, but like the others who put their jobs on the line to live with integrity, he is discovering his goal by the posture that it takes to get there.

In contemporary society there is something mystical about the word research. It implies that what researchers are doing is worthwhile but even more, it suggests that only a select few can do it. This mystique about research is unfortunate, for it tends to prevent the careful assessment of the value of research, both to the realm of ideas and to the betterment of the human condition. This is especially true of educational research which, I believe, has been mostly worthless, contributing little to the improvement of the teaching-learning process. It is one thing, however, to deplore the present state of research but quite another to dismiss its potential value.

FAILURE OF EDUCATIONAL RESEARCH

There seem to be two primary reasons why educational research does not improve the condition of education. The first is that most educational researchers do not understand what research does. The second is that most educational researchers are preoccupied in either testing hypotheses whose validity is already known through common sense, or whose results have so little transfer value to similar situations that their findings are worthless. What is generally called educational research is usually a form of *hypothesis testing;* that is, the researcher forms a hypothesis about a phenomenon or a certain set of phenomena and then designs an experiment to test the validity of the hypothesis. In obtaining the results of this hypothesis testing, the researcher is able to state with some certainty whether his hypothesis should be accepted or rejected. As the evaluator of such a piece of research, you must decide if you accept the findings. Such acceptance is predicated on a long list of "ifs."

(1) *If you believe that the experiment actually tested the hypothesis in question, you may accept the findings.* What is meant here is that the design of the experiment may not be appropriate for the measurement of the hypothesis in question. For example, in a series of experiments in 1901, Thorndike and Woodworth tried to show that training in one mental function does not really improve performance in another related function.[1] This research was undertaken because of the transfer-of-learning point of view held by many educators in the late 1800s and the early 1900s: if children learned certain disciplines, especially Latin and arithmetic, their abilities to learn other subjects, as well as their powers of thinking in general, would be improved. The first step in investigating this question was to find out if one mental function influenced another—function being defined as ability to do spelling, multiplication, etc. Without going into the

---

[1] E. Thorndike, and R. Woodworth, "The Influence of Improvement in One Mental Function upon the Efficiency of Other Functions, *Psychological Review* 8 (1901): 247–61, 384–95, 553–64.

details of the studies, the summary statement made by Thorndike and Woodworth was:

> "The general attitude which comes from the examination of all the facts we have demonstrated, a set of precisely formulated judgments, is what we have aimed to produce."[2]

It might be pointed out, however, that this general attitude was formed on the basis of data of five subjects in the first experiment. It is a statistical fact and good common sense that a small number of people used for an experiment may not truly represent the population at large. The results that Thorndike and Woodworth found, therefore, may simply represent idiosyncratic response patterns on the part of his subjects. Moreover, a later work by Harlow clearly indicates transfer of training between similar tasks and between dissimilar tasks—learning how to learn.[3]

(2) *If the subjects used in the experiment were representative of the population for whom the hypothesis was designed, you may accept the findings.* For example, Edward Tolman, a famous rat psychologist, wrote an article in 1947 entitled "Cognitive Maps in Rats and Men."[4] Based on some of his and others' rather extensive experimentation with rats, he draws some conclusions about human behavior from the findings of experiments on rat behavior. Such extrapolation of findings of the behavior of rats to the behavior of humans is a dangerous affair. Since humans have highly developed communication and cognitive systems, which rats don't even begin to approximate, applying findings of experiments on one species to another is of dubious value. I cannot accept Tolman's conclusions, for I do not believe that the sample of rats he experimented on is representative of the human population to which he generalized his findings. Although this example is an extreme one, it holds equally true where experimental findings on boys are extrapolated to girls.

(3) *If you believe that the statistical measures used to find out whether the hypothesis was substantiated or rejected were the appropriate ones, you may accept the findings.* The applicability of appropriate statistical models for certain data is often ignored. That is to say, each statistical model has certain rules that govern its use. If a statistic is used inappropriately, then the findings obtained are obviously questionable. In order to be able to determine the inappropriate application of statistics, you need to have a fairly sophisticated understanding of stochastic models.

---

2 Ibid., p. 563.

3 H. Harlow, "The Formation of Learning Sets," *Psychological Review* 56 (1949): 51–65.

4 E. Tolman, *Behavior and psychological man* (Berkeley: University of California Press, 1966) pp. 241–64.

(4) *If you believe that the confidence interval of the statistical tests used were set at a stringent enough limit, you may accept the findings.* In behavioral sciences, answers to experimental questions that involve statistical tests are reported as probabilities of occurrence or nonoccurrence. It is, therefore, the responsibility of the researcher to decide and report what probability of occurrence will be acceptable to him. It is common for the experimenter to specify a .01 or .05 significance level. In doing so, he is simply saying that if the data indicates that the figures obtained will occur by chance only 1 percent of the time or only 5 percent of the time, then he will accept the findings of his data at the specified level as giving support for the hypothesis. There is always the danger that the experimenter will reject his findings because he has made the confidence interval or significance level too stringent: this is called a Type 1 error. What happens in this case is that the experimenter rejects findings which in fact verify his hypothesis. The other danger is that he will set the confidence interval too low and accepts data as confirming his hypothesis when in fact they do not: this is called a Type 2 error.[5] So you see that these ifs, and many others which could be posed, make the outcome of any piece of research questionable to some and acceptable to others.

Confirmation of research vs truth

Research is only one of several ways by which man is able to obtain some kind of beliefs about his world and this last statement is what most educational researchers do not understand. It is common folly among many of the so-called hardnose researchers to believe that the empirical way of evaluating information is the only way of arriving at truth. All other ways are discounted as subjective and, therefore, worthless ways to deal with questions. Popper, in a book dealing with the growth of scientific knowledge, presents an argument against the mere testing of theories through hypothesis testing.[6] Popper's position is that the scientific method as described by Bacon and his admirers is rarely the way in which significant theories are formulated. He goes on to make the point that confirmations of a theory are easy to come by. Let me try to explain what he means. The inductive method of science, as described by Bacon, says that all science stats from observation. After observations have been made, hypotheses are formulated based on these observations. The hypotheses are then subjected to experimental testing and the ones confirmed begin to form a basis for the construction of a theory. The function of this inductive process is to

[5] For a more complete discussion of this topic, see W. Hays, *Statistics for psychologists* (New York: Holt, Rinehart and Winston, 1963), pp. 287–293.

[6] K. Popper, *Conjectures and Refutations* (New York: Harper & Row, 1963).

explain why scientific statements are true. Two factors mitigate against the value of this procedure. The first is that in the experimental testing of the hypothesis, the answers we obtain are not truths but only probability statements. Moreover, subsequent falsification of theories that were previously formulated and tested in the Baconian fashion exemplify the dangers of strict reliance on the scientific method for the formulation and testing of theories.

Another reason why research has not improved the condition of education—and to my mind a more important one—is that in science we are trying to find the laws of the universe—we are trying to give our world some order by finding what we hope to be the regularity inherent in the system. The value of finding this regularity resides in our use of laws to be able to predict outcomes of certain phenomena with the possibility, especially in education, of being able to modify those outcomes. Now if we rely strictly on observation to form our hypotheses and theories, we will be neglecting many powerful tools for obtaining notions about our universe— guesses, conjectures, and reason. In Baconian science, the expectancy is to find truth through observation, hypothesis formulation, hypothesis testing and confirmation. Popper's approach is also to find truth, but the expectancy that he holds is far more skeptical. Therefore, using his point of view, you get an idea, guess, conjecture and you test it, fully expecting it to be disconfirmed. The experiment, therefore, is one of the many critical tools which one can bring to bear on a scientific idea. This is a rationalist's approach.

> The rationalist tradition, the tradition of critical discussion, represents the only practicable way of expanding our knowledge—conjectural or hypothetical knowledge, of course. There is no other way. More especially, there is no way that starts from observation or experiment. In the development of science observations and experiments play only the role of critical arguments. And they play this role alongside other, nonobservational arguments. It is an important role; but the significance of observations and experiments depends entirely upon the question whether or not they may be used to criticize theories.[7]

This point of view, therefore, gives far more importance to the role of ideas and the ways in which theories are stated than to hypothesis-testing truth-seeking.

Traditionally, educational research has used hypothesis testing as a way to make science. The point is that hypothesis testing, if you take the rationalist point of view, is merely a critical tool which is brought to bear on a scientific idea. I myself fully endorse the use of hypothesis testing and observation in the examination of a theory in education but the use of hypothesis testing to formulate a theory seems like an uneconomical, if not

---

[7] Ibid., pp. 151–52.

an impossible, way to proceed. There are very few theories about in education. However, for an idea of what a fairly comprehensive one might look like, a perusal of Ausubel's theory of verbal learning would be worthwhile.[8] I will examine a summary of reading studies by Chall that tends to support this opinion.[9]

Nonproductive educational research

The second most obvious and wasteful fault of educational research is the preoccupation with hypotheses whose experimental outcome is self-evident. A good example is the study by Wright and Taylor in which they tested the notion of which was more effective in the learning and retention of materials, massed practice or distributive practice.[10]

The concepts of massed and distributive practice refer to the way in which material to be learned is rehearsed. Distributive practice indicates that material is learned over a period of time and that there are time intervals or rest periods between learning sessions. Massed practice indicates that material is learned all at one sitting. In experiments which investigate these phenomena it is often the case that different degrees of massed and distributive practice are given. That is, the experimenter may operationally define massed practice as ten twenty-minute practice sessions, with a two-minute rest period between each, and distributive practice as some kind of practice schedule which exceeds the massed practice schedule in the length of rest periods. As an aside, it should be noted that there are almost infinite variations possible in the design of such an experiment. This possibility offers the experimenter an opportunity to do lots of experiments and hence get lots of research articles published but, at the same time, provides little new information that will change educational practice. Moreover, one hardly needs experimental confirmation of the relative merit of massed versus distributive practice, when, in fact, any college sophomore could have told the experimenters that one retains information learned during cramming sessions for a shorter period of time and with less accuracy than one retains and reproduces information learned over a longer period of time. Notwithstanding the obvious answer to such questions, many educational researchers spend their lives examining them.

Another wasteful practice is the undertaking of research on a problem which, because of a possible range of conditions, has not applicability to past research, to future research, or to any theory or problem. The bulk of research on reading exemplifies this approach. For example, Chall's book

8 D. Ausubel, *The Psychology of Meaningful Verbal Learning* (New York: Grune & Stratton, 1963).

9 Jeanne Chall, *Learning to Read* (New York: McGraw-Hill, 1967).

10 S. Wright, and D. Taylor, "Distributed Practice in Verbal Learning and the Maturation Hypothesis," *Journal of Experimental Psychology* (1949): 527–31.

describes research studies primarily on the effectiveness of different kinds of methods of teaching reading. The conclusions of her book on the studies she reviewed are little more than tentative. As she says, "One of the most important things, if not the most important thing, I learned from studying the existing research on beginning reading is that it says nothing consistently."[11] One reason for this tentativeness is the lack of comparability between the studies. Here are some of the differences that prevent comparability between them: Some studies use one age range; others, another. Some equate the children in the control and experimental groups for IQ; others do not. Some run reading instruction for six months; others run it for four months. Some use readers with one kind of material; others, with another kind. Some studies measure reading performance using the Nelson Denny reading test; others use a homemade test. This list does not really present an accurate picture of comparing several studies. Usually a study has more than one variable that is different in another. Chall also cites many other factors that account for the lack of information to be gained from reading studies. Since this kind of research offers us little information of either a positive or negative nature, it does not aid us in deciding what reading method to use with what children under what conditions—all of which makes it a perfect example of Popper's science of infinite regress.

An alternative to failure

In one of the most enlightening papers on the subject of educational research, Bereiter makes the point that the lack of revelatory information gained for educational practice through experimental research resides not in the research methods used, but in the kinds of things investigated. As Bereiter indicates, the testing or construction of a theory through research is impossible, for "the simple truth is that after six decades of educational research we do not know enough about anything to base a theory on."[12] He goes on to make the point that the selection of a problem, because it is interesting (basic research), or because there is a pressing need (applied research), is an inadequate way to make any breakthrough in the investigation of the problems which a teacher has in the classroom. For example, the critical points to investigate are not the classroom problems per se, but ideas designed to solve them. And it should be noted that such ideas rarely have emerged from observations.

Consider the present educational failure of schools in urban ghetto areas, and consider the present examples of research aimed to solve such

11 Chall, *Learning to Read*, p. 87.

12 C. Bereiter, "Issues and Dilemmas in Developing Training Programs for Educational Researchers," in *The Training and Nurture of Educational Researchers,* ed. E. Guba and S. Elam (Bloomington, Ind.: Phi Delta Kappa, 1965), p. 97.

problems. First, there are those studies which deal with the educational problems of so-called ghetto children by making a theoretical statement. Such studies generally start with the theoretical statement that ghetto children are different than middle class children in achievement in some way or another—typical differences stated are reading or language. There are a host of descriptive studies which attempt to specify why and how these children are different.[13]

A descriptive study of the type mentioned here is one that seeks to pinpoint the differences over a range of characteristics of a population which appear to be different from the normal population. Test designers often wish to specify what the normal response to each item on their test is. In order to ascertain this, a sampling of responses is made on a population—usually middle class. If the test is to be standardized using normalized scores, the mean and standard deviation for the test scores are then calculated. Mean simply refers to the average of all the test scores. Standard deviation is a measure of the spread of the scores. Having performed these calculations, the test constructor can then specify what scores fall significantly above or below the mean for his population. A normal population, therefore, is one which has scores on a particular test that are not significantly different from the mean of the scores on that test.

If an experimenter finds, therefore, that the subjects whom he samples have a mean score significantly different from the mean scores on the standardized test, he can say that his sample is abnormal, and that differences do exist. For example, John's study examined patterns of verbal and cognitive behavior in 174 Negro children from three different social class backgrounds.[14] Her findings indicated that children from middle class backgrounds performed at more advanced levels than the children from the upper lower and lower classes.

Then there are a few studies that attempt to explain such differences theoretically.[15] In an article published in 1961, Bernstein outlined the importance of language in the socialization process. He presented a linguistic theory to explain social class differences in language structure which might account for differences in cognitive, social and affective development between social classes. Briefly, he proposed that there are two linguistic codes, elaborated and restricted. Most middle class children learn both codes whereas most lower class children learn only the restricted code:

[13] See especially, M. Deutsch, "The Role of Social Class in Language Development and Cognition," *American Journal of Orthopsychiatry* 35, (1965): 78–88 and Vera John, "The Intellectual Development of Slum Children," *American Journal of Orthopsychiatry* 33 (1963): 813–22.

[14] John, Ibid.

[15] B. Bernstein, "Social Class and Linguistic Development," in *Education, Economy and Society*, ed. A. Halsey, J. Flond, and C. Anderson (New York: Free Press, 1961), pp. 288–314.

Elaborated code is grammatically more complex, allows for elaboration of meaning and subjective feelings, and points to the possibilities inherent in a complex conceptual hierarchy for the organizing of experience. Restricted code is simple grammatically and does not allow precise statement of ideas or emotions. It is a language in which much meaning is assumed or implicit.[16]

In an experiment published subsequent to this article, Bernstein tested his theory.[17] His major predictions were confirmed by this experiment. Unfortunately, such confirmation goes only one step beyond the idea of individual differences and the concurrent remedy individualized instruction by pinpointing one of the exact differences, it doesn't tell us what to do about it.

Finally, there are the intervention studies which test strategies designed to offset the cognitive skill deficiencies, i.e. Bereiter and Engelmann.[18] The term intervention to the educational measure or other prescription which has been designed to improve a child's performance in some specific area such as reading. These are based either on some theoretical position or on some hunch. What is generally found in the last group of studies (the ones which might effect educational practice) is that some children do better because of the intervention and some do not.[19] However, even the children who have benefited from the one intervention strategy rarely continue to progress at a satisfactory rate in succeeding grades.[20] Hence we are left where we started—at the age-old and current problem in education: some children benefit more from some kinds of educational practices than others.

What Bereiter proposes as an alternative to the kinds of research described above is research based on a different kind of hypothesis. He states:

The weak inference pattern allows contrary hypothesis to survive side by side for generations. For instance, the hypothesis that readiness for reading depends on the myelination of neone fibers and the hypothesis that it depends on the acquisition of prerequisite skills lead to the same predicted age for readiness, and so they can peacefully coexist.[21]

16 Ibid., p. 82.
17 B. Bernstein, "Linguistic Codes, Hesitation Phenomena, and Intelligence," *Language and Speech* 5, no. 1 (1962): 31–46.
18 C. Bereiter and S. Engelmann, *Teaching Disadvantaged in the Preschool* (Englewood Cliffs, N. J.: Prentice-Hall, 1966).
19 Phillip Reidford, "Recent Developments in Preschool Education," in *Psychology and Early Childhood Education,* ed. D. Brison and Jane Hill (Toronto: Ontario Institute for Studies in Education, 1968), pp. 5–16.
20 M. Wolf and Anna Stein, "Head Start Six Months Later," *Phi Delta Kappan* 48 (March 1967): 349–50.
21 C. Bereiter, "Issues and Dilemmas in Developing Training Programs for Educational Researchers," p. 105.

The basic difference between a *weak inference hypothesis* and a *strong inference hypothesis* is that in testing the former, one has a fairly high degree of certainty that the hypothesis will be confirmed before it is tested, whereas in the latter it is extremely doubtful that the outcome will be as predicted, for this last reason. This differentiation is congruent with the position on the value of theories as stated by Popper. The following are his seven conclusions as to what constitutes a scientifically sound theory:

1. It is easy to obtain confirmations, or verifications, for nearly every theory—if we look for confirmations.
2. Confirmations should count only if they are the result of *risky predictions;* that is to say, if, unenlightened by the theory in question, we should have expected an event which was incompatible with the theory—an event which would have refuted the theory.
3. Every "good" scientific theory is a prohibition: it forbids certain things to happen. The more a theory forbids, the better it is.
4. A theory which is not refutable by any conceivable event is non-scientific. Irrefutability is not a virtue of a theory (as people often think) but a vice.
5. Every genuine *test* of a theory is an attempt to falsify it, or to refute it. Testability is falsifiability; but there are degrees of testability: some theories are more testable, more exposed to refutation, than others; they take, as it were, greater risks.
6. Confirming evidence should not count *except when it is the result of a genuine test of the theory;* and this means that it can be presented as a serious but unsuccessful attempt to falsify the theory. (I now speak in such cases of "corroborating evidence.")
7. Some genuinely testable theories, when found to be false, are still upheld by their admirers—for example, by introducing *ad hoc* some auxiliary assumption, or by reinterpreting the theory *ad hoc* in such a way that it escapes refutation. Such a procedure is always possible, but it rescues the theory from refutation only at the price of destroying, or at least lowering, its scientific status. (I later described such a rescuing operation as a *"conventionalist twist"* or a *"conventionalist stratagem."*) One can sum up all this by saying that *the criterion of the scientific status of a theory is its falsifiability, or refutability, or testability.*[22]

If the hypothesis is confirmed, the result will be something of an information breakthrough. For example, if we tested the notion that children of comparable ability would perform better in a classroom that was poorly lighted and the hypothesis were substantiated we would simply obtain a positive correlation between good lighting conditions and performance—weak inference. However, no one would be surprised. Moreover, such a correlation would not lead to any revolution in the teaching-learning process.

[22] K. Popper, *Conjectures and Refutations,* pp. 36–37.

As Bereiter says,

> The choice between weak and strong inference patterns is not a matter of truth but a matter of economy. Weak hypotheses are simply not worth bothering with regardless of how attractive they may be.[23]

A researcher who tests strong inference hypotheses does several very important things for educational research. He cuts down on the volume of research studies which appear in technical journals whose findings have no effect upon educational practice. He encourages risk taking in research, for the probability of his investigations being confirmed is extremely low. Since the probability of his hypothesis testing is low, a confirmation of one of his experiments should provide information of a revelatory nature; that is, his finding might not concur with the opinions commonly held about it and therefore a positive result would force a change of thinking and practice about the phenomenon in question. However, the major effect of encouraging research that tests strong inference hypothesis should be to put a high premium upon divergent thinking in educational research.

Reasons for low risk research

At the present time, people in two types of institutions conduct the bulk of educational research: government-financed educational research organizations, and universities. The former usually have a specific area of focus; for example, the Southwest Regional Laboratory (SWRL) devotes a good deal of effort to the *development* of language and reading programs for public schools. These programs are tested in a selected sample of schools and once their effectiveness has been found satisfactory, the programs are adapted for wider dissemination. This is one very common type of research being done in education. It is improbable that any major breakthough in educational ideas or practices will result from it, although a general upgrading of the quality of content and instructional techniques may well take place. The point is that this kind of curriculum research is a response to a need. School officials are unhappy with the progress of many students in reading, and organizations such as SWRL try to prepare programs to increase the rate and quality of children's reading progress. It should be emphasized that such product development and testing is far from revolutionary practice. Such research could be put into the category of the science of infinite regress. The development of, say, better reading programs (better as measured by criterion- or norm-referenced tests) is a worthwhile endeavor. Nonetheless, no evidence exists that shows that any particular cur-

---

23 Bereiter, "Issues and Dilemmas in Developing Training Programs for Educational Researchers," p. 105.

riculum package dramatically reverses the high failure rate evidenced by minority group students in any particular subject. It is highly probable that a significant proportion of our school population will continue to fail until a new idea which dramatically revises the face of educational practices is thought of.

It is of interest to assess why this condition prevails in such institutions and why, therefore, such government financed educational research does little to improve substantially the teaching-learning process. Both Federal and State governments operate on a year to year fiscal policy, and usually ask for an accounting of sponsored institutions on a yearly basis. The rationale, of course, is that these institutions should have something to show for the government money which they have spent each year. Reports prepared by such institutions for the government are scrutinized by the government granting agency which, in turn, must make this information available to the taxpayers' representatives. This practice is probably the major reason why strong inference hypothesis research is not popular with government-financed educational research organizations, with the government, or the people. All concerned want or need some evidence that the year's expenditure has resulted in some tangible improvement in education. In my estimation, the product improvement or process improvement is hardly what will make a major difference in education, but all parties concerned are caught up in this dilemma of accountability.

The situation is equally unproductive in the universities, but for different reasons. In most of the major schools of education in this country, faculty members are hired primarily to conduct research. Their jobs depend on the research articles they publish; hence the phrase "publish or perish." Generally, evaluations of a faculty member's status is conducted yearly or every two years. What is assessed is the quality and quantity of articles published. Dependent on this evaluation is the future of the faculty member —his job, pay raises, and promotion. Few educational research journals are interested in publishing studies whose results indicate that the hypothesis investigated has not been confirmed. Hence, strong inference hypotheses do not have much popularity among most educational researchers in universities. The logical question is, why don't such people conduct strong inference research after they have been promoted to tenured positions? There seem to be two reasons for this: the first is money, and the second is habituation. Without a steady stream of published studies, even after one achieves a tenured position, the chances of salary increases are diminished. As is usual in an academic career, three to four years of research production are required before a faculty member is considered for tenure. If someone spends his graduate education years—usually four—and then four more doing weak inference research, it is doubtful he will suddenly switch to strong inference just because he has gained tenure.

Methodology in research

Before we get into examples of strong inference hypotheses and the ways in which I believe the present practices in education could be radically changed by research, a brief lament on the uses of methodologies and statistics is in order. Two common kinds of studies are often undertaken in behavioral research: clinical studies and population sampling studies. Case studies are generally used in clinical psychology. The procedure is to identify a subject, usually disturbed, and then to make extensive verbatim reports of conversations he has held with a therapist. In addition, scores on tests administered to the client are reported. These data—the interviews and the test results—are analyzed by one or more people. Such an analysis is often done by comparing similar case studies with the evidence uncovered in the case to be discussed. When the case study method is used to formulate a diagnosis for a specific patient, it would seem to be a reasonable method to use. In my estimation, however, misuse of this method occurs when the findings of a few case studies are extrapolated to the population in general. Again the complaint is that a few isolated people (cases) do not represent the population at large. Yet two of the world's most influential psychologists gained their professional reputations on just such a practice—Freud and Piaget. Piaget's stage theory of intellectual development was formulated on data collected mostly from his children.[24] Piaget and his supporters (Inhelder, Bovet, Sinclair, Smock) have generalized findings from a few case studies, have constructed a theory, and dogmatically defend the theory as law.[25] However, many research studies conducted to verify Piaget's theory do not confirm his findings.[26] One may complain about Freudian theory on the same grounds.

For example, Freud made the point that the oedipal complex develops in boys universally at varying degrees of intensity. The oedipal complex

[24] Jean Piaget, *The Psychology of Intelligence* (Paterson, N.J.: Littlefield, Adams, 1960).

[25] Barbel Inhelder, M. Bovet, H. Sinclair, and C. Smock, "On Cognitive Development," *American Psychologist* 21 (1966): 160–64; Jean-Piaget, Idem, Foreword, in *Young Children's Thinking* by Millie Almy, E. Chittenden, and P. Miller (New York: Teachers College Press, 1966) pp. iii-vii; and Jean Piaget, "Review of Studies in Cognitive Growth," *Contemporary Psychology* 11 (1967): 532–33.

[26] D. Brison, "Acquisition of Conservation of Substance in a Group Situation," (Ph.D. dissertation, University of Illinois, 1965); S. Engelmann, "Cognitive Structures Related to the Principle of Conservation," in *Recent Research on the Acquisition of Conservation of Substance,* ed. D. Brison and E. Sullivan (Toronto: Ontario Institute for Studies in Education, 1967), pp. 35–51; R. Kingsley and V. Hall, "Training Conservation through the Use of Learning Sets," *Child Development* 38 (1967): 1111–26; G. Kohnstamn, "Experiments on Teaching Piagetian Thought Operations" (Paper presented to the Conference on Guided Learning, Cleveland, January 1966); E. Sullivan, "Acquisition of Conservation of Substance through Film Modeling Techniques," in *Recent Research on the Acquisition of Conservation of Substance,* op. cit.

refers to a boy's jealously of his father's relations with his mother. Freud's opinion in this matter was based on two sources of evidence—Western literature and observation of his own patients (case studies). However, the evidence of studies conducted in cultures other than Western clearly indicate that the development of the oedipal complex is not a universal phenomenon.

Population sampling studies need to be scrutinized for different, although just as serious, reasons. The practice in this kind of research is to draw a random sample from a population of subjects whom the researcher wishes to examine. For example, if the experimenter wishes to examine the effects of some treatment on kindergarten children, he would randomly select a number of subjects from the entire population of kindergarten children. He then makes the assumption that the sample he has drawn represents the entire population of kindergarten children in every respect. This assumption is perfectly legitimate, and has been shown to be a reliable practice in countless studies. The major criticism that can be made of studies using this sampling procedure is the way in which the data findings are analyzed. What is usually done is that the sample is randomly assigned to experimental and control treatment conditions. Both the experimental and control groups are given pretest measures, then treatment is administered to the experimental group, but not to the control group; finally, both groups are given posttests. The objective of such an experiment is to determine whether a treatment given to one of two equivalent groups of subjects makes a difference on the posttest scores. There are a large number of variations in this kind of experimental design,[27] however, the issue is in what is being measured and how the data are treated. For example, in a study I conducted, two kinds of subjects were given training.[28] The object of this training was to induce a concept, in this case, conservation of substance. However, given the type of analysis I was forced to conduct (this was my doctoral dissertation) on the data minimized the possibility of uncovering useful information on the processes which took place. This is what I did, and it was not an unusual but a standard process: I took the data for the experimental group and the data for the control group and I calculated means (averages) for each. By running analyses on the mean scores for each group, I lost the information that scrutinizing each case would have yielded. My prime concern was to find out if the educational treatment I gave to the experimental group would lead them to acquire the concept of conservation of substance. The pretest and posttest of this concept was a four-item test. Only subjects who had one or less correct responses to the four-item pretest were allowed to participate in the experiment; hence, all

[27] See J. Popham, "Simplified designs for school research," mimeographed (Southwest Regional Laboratory, 1967).

[28] Philip Reidford, "An Investigation of the Skills Prerequisite to the Acquisition of Conservation of Substance" (Ph.D. dissertation, University of Toronto, 1969).

subjects' pretest scores were either one or zero. When the differences in the pretest and posttest mean scores between the control and experimental groups were analyzed, a significant difference was found in favor of the experimental group. Hence, the hypothesis was confirmed, and I reported that the experiment was a success.

Actually, the experiment was a failure. The actual mean gain made by the experimental group from pretest to posttest on the four-item test was .61. This simply means that most of the experimental subjects did not learn the concept. By looking at the mean gains in performance, rather than looking at individual performance score, a highly distorted impression of the success of the experiment was created.

Support for research

Aside from the very critical issue of the kind of educational research which needs to be done, there is another order of problems which besets all researchers.

Research costs money and therefore the educational researcher must seek funds to support his work. The most usual way to do this is to write a research proposal and submit it to an appropriate government agency or a foundation. The writing of such a proposal is a time-consuming activity. However, usually even more time-consuming is the review process of the foundation or government agency. Having been granted the money needed to do the research, the researcher must then find sources from which he can draw the subjects who will constitute his experimental sample; but where does he go to obtain subjects? In the case of research in social sciences this can be one of the most frustrating experiences in the research planning procedure. If a researcher approaches a school in which he wishes to do research on some aspect of children's behavior, he will be questioned as to his ethics in dealing with the children. In many cases, he actually will be asked to present documentation that his research will not harm the children in any way, and he might even be asked to show that the research will benefit the children. School officials will probably present the researcher with scheduling difficulties, for their concern is the education of children and class time missed for any purpose, including research, is often viewed as harmful.

If the researcher were dealing only with a school principal, his task of obtaining subjects and appropriate times to work with them would be fairly difficult; however, the usual process for gaining access to students in a school is not so simple. Often a research proposal must be approved by a school board, who then instructs the superintendent to find an appropriate school or schools. The superintendent then requests several principals whom he knows to be sympathetic to research to cooperate. The principals willing to do so must then present the research idea to supervisors and classroom teachers to obtain their aid. Finally, in extreme cases, the school must request the parents of the children to sign a form permitting their children to participate in the research. Not only do these clearance procedures take the time of school officials but also they require that the researcher explain to each level of the school system his research proposal.

Although such procedures as outlined above seem tedious and exhausting, the worst is yet to come. When dealing with human subjects in research, it is highly probable that the original research design will have to be modified during the course of study. For example, some children might be absent at the time when a critical testing or training period is scheduled; some of them may become tired or fearful of the experimental procedures, and they will have to be dropped from the experiment. In addition, there are a myriad of things that can go wrong. Testers can get sick. The experimental personnel can make errors. Unforeseen data contamination can take place. For example, if the experimenter is subjecting two groups of children to two treatment conditions and if these two groups are in the same classroom in school and talk to each other, the effects of the differences between the two groups might be significantly reduced by their interchange of information.

Given all the possible things that make educational research a difficult and somewhat fortuitous undertaking, it is understandable why more long-range studies are not conducted. Ideally, as educators, we are not just interested in the short-term effect of an intervention treatment, but would like to trace its effects over a fairly substantial period of time. This is particularly true where research is done to determine developmental differences in children at different ages, so that education may be designed to profit from age characteristic idiosyncracies.[29]

There are two types of research which are designed to accomplish the two aims mentioned above—longitudinal studies and cross-sectional studies. There are several advantages and disadvantages to each methodology, and the following is an explanation of these.

Longitudinal refers to a research methodology in which subjects are identified as a population sample to be studied. Then the researcher collects data on these subjects over a long period of time, presumably for several years. One of the advantages of longitudinal studies is that individual growth curves can be plotted for each child. In addition, maintaining the same sample over a number of years allows the researcher to run many different studies at opportune developmental periods. Moreover, a researcher is better able to analyze the interrelationships between growth and maturation as the children grow older. This methodology also permits the researcher to investigate the effects of special events (e.g., initial school entry, death of a parent, pubescence) which do not occur at the same ages for all children. The disadvantages of longitudinal research are that it is expensive, demands

[29] See, for example, Piaget, *The Psychology of Intelligence.*

continuity of research personnel, and publication of findings is postponed. The main problem, however, is to find a sample of children who can be used in such a study. Such samples must not change their residences or a loss of data will result. Illness may also result in the loss of subjects. Finally, any unusual event during the years when the experiment is being run, such as war or depression, may result in obtaining atypical data.

The cross-sectional approach samples children of varying ages in order to obtain developmental and maturational information. The difference between longitudinal research and cross-sectional research is that the former examines the same children at different times in their chronological development whereas the latter examines different children of different ages. The advantages of the cross-sectional methodology are it is relatively easy to obtain large samples of children of different ages for short periods of time; the data obtained may be analyzed and published immediately since a number of different ages can be sampled at the same time; and continuity of research personnel is not needed. There are disadvantages to this methodology, however. The different age groups sampled must be comparable. Such comparability is at best only approximate, for each generation growing up is subjected to different external influences (e.g., in one age McCarthyism, in another, radicalism; in one folk culture, in another, rock music). Moreover, sampling in school probably overlooks children who have dropped out or who are in special classes or who are several grades behind, whereas such subjects would probably be represented in a longitudinal study.

What does research have to offer education

In spite of the many problems encountered, research on humans seems to offer a way for improvement of the human condition. Research is a way to aid us in arriving at certainty about an idea but, as such, it is no more than a decision-making tool. Such questions as what people should learn, what are the goals of education, and what political system engenders the most freedom and productivity will not be answered by research. After we have made a philosophical speculation about such questions, we can, presumably, test the speculation by using research methods, and thereby obtain a probability answer to our question. As pointed out before, however, research, or the experimental testing of hypotheses, is only one of the ways in which we obtain evidence on which to base a decision.

The fact that our schools fail to make profound intellectual and social changes in children whose backgrounds do not provide them has little to do with research methodology.[30] In my opinion, educational impact has not taken place as is dramatically indicated in the Coleman report because educational researchers have been too timid, unimaginative, and consequently have asked irrelevant questions.

---

30 J. Coleman et al., *Equality of Educational Opportunity* (Washington, D.C.: U.S. Department of Health, Education, and Welfare [OE-38001], 1966).

There have been a few notable exceptions, and I am thinking of B. F. Skinner and A. S. Neill. Neill is the founder of Summerhill, a famous free school in England. After having taught in what he terms "ordinary schools" for a number of years, he decided that the school should fit the child instead of the child fitting the school. Therefore he founded Summerhill, a school with a child-centered, not teacher-centered, ethos. Each member of the school—administrator (Neill), teacher, and student—was given one vote and each person, no matter what his status, was accorded equal rights within the school. Students could go to class or not go to class as they desired. Summerhill, according to Neill, is a continuing success. His criteria for measuring this success were happiness, sincerity, balance, and sociability, and he found that children at Summerhill enjoyed these qualities and enjoyed them because of the atmosphere of the school. Furthermore, the children were learning. Even the British school inspectors gave Summerhill a fairly favorable report.[31]

Summerhill is an imaginative and bold research idea. Neill had the idea that child-centered education would produce happier, more sincere people who would learn not because they were forced to, but because they wanted to. The way he tested his idea, or theory, is impressive. He didn't set up one experimental class and one control group and test the effects of treatment after a short period of time. Probably he didn't do this because he was not trained as an educational researcher and formalized methodology is not his way of life; or perhaps he foresaw that the outcomes of such an experiment would reveal very little. It should be remembered that most educational researchers consistently take the more timid approach of running a limited empirical study. Neill might well be criticized for not having administered pretests and posttests to his students. Such testing presumably would have revealed whether or not there were significant changes in these students after a specified amount of schooling. However, inasmuch as reliable measures of happiness, sincerity, and balance do not exist, the only measure that fits his criteria is sociability. Neill's criteria for success rules out the possibility of running a comparative study between his school and another type of school. The other type of school would undoubtedly not have had the same criteria.

Yet in spite of the design and measurement problems of Neill's continuing experiment, he has had great influence. Tributes to his program come from such diverse sources as Ashley Montagu, Henry Miller, Carl Rogers, and Herbert Read. It is probably not rash to predict that Summerhill has and will have a more profound effect on schools and the people who attend them than all of the reading studies reported in Chall's book.[32]

Another outstanding contributor to the dramatic changes in educational practice is B. F. Skinner. Skinner's work and point of view has one

[31] A. S. Neill, *Summerhill:A Radical Approach to Childrearing* (New York: Hart, 1960).

[32] Chall, *Learning to Read.*

very important aspect which is also reflected in Neil's work. They both believe that to achieve significant changes in man the total environment must be changed. Skinner is probably most famous for identifying operant conditioning. Briefly, what Skinner has shown is that behaviors which are positively reinforced become stronger and strongly resist extinction, whereas behaviors which are not reinforced, infrequently reinforced, or negatively reinforced, extinguish. The substantiation of Skinner's operant conditioning model was originally made on pigeons. Skinner designed a box whose main features were a disc that could be pecked and a cup into which food could be dropped. The operant conditioning procedure was to put a pigeon into the Skinner box and shape its behavior. That is, when the pigeon drew closer to the disc that Skinner wanted it to peck, it was rewarded by a pellet of food. Gradually, by rewarding the pigeon with food each time it approached the disc, the pigeon came to peck the disc. This process Skinner calls shaping behavior. Once the pigeon knows that it will get a pellet of food when it pecks the disc, its behavior becomes predictable. There is a great deal more to Skinner's experimentation that I don't have time to go into here; however, what is important about this discovery is what it led to.

Skinner makes the point that we can shape any behavior we wish to. He himself raised his infant daughter in a controlled environment—a variation of his Skinner box. Skinner's contribution to education is in the field of shaping behavior through controlling and programming the environment. What he found out in his experiments with pigeons was that by rewarding small steps which led to the end behavior desired, one could teach a pigeon to perform almost anything within that species' limitations. In generalizing this finding to humans, Skinner argued that the same was true. If you can specify the end task to be learned, then you can break the task into small progressive steps. If, at every step, reinforcement is built in for a right response, then a student who has mastered each small step should be able to perform the end task. This description is essentially the principle under which linear programmed instruction operates, and despite some difficulties with it,[33] its discovery has resulted in some great benefits for education. Programmed instruction has proved to be a valuable mode of instruction and serves in many institutions as an adjunct to teacher-instructed courses. Even more important is the idea that one can specify exactly how to teach someone a task. By using the principles of programmed instruction, teaching no longer needs to be simply an intuitive process—one can actually specify exactly how to teach a concept. Because this can be done, teachers are admonished to be more painstaking in planning their teaching.

Both examples described above are bold, both have emphasized change in the total environment, both have had considerable impact on the schools

[33] Robert Gagné "Military Training and Principles of Learning," *American Psychologist* 17 (1962): 83–91.

on the way people think about education and upon the children who are exposed to these methods.

Future research

I think that the point has been strongly made in this chapter that most of the research that has been done in education has done little to change educational practices. Earlier in the discussion, an attempt was made to speak to the value of strong inference hypotheses rather than the more common practice of experimenting with weak inference hypotheses. The question arises as to what a strong inference hypothesis is, and several high risk hypotheses that have a low probability of being confirmed are described below.

A "steam engine" for thinking

When Napoleon moved his troops from Paris to Rome, his potential speed of movement was no greater than that of Alexander the Great. In spite of the fact that centuries had elapsed between the time when these two men lived, the speed of the horse and of men determined their traveling time. Yet only a few years after the demise of Napoleon, generals could move their troops approximately five times as fast. What had happened? Man had discovered a way to increase the speed of travel—the steam engine. And with this discovery, the world became smaller; the nature of war changed. A qualitative and quantitative technological event had occurred which drastically altered the social, economic, and political practices of the world.

In the area of transmission and reception of information, people in the twentieth century are restricted by the same limitations as those of the ancient Greeks. We receive and transmit language at a rate which is probably the same on the average as that of classical times. The question is, why? There is nothing physiological to prevent us from speaking faster and understanding spoken speech at a greater rate. Habit is a hard thing to break—especially 3000 years of habit. But what would be the advantage of transmitting (speaking) and receiving (hearing) language at three times the normal rate? To begin with, people who have nothing to say might talk less although there is a possibility that they would be three times as redundant. More importantly, however, is the possibility that intellectual processes are interrelated and that a change in the quality of one might have an effect on another. For example, suppose that the rate of thought is a function of the rate of verbal reception and the rate of verbal transmission, then if we were to increase the rate of transmission and reception by three times the normal rate, might it not be a possibility that thinking rate would also increase? If this were to happen, just think how schools would change. But even more, the situation would be somewhat analogous to the invention of the steam engine; that is, there would be a qualitative modification of all intellectual and social life. Even if an increase in transmission and reception rates did not effect the rate of thinking, our increased quantitative ability in input and output alone would give us the potential to process three times as much information as we presently do, which is becoming increasingly desirable, given the continuing information explosion.

We presently have all of the necessary technology which would allow us to accomplish this. There is a machine called the speech compressor that increases the rate of speech intelligibility up to three times the normal rate without increasing the pitch. Moreover, it would be relatively simple to construct a word meter that could be used as a device in training people to talk faster.

The above is a strong inference hypothesis. Its confirmation would radically change the human condition and education. Its chances of success are probably quite slim, not because man could not learn to transmit and receive at a faster rate, but because the attitudinal resistance to such an innovation would be overwhelming.

Teaching reading

As Chall's book illustrates and as the Coleman report confirms, a large percentage of the U. S. population fail to learn to read adequately.[34] The reasons given for this failure range from the lack of phoneme-grapheme correspondence to poor eye movements.[35] This high failure rate on the part of the school to teach reading gives impetus to costly research which attempts to discover better ways to teach reading. Since our school system is print-oriented, all those who fail to read at a reasonable level of competency fail at school and subsequently fail in life; that is, they are denied the opportunity to explore ideas and to compete for well-paying jobs. Effectively, therefore, we are denying an education to all those students who fail to learn to read and therefore we perpetuate and widen the social and economic inequalities which presently plague our society.

It seems to me that if we were going to find a way to teach reading effectively to all, we would have found it by now. Why not consider another possibility. Ask the question—is there any reason why we need to know how to read? Let us try this hypothesis: Suppose all of the information presently recorded in print were recorded on audio tape. Suppose, also, that we shorten the initial school year by one week so that we could use that money to supply each student with a small, heavy-duty tape recorder. Immediately,

[34] Chall, *Learning to Read*.

[35] J. Carroll, "The Analysis of Reading Instruction. Perspectives from Psychology and Linguistics," in *Theories of Learning and Instruction*, Sixty-third Yearbook of the National Society for the Study of Education, part I, ed. E. Hilgard (Chicago: National Society for the Study of Education, 1964) pp. 336–53.

we have eliminated the main function of grades one through four, the teaching of reading. All children would now have access to all information. Moreover, we can concentrate in the early elementary school on the development of problem-solving conceptual skills as well as a host of other interesting ideas and processes that we now give second shift to because of reading problems. I can't think of one powerful reason why this shouldn't be put into immediate practice. Technologically, we can handle it. The economic demands of a new tape toting market would ensure industry's avid cooperation for the usual profit motives.

The implementation of the above ideas would have sweeping educational, economic, and social impact. No longer would a large percentage of children experience early failure. School time could be spent opening up the world of ideas. With communication success would come educational success. This, of course, leads to social and economic success. Is it moral for us not to initiate such an innovation?

Now suppose the two strong inference hypotheses outlined above were initiated concurrently?

I would like to challenge you to think of some strong inference hypotheses which, if confirmed, would greatly change educational practice.

Education for change

In a bold and exciting book, Postman and Weingartner make the point that change is occurring so rapidly that we no longer can foresee the information that will be necessary for a student to have in order to be sucessful in his world.[36] They go on to say that what we should be doing, therefore, is to train students to deal with change. They outlined a method for doing this. What they suggest is that the child throughout his education be encouraged to examine ideas, to discuss them, and to evaluate them critically. They point out that since a teacher cannot know what the world will be like in fifteen years, it is far more important for the teacher to act as a facilitator of discussion, a resource for finding information, and a stimulator of problem-solving.

This is a powerful hypothesis. The chances of such a plan being implemented on a longitudinal bases are slim, for it entails meddling with people's lives for a long period of time. And there always is the possibility that the experiment will fail.

As with Skinner and Neill, all of the above ideas demand manipulation of more than a single experimental variable. Rather, they hypothesize that great quantitative and qualitative changes come from dramatic modifications of our environment. Another characteristic of these ideas is their

---

[36] N. Postman, and C. Weingartner, *Teaching as a Subversive Activity* (New York: Delacorte Press, 1969).

simplicity. And finally, all of the ideas will find great resistance in the population at large, for they overthrow customary ways of doing things, and custom is always reluctantly relinquished.

SUMMARY

The main idea presented in this chapter is that weak inference research that is presently being conducted in the field in the field of education holds little promise of uncovering information which will substantively effect educational practice. An alternative basis upon which to make fruitful discoveries was presented—strong inference research. However, even the suggestion of substituting strong inference hypotheses for weak inference hypotheses is a strong inference hypothesis! That is to say, the implications of making this change in the field of education research demand sweeping changes in educational practices. For example, if strong inference research were adopted by most researchers, college professors could no longer be promoted on the basis of number of publications but only on teaching and work in progress. The number of research journals would have to be reduced, for fewer articles would be written. In addition, the present practices of giving research grants would have to be reviewed. Accountability for progress in research could no longer be expected by foundations and government granting agencies at the end of each fiscal year. But the most important implication of the strong inference point of view resides in the nature of any strong inference hypothesis that was confirmed. Schools could no longer ignore educational research, for the scientific revolution, which I feel would result in such confirmation, would provide such powerful evidence for modification of educational practice that the public would not allow it to go unnoticed.

index

Information-oriented approach to environment, 182, 183
Information-processing approach to environment, 183–84
Institutional interaction, 94–95
Integration, defined, 210–11
Intelligence, development of, 238–42
Interaction-oriented approach to environment, 182, 183
Internal systems, external and, 83–84
Interpersonal relations:
    authenticity in, 250
    in therapeutic environment, 224–25
IQ, socioeconomic status, going to college and, 75

Jews, role of, in literature, 159–60
Joyce, Bruce, 167–200

Knowledge:
    learning and, 241–42
    soft and hard, 137–41
    technology and, 230–33
    wisdom and, 5–6

"Laissez-faire freedom," 31–33
Latent functions, 84–85
Layers, 192–93
Learning:
    cooperative, 122–23
    Gagné's learning model, 109–10
    knowledge and, 241–42
    psychological, 115–16
    about the world, 127–28
Literature, 135–63
Low risk research, 268–69

Manifest function, latent and, 84–85
Mexican-Americans, 68
Middle-class standards, defined, 88–89
Minority groups, 68; see also Blacks; Jews
Missions, 180–87
Missions-means matrix, 182
Mobility, see Social mobility
Moral decisions, 243–46
Motivation, 217, 223–24
Multilayer curriculum, 194–95

Nakata, Kouji, 227–53
Negroes, see Blacks
Neighborhood concept of education, 61
Nihilation, action and, 24–26, 34
Nonproductive research, 263–64

Norms, defined, 78–79

Objectivity:
    of history, 67
    sociologists and, 75–77
Organizational development, 247–51

Parent-surrogate friend relationship, 209–10
Pathos, tragedy and, 149–50
Peer groups, 90–91
Personal change, literature and, 150–62
Personalist approach to environment, 182
Philosophy, 13–46
Planning of curriculum, 169, 174
Pleasure, critique of, 35
Poor children, contempt for, 54–55
Post-industrialism, 233–38
Poverty (1900s), 53
Privacy, threatened, 235
Programmed instruction, 110–12
Progressive education, 46–47
Projection, function of, 212–13
Psychological learning, 115–16
Psychology, 103–32
Public education, 50
Public schools (1900s), 53, 57–59

Racism:
    notions contained in, 97
    in schools, 88–89
Rationalization, as defense, 213
Reaction formations, defined, 213
Reading, research and teaching, 278–79
Reconstruction, see Social change
Reconstructionists, counselors as, 217–18
Reform movements, 50, 51–67, 97, 98
Regionalism, 48
Regression, effects of, 213
Reidford, Philip, 103–32, 257–79
Reinforcement, defined, 108–9
Reinterpretation of history, 49–50
Relating to others, 130–32
Repression, effects of, 212
Research, 257–79
Robischon, Thomas, 13–40
Role play, defined, 127
Roles:
    advisor-predictor, 207–8
    defined, 80
    disciplinarian, 208–9

Roles, (cont.)
 evaluation of, 82
 students as, 81

Sanctions, defined, 82
Schools:
 as bureaucracy, 7, 8
 business (1900s), 56–57
 decentralization of, 97
 economic system and, 87–88
 efficiency of, 222–23
 family and, 89–90
 hierarchy in, 81
 population of (1908), 64–65
 public, 53, 57–59
 social change and, 92–99
 as social system, 91–92
 See also Education; High Schools;
  Learning; Teachers
Science, values and, 106–7; *see also*
  Technology
Scientific revolution, social change and,
  95–97; *see also* Technology
Self-estrangement, sources of, 81; *see
  also* Alienation
Silence strategies, described, 129–30
Social change:
 changing social patterns and, 236–38
 guidance and, 204
 humanistic movement and, 98–99
 schools and, 92–99
 student's role in, 4, 5
 technology and, 95–97, 233–38
Social life:
 interdependence of, 95
 in literature, 156–59
Social mobility:
 effects of, 92–93
 status and, 83
Social structure, defined, 78
Socialization, 19–22
 differential, 88
 education as major means of, 37–38
Sociologists, objectivity and, 75–77
Sociology, 74–99
Soft knowledge, hard and, 137–41
Spirit of inquiry, developing, 251
Stage development, described, 112–15
Status:
 defined, 82–83
 going to college and, 74–75

rates of deviance and, 83
Strong inference hypothesis, defined,
  267
Student problems:
 psychology applied to, 211–14
 sociology applied to, 214–16
Student unrest, sources of, 3, 81
Students:
 role of, in social change, 4, 5
 as roles, 81
 suicides among, 23
Subservience, effects of, 219
Suicides among students, 23

Teachers:
 quality of (1910), 53
 role of, in curriculum, 174–75
 training of, 8
Technology:
 curriculum and, 174
 knowledge and, 230–33
 moral values and, 239–40
 social change and, 95–99, 233–38
Tests, limitations of, 137–38
Tragedy, pathos and, 149–50
Training of teachers, 8; *see also* Vocational training
Trust, emphasis on, 250
Truth, research vs., 261–63
Tutorial mode of curriculum
  (idiosyncratic curriculum), 189–91
 in operation, 192–93

Unemployment rates (1966), 141
Unidimensionalism, effects of, 221
Utilitarian ethic, 31–38
 critique of value in, 33–38
Urbanization, effects of, 92

Values:
 defined, 79–80
 literature and, 147–49
 science and, 106–7
 technology and, 239–40
 utilitarian ethic and, 33–38
Vocational training, 55–64
 industry's need for, 55–58

Weak inference hypothesis, 267
Wisdom, 5–6
Writers, 143–47

5228 00004 7578